Selected and Introduced by
John Berninghausen and Ted Huters

Revolutionary Literature in China

AN ANTHOLOGY

M. E. Sharpe, Inc., White Plains, New York

<u>Revolutionary Literature in China</u> was first published in two
issues of the <u>Bulletin of Concerned Asian Scholars</u> (Volume 8,
Nos. 1 and 2).

Library of Congress Catalog Card Number: 76-51581
International Standard Book Number: 0-87332-103-0

Printed in the United States of America

Contents

John Berninghausen and Ted Huters   3   Introductory Essay

Zhou Shou-juan   12   We Shall Meet Again/*short story* (1914)
— translated by Perry Link

Ye Sheng-tao   18   People Who Insult People/*essay* (1921)
— translated by Perry Link

Zheng Zhen-duo   19   A Literature of Blood and Tears/*essay* (1921)
— translated by Perry Link

Ye Sheng-tao   20   On the Bridge/*short story* (1923)
— translated by Donald Holoch

Guo Mo-ruo   27   Revolution and Literature/*essay* (1926)
— translated by Lars Ellström

Cheng Fang-wu   33   From a Literary Revolution to a Revolutionary Literature/*essay* (1928)
— translated by Michael Gotz

Mao Dun   37   From Guling to Tokyo/*essay* (1928)
— translated by Yu-shih Chen

Qu Qiu-bai   44   Who's "We"?/*essay* (1932)
— translated by Paul Pickowicz

Qu Qiu-bai   47   The Question of Popular Literature and Art/*essay* (1932)
— translated by Paul Pickowicz

Ding Ling   52   A Day/*short story* (1930)
— translated by Gary Bjorge

Mao Dun   56   In Front of the Pawnshop/*short story* (1932)
— translated by John Berninghausen

Zhang Tian-yi   62   Hatred/*short story* (1932)
— translated by Shu-ying Tsau

Ma Ke   71   Man and Wife Learn to Read/*one-act* Yangge *play* (1945)
— translated by David Holm

Qin Zhao-yang   81   Silence/*short story* (1957)
— translated by Jean James

Zhou Li-bo   85   The Guest/*short story* (1964)
— translated by Joe Huang

Hao Ran   92   Debut/*short story* (1966)
— translated by Wong Kam-ming

John Berninghausen and Ted Huters   98   Short Annotated Bibliography

103   Contributors

Revolutionary Literature in China

Introductory Essay

By John Berninghausen and Ted Huters

During the past sixty years, one of the world's great cultures has been transformed by a profound revolution which touches virtually every aspect of life in that society. As China continues the struggle to fully control her own destiny and to put her revolutionary ideals into practice, the rest of the world looks on with no little fascination tinged with a certain amount of envy, residual misunderstanding, skepticism and admiration.

Perhaps the aspect of the Chinese revolution least understood and appreciated in the rest of the world is the development of a new art and literature. Although the widely differing reactions to revolutionary literature and art among outside observers interested in the current state of the arts in the People's Republic of China range all the way from total hostility to sycophantic praise, a more typical response is a bewildered shrug of the shoulders. Even among the scholars in the West who study Chinese literature, only a very small number have devoted serious attention to 20th century Chinese literary works. Insofar as modern Chinese literature comprises only one small sliver of a literary tradition three thousand years old, this is not all that surprising. Yet the greatly increased interest among both scholars and the general populations of other societies in China's undeniably impressive political and economic achievements has generally not been accompanied by a corresponding increase in the attention given to the developments which have taken place in her art and literature.

One obvious problem which confronts those of us who would like to better understand modern Chinese literature but who cannot read it in the original language is the lack of readily available translations. It is the basic purpose of this special issue of the *Bulletin of Concerned Asian Scholars* to present a selection of significant short stories and critical essays in complete translations which will illustrate something of the process by which the *revolutionary* literature of contemporary China developed. Every attempt has been made by the editors of this special issue to obtain translations of works heretofore unavailable in English and most of the pieces being published here are appearing for the first time in any of the major European languages.

In the same way that the social and economic transformation achieved in China through political revolution represents a historical response to certain problems and conditions which are peculiar to China, as well as a response to some of the problems and conditions common to many societies, likewise revolutionary Chinese literature has developed within a Chinese context and is directly linked to China's unique history and cultural heritage. Its development was, needless to say, simultaneously influenced by historical events and literary phenomena external to China.

A Chinese short story in which "boy meets girl, boy and girl fall in love, boy and girl are separated by cruel fate, boy and girl die of broken heart" will likely share some features and concerns typically found in short stories which treat a similar theme regardless of language, historical background, dominant value system, social order, literary traditions or class origin of author. By the same token, a 20th century Chinese novel about a protagonist engaged in revolutionary struggle to overthrow the existing social order and establish a new society based on Marxian socialism will, just as novels written in other societies which deal with similar themes, encounter certain types of artistic problems; a Chinese novel is, after all, still a novel, and this particular type of novel will tend to solve those problems in ways that are usually similar to solutions worked out in non-Chinese novels of like theme. On the other hand, no matter how similar their thematic content, ideological orientation or literary techniques, the *cultural differences* (including those of different literary experience and expectations) will have a significant influence on literary works written in different languages and societies and will automatically produce differences in meaning and methods of expression.

The writers (story-tellers) and the audience for whom they create the literary communication have received a particular conditioning via their shared historical, cultural and literary experiences. These experiences are conceptualized, remembered and evaluated in ways which are at least partially *unique to that specific culture and its language.* In order to begin to better understand the development of revolutionary literature in China and its relationship to modern Chinese society and the Chinese revolution, we have to keep the following two points firmly in mind:

1. Modern Chinese literature, revolutionary as well as non-revolutionary, is an outgrowth of traditional Chinese literature and is related to modern Chinese society in ways that parallel the relationship of traditional Chinese literature to its society.
2. Revolutionary Chinese literature reflects the revolutionary changes which could only have occurred in this century and which are not unrelated to the

modern experiences and revolutionary struggle of other societies in this century.

While the Bolsheviks in Russia were seizing power and setting up the first government based upon a Marxian revolutionary ideology, Liu Ban-nong's poem, "A Paper Window Between," was published in Beijing (Peking). Written in the vernacular, this fairly prosaic piece of verse was a harbinger of the changes then taking place in China's intellectual and artistic circles. Besides its thematic concern with the irony of social injustice, of the irrational yet vast disparity between the lives of people living only "a paper window" apart, the fact that a Chinese intellectual and poet raised on the elegant diction of classical Chinese would intentionally abandon the conventional language and clichés of traditional poetry in favor of such commonplace words was symbolic of the momentous shift in literary purposes and sensibilities then taking place. And although these experiments in new modes of expression were to go through several stages, the pressing needs of China in the early part of this century and the example of the October Revolution in Russia and the successes of the Communist Party of the Soviet Union in strengthening and industrializing Russia helped to pull modern Chinese writers in the direction of a consciously revolutionary literature.

Only six years before Liu Ban-nong wrote his little poem, the Manchu imperial dynasty (Qing dynasty, AD 1644-1911) and more than two thousand years of China's imperial system of government had finally collapsed. At this time, China was still a semi-feudal society besieged by pressures from imperialist powers in the West and a modernizing, expansionist Japan. Her cultural pride in that long and successful history as the dominant civilization in East Asia made the shame and frustration of her relative backwardness and weakness all the more painful.

Many Chinese still clung to the belief that a new dynasty would emerge to re-establish social order and national self-esteem by resuscitating the old familiar imperial government, the examination system which had offered upward social mobility to a small educated minority *and* the Confucian ideology upon which the whole system had been justified. But the young intellectuals, filled with admiration for Western democracy, scientific progress and industrial society, were sure that the time had come to make a complete break with the past. They were now convinced that China could not progress without liberating herself from the antiquated values, traditional ideas and customs, moral philosophy and ethnocentric world outlook embodied in and inevitably preserved by classical Chinese language. Instead of seeking consolation in the shared memories of China's glorious past and presumed cultural superiority, they yearned to escape from that past. The young writers wanted to create a new literature written in an entirely new mode of expression, a literature that would let in fresh breezes of the new, the modern, the progressive, the Western, the advanced. This new literature was to avoid the dead weight of China's long past, they thought, by virtue of its "modernized" new literary language, *baihuawen*, and its conscious introduction of a wide variety of Western ideas, themes and styles of writing. Trained from early childhood in the written language of their cultural heritage, *wenyan* (classical Chinese), these younger writers who were reaching adulthood at the time of the First World War in Europe faced the extra problem of creating a new

medium of literary expression at the same time they sought to utilize their new literature for articulating new visions, new values, new themes. The *baihuawen* which they helped to champion as the new language of journalism, education, commerce and politics as well as literature was based on the *vernacular* language of the educated elite living in those urban areas most influenced by contact with the West. A new generation of disenchanted young intellectuals and students rallied to this new form of Chinese as a long overdue liberation from the stereotyped phraseology and outworn diction of *wenyan*, finding almost as much excitement in the medium itself as in the messages about personal freedom, emancipation from feudalistic culture or radical solutions for the nation's backwardness which it expressed.

Most of the educated youth in the cities firmly believed that the new *baihua wenxue* (vernacular literature) would be able to serve society's needs by communicating to the people of China the heady optimism and excitement engendered by the collapse of the old order which they felt. At the same time they supposed that the new literature would awaken the masses to the sorrow and shame of China's current weakness and poverty, would help to promote radical change guided from within China rather than by forces external and inimical to it. However, as is pointed out in the essays by Guo Mo-ruo, Cheng Fang-wu, Mao Dun and Qu Qiu-bai which follow, the new *baihuawen* rather quickly proved to be something of a failure since it was often too difficult for most ordinary readers to comprehend and was far too "Westernized" to appeal to popular taste.

The movement for *baihuawen* as the desired alternative to *wenyan* had been greatly spurred by the May Fourth Movement which began in 1919. In that year, China's hopes for international recognition of her national interests were shattered at the Paris Peace Conference and the Chinese government in Beijing was simultaneously exposed as capitulating to imperialist pressures exerted by the Japanese. The students in the Chinese capital took to the streets in mass demonstrations on the fourth of May. The subsequent patriotic, intellectual and cultural movements committed to rapid and thorough change are grouped together under the term "May Fourth Movement."

Although the May Fourth period is often thought of as covering the years between 1919 and 1937, it is useful to distinguish between the early May Fourth period and the later May Fourth period. With reference to the development of the new *baihua wenxue* (vernacular literature) which was an important element in the May Fourth Movement, we may define the works written during the decade of 1918-1927 as early May Fourth literature and the literature produced between 1928 and 1937 as late May Fourth works. But in terms of the development of *revolutionary* Chinese literature, it should be noted that it had antecedents in certain works written in the late Qing which contained strong elements of social consciousness and that the actual culmination of its historical and literary development did not occur until after the May Fourth period was over. In fact, the literary expression of protest against social injustice, especially in poetry, can be traced all the way back to some of the earliest works of Chinese literature. It was, however, only in the late May Fourth period that the *mainstream* of Chinese literature shifted course in the direction of consciously revolutionary objectives and methods. And it was only in the period after the 1937 invasion of China proper by Japan which drove the urban revolutionary writers into the hinterland that the militant revolutionary nature that is the distinguishing mark of literature in China ever since 1949 was finally defined and put into practice.

Certainly it was no accident that the traumatic course of Chinese history during those years and the expanding power and influence of the Chinese Communist Party coincided with the emergence of a truly *revolutionary* literature in the Marxian sense of the term. As can be seen in the essays by Guo Mo-ruo and Cheng Fang-wu which call for a revolutionary literature and which were written right at the transitional period between early and late May Fourth literature, the influence of the Bolshevik Revolution in Russia and of Soviet examples of revolutionary literature is quite unmistakable. Indeed, the definition and practice of revolutionary literature in China worked out during the past half century bear close resemblance to many aspects of revolutionary literature in the Soviet Union.

One of the problems which the writers who wish to create revolutionary literature always face is that of how it is to be defined. Some would define it as literature which seeks to deligitimize the present and the status quo in order to promote faster progress toward a better and more advanced future. Others might see revolutionary literature as literature which offers a militant or shocking repudiation of whatever conventional values and literary tastes are currently prevalent. For writers and critics of a Marxian persuasion, revolutionary literature must consciously endeavor to "raise the consciousness" of its audience—that is, it must promote and increase the audience's understanding of socio-historic reality according to the perspective of class struggle and the stages of historical development all societies pass through on their way to communism. Some Marxian literary theoreticians would also insist that revolutionary literature must seek to foster socially responsible behavior through the delineation of *model* characters by whom it is hoped the audience will be inspired and whom the readers will emulate. Revolutionary organizations, most notably various communist parties which have succeeded in taking state power and which see themselves as the vanguard of the proletariat, frequently conceive of revolutionary literature as being quite simply the literary embodiment of the proletariat's correct perspective and policies as determined by the communist party vanguard. Furthermore, the literary artistry employed in the pursuit of this *didactic* raison d'être, although important, is clearly considered subordinate to ideological concerns. Therefore style and technique are to be evaluated primarily with reference to how effectively and accurately they have assisted the didactic function of conveying an appropriate ideological content to those readers defined as the audience to be served by that work.

In the industrially advanced societies of the West, the fundamental direction in which the cultural and literary environment has been developing during the last hundred years involves a negation of any explicit moral vision and didactic function for creative literature. In these societies, the majority of modern writers have focused more on the exploration of individual subjectivity and have tended towards psychological relativism rather than 'social realism' or a literary rendering of the shifting relationships among various social groups (classes) as they move through history. Of course, there were many

significant exceptions to this overall tendency in the advanced capitalist countries, particularly the literature of 19th century Europe that Georg Lukács termed "critical realism" and the social protest literature of the first thirty-five years of this century. But most of us have been strongly influenced by the more recent trends which have been dominant in our native literary terrain and we are thus likely to have a certain distaste for explicitly didactic art and literature. By the same token, the differences in ideological standpoint between most readers in capitalist societies and the majority of readers in socialist China will presumably interfere with our enjoyment of revolutionary Chinese literature.

It would, however, be a serious mistake for us to imagine that revolutionary literature in China was and is nothing more than an importation from Russia without any antecedents in traditional China or affinities with traditional China's cultural and literary heritage. It is important therefore to suggest some of the linkages between the nature of traditional Chinese literature and modern revolutionary literature in that country.

China's literary aesthetic developed out of a long and complex involvement between literature and ethical-moral-political concerns. Just as we have difficulty drawing any sharp line of demarcation between politics and morality in modern Chinese society and art (i.e., what is good politically is moral and what is moral is politically desirable or 'revolutionary'; what is good for the person is good for the people, what is good for the people is good for the individual), traditional Chinese thinking tended to view politics and morality as part of a unified whole. In the main, Chinese literature gave primary emphasis to didactic content and function. It is thus not at all easy for most of us to put ourselves in the place of a Chinese audience for whom a conscious concern with ethical and political issues as well as explicitly didactic intent seem quite natural and desirable aspects of any literature serious enough to be considered worthwhile. A concentration by the literary work on the psychological motivation of individual characters or on the ambiguities of ethical dilemmas, to say nothing of the subjectivist attack upon the concept of knowable or 'objective' reality which is characteristic of many modernist works in the West, would doubtless strike a Chinese audience as unnatural and unwholesome if not downright meaningless.

In responding to and assessing revolutionary Chinese literature, or any other literature for that matter, one must keep in mind the fact that authors are required to work in concert with the experiences and expectations of their audience. And not only have those expectations been formed by historical processes but also by the shared experiencing of literary works. In the case of the Chinese audience, the exceedingly long course of China's cultural history has allowed centuries and centuries of shared aesthetic experience to accumulate and this produced an audience united by a high degree of aesthetic and ethical homogeneity. Certain fundamental ideas which underlay the Confucian ideology had direct bearing upon this relationship between politics and literature in traditional China.

Although a simplification, one essential difference between China's cultural heritage and our own is to be found in our differing conceptions of man's relationship to the cosmos. The Chinese viewed human society as having been created by mythic culture heroes, not gods, who were believed to have brought civilization into being by "inventing" morality.

In the Confucian tradition, a dominant source of social norms and state ideology during most of China's history, it is the possession of morality and culture and history which constitutes man's basic nature and separates man from all other creatures, not the possession of an immortal soul. There came into being rather early on a sustaining myth of a utopia which was thought to have existed at the dawn of Chinese civilization, a 'golden age' held to have provided models for all that man would ever need to know. Everything in which the Chinese could take pride was thought to have originated in that 'golden past.' In fact, the central question of all human history was regarded by the Chinese as one of how to restore the past utopia or, at the very least, how to retard any further decline from it.

History, the recording of events and commentary on their import for human society, thus acquired special status as the key to the state ideology. As a record of the ancient culture heroes and the sages, it contained models for moral and hence quintessentially human behavior. This gave rise to the paradoxical twin obsessions which characterize the approach to history in traditional China: a passion for recording, preserving and meticulously reconstructing the past in order to transmit it to later generations and an equal passion for protecting society and future generations by exercising moral censorship over the historical record. This latter function was carried out by the highly educated elite, whether or not acting in an official capacity. Control was maintained by means of careful selection and editing of that part of the record which was deemed safe and appropriate to be passed on to posterity. The importance in which history and written records were held can be seen in the periodic phenomenon of the literary purge, which more than once reached the point of executing the author of heterodox ideas or interpretations, sometimes killing off all his relatives for good measure.

Since there was no outside or transcendent force upon which to lay the blame for immoral or irrational human behavior, the actions of men could only be interpreted on the basis of a matter-of-fact record of events. Given the lack of supernatural intervention as an acceptable explanation for human affairs gone awry, and given the widely accepted belief in a utopia of the past and the perfectability of human nature, human actions which did not conform to accepted values and social norms could only be ascribed to some sort of straying from "moral reason." There was, therefore, little basis for extending sympathy to individuals gone wrong or for a sympathetic literary portrayal of characters who did not conform to the accepted morality. Moreover, since the key to moral behavior was held to be immanent in the written recording of human affairs, past and present, giving expression to any "immoral behavior" (whether in the writing of history or of belles-lettres literature) was vulnerable to attack as posing a distinct threat to the stability of society and as potentially subversive to the state unless that supposed immorality was balanced with conventional and implacable punishment. Culture, then, functioned both as conclusive evidence of moral reason being present in the world of men *and* as the enforcer of strict accountability for all humans which would uphold that moral reason.

Since the enduring hold of traditional culture is explainable by the dual functions of describing and prescribing social interaction which it fulfilled, it should hardly surprise us that literature, the supreme expression of culture, became a closed system in which didacticism came to be intertwined with representation at every level. Not only does the overall thematic structure of literary work reveal this mixture, but even the constituent elements of significance and style within a work, e.g., proverbs and simple metaphors, frequently combine description and prescription. Or to put it another way, the blend of moral purpose (*didacticism*) and the depiction of reality (*representation* or *mimesis*) is so pervasive in most works of poetry, history, philosophy, essays, official documents, and letters (traditional *high literature*) that to attempt to split the two elements apart seems to distort the meaning of such works. Similarly, the moral vision and the mimesis which are bound together in revolutionary Chinese literature of the modern period cannot easily be separated.

As in other traditional societies, access to the more sophisticated forms of artistic expression, especially those of written literature, was limited to a very small segment of the population. Only the elite could afford to provide their sons with the long and expensive education in the complexities of Chinese language and the corpus of literary works required for success in the Imperial Examinations and a proper appreciation of sophisticated art forms. In large measure the formal and informal education of the 'scholar-gentry' class whose members staffed the government and state apparatus involved a rigorous indoctrination in the Confucian ideology, the moral reason, upon which the authority and legitimacy of the state were seen to rest. This ruling-class elite had an obvious vested interest in the maintenance of those values which permeated their literature and which justified the hierarchical structure of the social order from which this class greatly benefited.

Much as this system and these members of the educated elite sought to limit new patterns of social behavior and to resist philosophical and aesthetic innovations, new cultural forms did develop and spread during the many centuries of China's cultural history. By the time of the Song dynasty (the Sung, AD 960-1280), urbanization began to create a new class of semi-educated people who could enjoy a certain modicum of leisure. A body of less complex, less arcane forms of literature, both oral and written, was created for this new audience. However, these new, more popular tales, lyrics, theatrical works, and songs failed to express a significantly different world view. This fact represents an obvious difference from the historical experience of Western Europe in a later period of urbanization when the new forms of literature which arose to serve the emerging bourgeois audience did express a world view greatly different from that expressed in the literature of the feudal aristocracy.

The failure of an independent Chinese bourgeoisie with its own ideology to develop at that time was of lasting significance in China's historical development and was clearly reflected in the realm of art and literature. The popular works which came into being at this time and the widely enjoyed works of vernacular fiction written later during the Ming (AD 1368-1644) and Qing dynasties for the expanding urban audience were, if anything, even more imbued with the traditional values and didactic purpose of the old literature than was the "high literature" of the ruling class elite in the Ming and Qing.

This remarkable tenacity displayed by traditional norms and assumptions which persisted in the literature aimed at a popular audience in the cities was a source of frustration for the serious writers who were interested in getting their revolutionary message across to the general public during the first three decades of this century. (See their attacks upon "butterfly" literature accompanying "We Shall Meet Again" and Qu Qiu-bai's advocacy of resorting to "gossip literature" in "The Question of Popular Literature and Art," ff. 27.) We need only look at the first story in our collection, "We Shall Meet Again," to find that despite its superficial elements of modernity, i.e., the presence of a foreigner, his romantic involvement with a young Chinese woman, the descriptions of their kissing, etc., the story is still basically within the tradition of short stories written since the Song for the less sophisticated urban audiences and reveals a strong loyalty to traditional values in 1914.

As Link points out in his introduction to "We Shall Meet Again," this genre of popular fiction, even though giving promise of social consciousness and progressive tendencies at the turn of the century, became more and more a vehicle for entertainment and escapism in its appeal to a rapidly expanding readership during the years leading up to and throughout the May Fourth period.

Of course, the problem posed by the popularity of escapist literature is far more significant than any mere failure of "butterfly literature" to be impressed into the service of a serious moral vision and didactic intent. The problem which none of the essays presented herein seems to have been able to answer was whether "high-minded," serious literature of the May Fourth Movement with its frequently difficult style, cultural iconoclasm, and sometimes radical message could *compete* for readers with those works written by equally skillful if less profound authors who were willing to produce anything just as long as it would sell. Of the four critical essays included, all by serious revolutionary writers, only Mao Dun's "From Guling to Tokyo" touches upon the knotty problem of the reading public having little taste for "slogan literature" on the Soviet model. Of course, this particular essay was composed while the author was still in the grip of disillusionment and pessimism brought on by the drastic reverses suffered by the left-wing revolutionary forces and the CCP in 1927. Mao Dun was also bridling at the harsh attacks leveled against his realist novels by some Communist critics.

Revolutionary literature originates in the effective and evocative verbal expression of social reality crafted in literary form by people living in an unjust society. (The term "unjust society" allows for the possibility of a revolutionary literature emerging in response to systemic injustices existing in societies at any stage of development, including societies already on the road to socialism.) In its first stage of development, revolutionary literature and art are distinguishable from non-revolutionary art and literature by the conscious expression of the unhappiness, suffering or exploitation of people caused by social injustice. Furthermore, the expression of this suffering and unhappiness in literary form is intended to increase the audience's awareness of inequity and to persuade it that such inequity is a consequence of the way in which society is organized. Revolutionary literature must reject any fatalistic acceptance of social injustice as inherent in the "human condition." Moreover, it must affirm that the alleviation of social injustice by a fundamental restructuring of

unjust societies is both possible and desirable.

Lu Xun (Lu Hsun), the first great modern writer in twentieth century China, tells the following anecdote in the preface to *Nahan* (Call to Arms), his first published collection of fifteen short stories which he wrote between 1918 and 1922: at about the same time as Liu Ban-nong published his poem in 1917, an old friend visited Lu Xun and urged him to write something for the magazine *New Youth*, which was the leading organ of the disenchanted intelligentsia and anti-Confucian cultural rebels of the day. Lu Xun responded to this request with a parable:

Imagine an iron house without windows, absolutely indestructible, with many people fast asleep inside who will soon die of suffocation. But you know since they will die in their sleep, they will not feel the pain of death. Now if you cry aloud to wake a few of the lighter sleepers, making those unfortunate few suffer the agony of irrevocable death, do you think you are doing them a good turn?

To which his friend responds:

But if a few awake, you can't say there is no hope of destroying the iron house. *

This is true, thinks Lu Xun, hope can never be totally blotted out and he agrees to write a story for publication. This turned out to be the famous "Diary of a Madman" (dated April 1918) which marks the opening salvo against the old literature and Confucian cultural values in the form of an imaginative and highly successful piece of literary art. Most of his short stories written during the early May Fourth period convey a bittersweet awareness of China's dilemma and the negative aspects of its enduring traditions. But in the early years of the modern literature movement, writers like Lu Xun and Liu Ban-nong were often unsure about how successful revolutionary insights or values would be in rousing the people from their stupor. The time had not yet arrived when the early revolutionary writers were able to believe that they had solutions to the problems China faced and their fiction, poetry, essays and plays do not offer much in the way of "blueprints for the future."

Ye Sheng-tao's 1923 story "On the Bridge" does not concern itself, however, with the question of whether or not the Chinese people can be aroused to face up to their problems. For his young protagonist, the issue has already been resolved by the implicit assumption that they can be; the question has become one of how it is to be done. It is interesting that this story focuses upon the individual, much of it taking place within the consciousness of the alienated young man who has decided upon an act of political terrorism. "On the Bridge" reflects the influence upon early May Fourth literature of nineteenth century European Romanticism and realism. But we can also find the traditional Chinese notion of benevolent human reason which lies not far beneath the surface of this story. The obvious implication is that people will wake up, become more human and susceptible to reformation if only the means to smash the tyranny of ennui and senseless custom can be found. Whether the means taken

---

* *Selected Stories of Lu Hsun* (Peking: Foreign Languages Press, 1972), p. 5.

by Zu-qing are the right ones or not cannot be determined from this story. Later on, revolutionary writers will take more pains to answer the question of which means are the right ones.

The contrast presented between Ye Sheng-tao's story and the earlier "butterfly" story with regard to traditional ideas and values could hardly be greater. Gui-fang murders the foreigner she loves, Freeman, in order to maintain her cultural identity and her ties to all the Chinese values her uncle forcefully articulates. This is almost diametrically opposed to Zu-qing's decision to assassinate a rich man. Zu-qing's planning and implementation of his existential act of will are intended to further remove him from his inherited cultural identity and are also justifiable by virtue of their "revolutionary" potential.

In his 1921 attack on the advertisement for the Saturday Magazine, a leading publisher of popular "butterfly" fiction, Ye Sheng-tao (then known as Ye Shao-jun) stated the following point of view: "Only literature has the power to serve as the tie which binds together the best in the human spirit. . . ." Zheng Zhen-duo, Ye's fellow member in the Literary Research Society, an important literary coterie, vents his sense of outrage against popular entertainment fiction for showing little concern over the struggle to save the nation.

Cheng Fang-wu and Guo Mo-ruo were both members of the Creation Society at this time, a literary clique which began in the early twenties as the leading promoter of European Romanticism but switched over to a passionate espousal of Marxism and a Marxist approach to literature in the mid-twenties. From this time onward, the more progressive young writers tended to either join or have some contact with the Chinese Communist Party, and the Marxists took the initiative in the debates over what revolutionary literature should be. Qu Qiu-bai was for a short time the leader of the Chinese Communist Party and had previously been to the Soviet Union where he had studied Russian. He became one of the earliest and most adamant spokesmen for a literature aimed at the masses and written in a language comprehensible to the masses. As a Communist Party member, he also had definite ideas about what ideological values the new mass literature should transmit to the masses. Mao Dun, on the other hand, although he had had very early contact with the CCP in Shanghai and like Guo, Zheng, and Qu had participated in some revolutionary activities during 1925-1927, apparently moved away from the CCP after the collapse of the Wuhan revolutionary regime in the summer of 1927. He began to write novels at that time which had quite an impact in portraying the demoralization and moral ambiguities confronting bourgeois youth in the large cities. But the Communists and the writers who supported them simply were not that interested in explorations of bourgeois alienation and the moral ambiguities of revolution. Fighting for survival after the devastating effects of the rupture with the Guomindang and Chiang Kai-shek's White Terror which began in April 1927, the Communist writers and literary critics were much more concerned with the important service literature could render in communicating their revolutionary ideals to the Chinese people and in discrediting the feudal and bourgeois elements in society (particularly among the disaffected bourgeois youth they hoped to win over to revolutionary activism) than they were in achieving new aesthetic heights. Not only were they pushed by the dangerous and even desperate situation in which they found themselves toward the theories of "proletarian literature" and its emphasis on political utility, but the didacticism of this new revolutionary literature coming out of the Soviet Union struck a responsive chord in the hearts of serious-minded young Chinese revolutionaries. More interested in fashioning a theoretical framework which would illuminate the historical and social nature of all literature, Guo and Cheng went on the attack and condemned the revolutionary literature of the period for having been written by bourgeois intellectuals. In this process, we should not fail to note, they introduced dialectical argumentation to the discussion of what "revolutionary literature" is and should be.

Mao Dun declined to identify his literary works as "revolutionary" since they failed to offer any solution for the problem of how the revolution was to be achieved. But he defended the realism of the bourgeois revolutionary writer who writes about the bourgeoisie and what he knows from personal experience. The differences we find between Mao Dun and the more militant CCP members like Qu, Cheng, and Guo on this point are indicative of the split among revolutionary writers between "realists" and "romanticists." As we have already pointed out, Chinese literature usually has not admitted to any clearcut distinction between the representation of reality and presentation of "correct" moral vision. However, writers can always emphasize one at the expense of the other. Mao Dun as a revolutionary realist seems to have been willing to sacrifice closer conformity to the defined moral vision, i.e., Marxist ideology, for the sake of closer conformity to the representation of the reality he personally experienced.

At the beginning of the 1930s, most of the revolutionary and progressive writers centered in Shanghai finally united in the League of Leftwing Writers which they formed in the spring of 1930 under the leadership of CCP members. Qu Qiu-bai was one of the most influential Communists in the League and by 1932 he had defined the fundamental problem of revolutionary literature as concerning "the use of artistic forms to convey revolutionary political slogans." This formula, directly conflicting with Mao Dun's advocacy of describing what one actually sees as opposed to using slogans and formulas in literary content, is basically in the Leninist mold and presages the policies on art and literature enunciated by Mao Ze-dong at Yan'an (Yenan) a decade later. Like Qu, Chairman Mao insisted upon proletarian leadership for the new literature and that the writers must link up with the ordinary people, work with their hands, learn the language of the underprivileged and aim their literary works at the mass audience. Unlike Qu Qiu-bai, however, Mao did not have a condescending attitude towards the peasants and was able to see that the new revolutionary literature of China would have to make many accommodations with traditional agrarian folk art which was still very influental and popular among the large rural populace. (Ironically, Qu was severely criticized and even vilified during the Cultural Revolution in the 1960s despite the fact that he gave his life for the revolution in 1935 when he was executed by the Guomindang. Nor is he credited nowadays in China with having made any particular contribution to the development of revolutionary Chinese literature.)

At the Yan'an Forum on Art and Literature held in the

Communist-controlled area in 1942, Mao Ze-dong had become very concerned about the tendency among the unruly revolutionary writers from the cities like Ding Ling, Ai Qing and others to write works which were not altogether positive and uncritical about life under CCP government. He felt he had to put a lid on their "writing about the dark side of things." He was also acutely aware of the inability and disinclination that these urban intellectuals had for linking up with the illiterate and semi-literate peasants in whose area they were living. The notion that revolutionary writers should do just that had been mainly a theoretical position of Communist Party writers and critics a decade earlier. But now in Yan'an it had become a practical necessity. Not only were the Communists facing the difficult problem of governing a large and beleaguered area in North China at that time, but they could hardly afford to allow the negativism of intellectuals accustomed to the "luxury" of critical independence and biting satire to lower the morale of the general population in their area. As the majority of these people were peasants who had never been to a large city or even seen the inside of a school room before the Communists brought some minimal education to them, nothing could have been less useful or relevant to them than stories such as Ding Ling's "A Day."

Ding Ling was probably the most famous woman revolutionary writer yet produced in twentieth century China. At first, much of her fame was occasioned by her unconventional life style in Shanghai where she lived with Hu Ye-pin, a young CCP writer who was executed in 1931. But from her early works which treat the psychology of the alienated young women in the twenties, Ding Ling's work turned to more radical and political topics such as the plight of the peasantry. She joined the CCP after the execution of Hu Ye-pin, spent some years in Guomindang jails and then wound up in Yan'an. Although published at the beginning of the 1930s, "A Day" seems to be artistically and thematically closer to "On the Bridge" than to either "In Front of the Pawnshop" by Mao Dun or "Hatred" by Zhang Tian-yi. Like many modernist works of European and American fiction produced in this century, "A Day" has no little difficulty in solving the technical problem of how to portray boredom and alienation without boring and alienating the reader. It serves as a cautionary example for the modern Western reader who may be tempted to attribute any and all failings encountered in modern Chinese literature to its didacticism, highly charged political content or explicitly revolutionary vision. Much less "revolutionary" or didactic than the stories included here by Mao Dun, Zhang Tian-yi or Zhou Li-bo, for instance, and perhaps more familiar to our "modernist" sensibilities and aesthetic expectations, "A Day" is nonetheless clearly inferior in terms of aesthetic quality.

The second stage in the development of revolutionary Chinese literature was reached after the formation of the League of Leftwing Writers and the increasing focus upon *economic and structural* aspects of social injustice. Stories like Zhang Tian-yi's "Hatred" and Mao Dun's "In Front of the Pawnshop" were carefully crafted to impress upon their essentially educated, urban audience the fact that a majority of China's people were living in poverty and under the oppression of feudalistic social organization in the countryside. Furthermore, these works were designed as a warning to the bourgeoisie that not only was the situation morally unacceptable but that it was becoming economically untenable. In the late May Fourth period of 1928-1937, modern Chinese literature became increasingly 'revolutionary' and more relevant to *Chinese* realities. It did so by moving away from earlier Romanticism, individualism, avant garde (i.e., Western) experimentation and a preoccupation with urban alienation towards the graphic depiction of poverty and famine in the rural areas and vicious satirizing of the corrupt gentry and Guomindang bureaucracy, urban and rural.

It was during this second stage, when the individual writer was still free to respond in his own personal fashion to the severe contradictions he or she perceived in society and with the passion of a revolutionary fighter to transform that independent vision into a work of art, that some of the best revolutionary literature was written. There was a definite improvement in the technical abilities of Chinese writers during the thirties to handle the new *baihuawen* which was by this time becoming both more standardized and more flexible. The irony of the situation is that the powerful tensions set up in writers like Mao Dun and Zhang Tian-yi by the human suffering they saw among the poor *and* by the uncertainties they felt vis-à-vis the apparent failures and weaknesses of the revolutionary forces provided much of the impetus for their best work. This may help to explain why so many revolutionary writers stopped writing literature once the revolution had succeeded in taking state power in 1949. Not only were they subject to more bureaucratic control over their artistic production than before, but some of the contradictions of society which had formerly fired their imaginations were now either being solved or were no longer permissible themes under the new social order.

The third stage in revolutionary Chinese literature occurred during the War of Resistance Against the Japanese which was fought from 1937 to 1945. With the loss of cities like Shanghai, Peking, and Canton to the Japanese occupation,

the writers were forced to move into the hinterland, escape to overseas havens, or live under Japanese control. Almost all of them adopted a new direction in their writing, now striving to make their art serve the war effort (just as happened in England and the U.S. during World War II). The more contact these writers had with ordinary Chinese people in the interior, the more anachronistic May Fourth literature with its Western influence and Westernized *baihuawen* seemed to be. Once the urban writer committed him- or herself to assist in mobilizing the patriotism and nationalism of the common people, he or she was forced to adopt more popular and easily assimilated forms of literary expression. Lo and behold, for all the earlier attempts to dump China's cultural heritage, it turned out that the soldiers, workers, shopkeepers, and peasants—in fact, almost everyone but the intellectuals—still preferred the more familiar and traditional folk arts to the urban and relatively 'sophisticated' May Fourth literature.

"Man and Wife Learn to Read" is an excellent example of this pivotal third stage in the process by which revolutionary literature grew up in China. This work from the Yan'an period utilized a rural form of drama incorporating song, dance and rhythmic chanting, the *Yangge* (Rice Planting Song). It fairly crackles with the energy being released by the profound changes in the countryside such as the campaign for literacy. Writers were now supposed to see themselves as just another type of worker or soldier within the ranks of the revolutionary forces and to express in literary form the reality of the immense social and political transformation which was taking shape right before their eyes. And as had been the case for Chinese writers previously, the revolutionary writers in Yan'an were expected to be simultaneously descriptive and prescriptive in their treatment of this new reality. They were thus, it goes without saying, expected to portray the new social order and the Communist revolutionaries in a favorable light.

It was during the Yan'an period that the careful attitude toward the written word which has characterized Party policy ever since achieved its final shape. With revolutionary literature, now recast in popular forms, given official status as a propaganda vehicle, came the dual requirements of purging the traditional forms of Confucian content and of ensuring that the new art works satisfied contemporary political needs. The rigor with which the resulting literary policy has been carried out shows that the tendency to assume a crucial influence on human destiny for the written word has not disappeared from Chinese consciousness. The vigilance which led to the eventual repudiation of almost all works written during the earlier stages of the revolution is, however, emblematic of the determination to continually reassert the power of human will and not to let the dead hand of the past, as represented by prior, "sacred" literary texts, control human life. This is the literary manifestation of the continual struggle and transformation of the conditions of existence that lie at the heart of the Maoist ideology.

In practice, however, while didacticism per se does not necessarily enhance or impair literary value, the constant process of revision and repudiation of literature created as contingent upon a transient phase of the revolutionary dialectic has effected a double bind on Chinese authors. To begin with, in linking a work too closely to specific issues, the very elements which made a piece of literature topical in the

first place will tend to diminish that work's significance once the historical situation has changed. Secondly, there is the more general danger that ideological censorship or politically motivated "moral criticism" can be used by those in power to suppress expression of divergent opinion and to inhibit literary experimentation. Such obstacles to the further development of revolutionary literature are hard to avoid where there exists a disinclination to recognize any qualitative differences between literature and polemical exhortation. If revolutionary literature is required merely to follow the development of the political dialectic, it loses its capacity for independent criticism.

The last three stories presented are all from the post-Liberation period (i.e., after 1949). Qin Zhao-yang's story "Silence" is the product of an interlude in which the Party relaxed its tight control over public debate and over literature which sought to expose serious problems in post-Liberation China. Written during the "Hundred Flowers" period (late 1956–early 1957) when a public airing of substantive criticisms and expressions of dissatisfaction was tolerated and even encouraged by the Central Government, stories like "Silence" reveal the persistence of the critical tendency in many revolutionary writers and intellectuals. There can be little doubt that many of these writers and intellectuals were unhappy with the revolution which was rapidly dismantling the privileges enjoyed by people from their elite class background and were indeed guilty (as the CCP literary watchdogs were so quick to charge) of using literature to oppose further intensification of the revolutionary process. However, it seems equally indisputable that many of these critical writers were still essentially the same dedicated revolutionaries who had risked their lives under the Guomindang to write revolutionary literature. They now hoped to serve the revolution loyally by exposing its inadequacies or mistakes or injustices to public view. To their sorrow and that of many readers, they were wrong. There was to be little or no toleration for a critical realism which contradicted *a priori* insistence on "revolutionary optimism."

In response to the criticism unleashed during the "Hundred Flowers" period which the Party decided was becoming too negative, too fundamental, too destructive, there was launched an "anti-rightist" campaign designed to stem the flood of criticism. Among the targets of this campaign were literary works which seemed to call the tenets of Marxism-Leninism and Chairman Mao's thinking into question. One of the most basic of those tenets is an abiding faith in the revolutionary activism, capability and initiative of the masses (*including* the peasant masses in Mao's version of Marxism), a faith clearly contradicted by Qin Zhao-yang's portrait of their passivity.

Perhaps one of the best writers after 1949 in China and one who did come from a peasant background is Zhou Li-bo. His 1964 story "The Guest" effectively integrates lively dialogue, a sense of humor and relatively believable characters such as Mother Wang and Da-xi with the ideological demands (i.e., moral vision) of the times. As such, it is one of the more successful examples of the fourth stage of revolutionary literature in China in which the nation has been liberated by the revolutionary forces.

With state power in the hands of the CCP and no need to temporize with non-Party rivals, revolutionary literature has the problem of maintaining the sense of dramatic struggle and confrontation now that former enemies have lost much of their credibility and many of the obvious targets of pre-Liberation struggles have become historical rather than current. This problem is all the more crucial for revolutionary Chinese literature at this stage, with its emphasis on the struggle between good and evil, since it must have powerful adversaries for its positive characters in order for real tension to be generated in the audience.

A typical solution to this problem has been to set post-Liberation works in the bad old pre-Liberation days when there was a surplus of truly fearful enemies to be dealt with. For works set in post-Liberation China, the writers tend to avoid creating believable yet strong villains who could serve as foils to their positive characters. Under the principles of "revolutionary romanticism" in which literature is required to present its audience with positive and heroic characters to be emulated and not supposed to weaken the impact of the *model characters* with ambiguities of personality, we often find completely preposterous dialogue (which sounds suspiciously like an editorial in last month's *People's Daily*) being put into the mouths of depersonalized characters. Zhou Li-bo partially finesses this artistic liability by putting the more hortatory words of Ju-ying into her letter to Da-xi. In Zhou's style, like that of Zhao Shu-li and Hao Ran, the leading writer of fiction in China since the Cultural Revolution of 1965-1969, we can find passages of lyrical description plus an artful utilization of rural vocabulary and local patois. Often these authors from a peasant background use literary or linguistic devices recognizable to the peasant audience as belonging to the oral tradition of story-telling. This is indicative of the lasting effects of the movement away from urban sensibilities and European influences which took place at the end of the late May Fourth period.

Since the Great Proletarian Cultural Revolution commenced in 1965, only Hao Ran has given some evidence of hopeful possibilities for *professional* writers to continue the process of developing revolutionary literature to higher levels of integration between revolutionary content and effective artistic form. Many of the best revolutionary writers from the late May Fourth period stopped writing creative works before or during the Civil War between the CCP and Guomindang of 1946-49. Several others continued to write up until the Anti-Rightist campaign of 1957 and then stopped. Virtually none of them have published anything since the Cultural Revolution.

There is a tension in all societies centering around the role of intellectuals. In the case of revolutionary China, this tension has been quite apparent since 1949. China has gone further than most societies in seeking to integrate the intelligentsia with the masses and in denying any privileged forum from which intellectuals and writers are allowed to criticize their society with more immunity than is possessed by other members of the society. Whatever our sympathy or antipathy for China's policies toward intellectuals and artists (especially writers), we should not ignore the existence of a contradiction between writing and promoting literature aimed at raising the ideological confidence, political consciousness and cultural level of the formerly disadvantaged minority versus writing and promoting literature characterized by the most sophisticated expression of the individual writer's innermost insights, personality, personal and political values.

In any overtly politicized state such as China, where governmental or Party policies will have a large degree of control over what is to be published, it is nonetheless difficult to completely control the production of literature. Too much control leads inexorably to formulaic works entirely too predictable and schematic to have much impact. This has been a big problem in China and continues to be one. On the other hand, we must recognize the revolutionary logic and potential impact of China's choice, one which has been to stress increased participation of ordinary people in the creation and appreciation of art and literature and to seek to "de-professionalize" the production of art and literature as much as possible.

As for what the future will hold, we do not know. There probably are unknown writers currently producing highly interesting and artistically advanced works of revolutionary literature in China of which we are still unaware. Such works may be lying in manuscript awaiting the day when they can be brought out for publication. That time may not arrive for another ten to twenty years until a whole new generation of Chinese workers and peasants has grown up with all the cultural advantages and higher educational level which the new socialist system is doing its best to provide. The multitude of contradictions in Chinese society between new and old, popularization vs. quality, criticism vs. praise will continue to exist and to be discussed as long as the Chinese Revolution retains its vitality. The Chinese themselves are the first to point out these difficulties. It is this continuing dynamism in areas other than the immediate sphere of literary production that leads one to hope that some of the problems can be resolved on a higher plane of literary quality.

March 1976

EDITORS' POSTSCRIPT

Although the analysis of non-Western cultures has long been neglected in the United States, in the field of Chinese literature there have been some hopeful signs in recent years that the study of twentieth-century Chinese literature is finally coming into its own. There have been only a handful of scholars in Europe, the English-speaking countries, the Soviet Union and Japan during the past fifty years willing and able to combine their erudition in the field of classical and pre-modern Chinese literature with an interest in the development of modern Chinese revolutionary literature. All of the younger scholars, teachers and researchers interested in twentieth-century Chinese fiction are in their debt, not to mention our indebtedness to the many Chinese scholars who have provided insights into various aspects of modern Chinese letters.

One exciting step forward came in August 1974, when a two-week workshop on modern Chinese literature was convened at Harvard University, followed by a one-week conference on "The Role of the Writer and the Evolution of Literature in Modern China," with more than fifty scholars from around the world participating. It was at that time that our long-held desire to contribute something from the realm of art and literature to the *Bulletin* finally took shape and commitments for translations were obtained. We would like to thank all those contributors who have made this special issue possible, with a special word of thanks to Jon Livingston, Steve Andors, Christine White, and Howard Goldblatt for all their assistance, criticism and encouragement.

Introduction to Zhou Shou-juan's "We Shall Meet Again" and Two Denunciations of this Type of Story

The May Fourth movement marked the beginning of the most important effort in modern China to build a new society by writing "new literature." But it was not the first such effort. In the early 20th century progressive young Chinese in Shanghai and Japan, hoping to make China as strong as the Western nations, had already reached the conclusion that the key to this effort was "new fiction." Their leading journal was called, in fact, *New Fiction,* and its editor, Liang Qi-chao (Liang Ch'i-ch'ao), explained in Issue One, 1902, that new citizenship, new morality, new religion, new government, new customs, new art, and new personal character all depend on new fiction. "If we wish today to improve order among the masses," he wrote, "we must begin with a revolution in the realm of fiction." *

Liang's audience was small, but its response enthusiastic. Half a dozen new fiction magazines soon appeared in Shanghai carrying stories which upheld the social idealism of the new reformers. There were translations from Western literature as well as original creations. Qian Xing-cun (A Ying), in his *History of Late-Qing Fiction,* distinguishes seven categories among the progressive themes of the time: the national revolution movement, the debate over constitutionalism, the movement to liberate women, the anti-superstition movement, the exposure of official corruption, the industrial and commercial struggle and opposition to the comprador class, and the movement to oppose the American exclusion acts. In many ways it was as if the May Fourth movement had appeared fifteen years earlier. Except for translations, almost all the new fiction was in *bai hua* vernacular syntax as opposed to classical syntax, though without the pronounced Western influence of May Fourth *bai hua. Bai hua* newspapers appeared, as did *bai hua* poetry, and hopes were high that this new vernacular writing would penetrate and help remould all of China.

But the late-Qing progressivism in literature quickly degenerated, which is why China's modern literary revolution is generally marked from the May Fourth period rather than from 1902. By the mid-'teens, the overwhelming emphasis of the new fiction had become entertainment. Love stories and scandal stories predominated, and the urge to use *bai hua* lost its vigor. "Progressive" elements were still included in many stories, but now more as a matter of form, or even as a stylish gimmick, than because of genuine interest in progress.

There were several reasons for late-Qing fiction's decline. First, the idea that vernacular fiction should be progressive or morally uplifting did not rest well with traditional assumptions. Fiction reading had always been viewed purely as entertainment, and often, especially among the elite, as less-than-healthy entertainment. Men read fiction in private, while women, if they read at all, would hide books under their pillows and never admit to reading. In the 'teens, the tendency to view fiction as mere entertainment was intensified by the particular historical dilemma of the group of authors who found themselves in Shanghai writing fiction. They were almost entirely from inland gentry backgrounds and were well educated. But their standard route to success had been cut off with the abolition of the civil service examinations. With few exceptions, they also failed to attain position or recognition under the new system of the Republican regime. Thus their pursuit of fiction often carried the hint of sour grapes, as they withdrew to the security of the attitude that life is just a game. They were confirmed in their pursuit of fun by the fact that they could be paid for it. Beginning around 1900, Shanghai publishers offered fixed rates (usually 2 yuan per thousand characters) for fiction manuscripts, and as modern printing and distribution methods spread, fiction became a substantial commercial commodity.

The 'teens readership of entertainment fiction resembled its authors in certain essential respects. Many were migrants to the city who held positions of marginal power in the semi-Westernized "modernizing" environment. They included clerks, shop assistants, students of the "new-style" schools, secretaries, petty bureaucrats, and so on. Like the authors, they were separated from their traditional bearings and insecure with their new ones. China's national crisis, life in the industrializing city, the pressure to adopt Western ways—it was too much. They needed escape, and that is what entertainment fiction provided.

The Industrial Revolution in the West had also been accompanied by the rise of "bourgeois" entertainment fiction.

---

* "On the Relationship of Fiction and the National Sovereignty," *New Fiction,* vol. I, No. 1.

Historians of Western culture often point out that sentimental love stories–such as Samuel Richardson's novels in 18th century England–typify the first stage in the emergence of new urban bourgeoisies. Shanghai entertainment fiction fits this pattern. Though there were several kinds–love stories, social-portrait stories, scandal stories, detective stories, righteous-hero stories, and many other kinds–the first and biggest hit was made by highly sentimental love stories.

The love stories swelled into a modern popularity "wave" in the mid-'teens, but they drew upon literary forms and themes which certainly were not new. Many were in classical style and made liberal use of *jueju* poetry. Others were in a mixture of styles based on vernacular and storytelling forms. All made great use of parallelism of words, of phrases, and of ideas which reflected the balanced reciprocity of the romantic relationship between lovers. Though a few of the leading stories which sparked the wave were done with considerable artistry, the flood of imitations which followed–literally thousands of stories–fell into a small number of very hackneyed patterns. The main type was "sad ending" romances, and they were clearly labeled as such so that a reader could know in advance what was in store.

When the young May Fourth writers appeared on the scene they revived the effort to build a strong and healthy

China by renovating its literature. This required that they oppose themselves most vigorously to the love stories and the other popular fiction which had grown up in leading cities. Such fiction commanded the interest of the bulk of the modern readership–and thus blocked May Fourth's access to the very people they hoped to reach and inspire with their own vital message. And not only did they block the way, they did active harm by lulling readers into a feeling of ease and escape right at a time when China's plight was so urgent. The popular stories upheld traditional morality, in fact often were object lessons in chastity, filial piety, continence, and other traditional virtues which the May Fourth generation saw as part of the reason for China's weakness. The old morality would have to be seriously re-evaluated, in their view, and its literary apologists, including the love story authors of the 'teens, would have to be replaced.

Accordingly, they launched a campaign. May Fourth journals of the early 'twenties, especially *The Literary Thrice-monthly* (Wenxue Xunkan), published a welter of short critical pieces lambasting the popular writers of the 'teens. Zheng Zhen-duo and Mao Dun led the way, but Lu Xun, Ye Shao-jun, Guo Mo-ruo, Ba Jin, and many others ignored whatever factional differences lay among them to join this cause. Borrowing symbols which the popular writers often used to describe pairs of lovers, May Fourth writers satirized them as the "Mandarin Duck and Butterfly School," a label which survives to the present day. In spite of the May Fourth attack, though, the fiction continued to survive, and so did its name. One finds it serialized in newspapers throughout the 'thirties and 'forties, and it is read even to the present day among Chinese outside the People's Republic.

The love story "Till We Meet Again" which is translated below was written in 1914 by Zhou Shou-juan, one of the most prolific writers of the 'teens and 'twenties. It was published in *The Saturday Magazine* (Libailiu), a leading organ of entertainment fiction which was named after *The Saturday Evening Post*. The story may in many ways be taken as typical of the highly sentimental love stories of the 'teens. It is a "sad ending" story, and it presents an object lesson in filial piety. It is unrepresentative in only one major respect, namely that the male lover is a foreigner. Precisely this element, though, graphically illustrates in this story an important underlying theme which runs through almost all the popular urban fiction of the 'teens and 'twenties. This theme is resistance to Western culture. Westernization is considered stylish in many superficial ways in the fiction–such as in shaking hands, using English phrases, etc.–but is firmly rejected at a deeper level, where such things as marriage and filial piety are at stake.

The two pieces which follow the story are examples of the May Fourth writers' attack on the popular urban fiction of the 'teens. The first is by Ye Sheng-tao, who himself had contributed to popular love story magazines in the mid-'teens. By 1921, Ye has wholeheartedly joined the new ranks of May Fourth; his attack singles out *The Saturday Magazine*, but also, because of his first-hand experience with such fiction, shows an appreciation for the nature of its appeal and for the steps required to struggle against it. The second piece is by the distinguished litterateur Zheng Zhen-duo. Written when he was only 22, Zheng's attack is more in the nature of an impassioned outcry.

Perry Link

We Shall Meet Again

By Zhou Shou-juan

translated by Perry Link

It was the last day in September, and the autumn leaves had turned red as the rosy clouds of dawn. The rays of the setting sun still illuminated the glittering evening landscape. As Marshall Freeman walked slowly out of the British consular offices, he raised his head for a look at the beautiful sky. Then, heaving a sigh, he stepped into a horse carriage; the driver cracked his whip, and the carriage rumbled off.

This Marshall Freeman was originally a Londoner, and was about twenty-six or twenty-seven years old. He was slender, handsome, and quite a beau. Ten years ago he had received a bachelor's degree from Oxford University. In 1900 he began serving as a clerk in the British Legation at Peking, and had been transferred to Shanghai as Secretary of the Consular Offices. The Consul thought very highly of him. He used him as his right-hand man, and would never be without him. And Freeman certainly did work hard—365 days a year without a miss. He left home every morning at eight on the wings of the morning sun, and returned only with the setting sun at five in the evening.

On his way home every day he passed through a park, where, every time he passed by, a Chinese girl of about seventeen or eighteen years could be seen leaning gracefully on her beautiful snow-white arms against the green railing of the park's sundeck. Her pair of eyes shone down like two clear little streamlets, and the corners of her mouth betrayed the hint of a smile. At first Marshall thought nothing of it. But later he saw that it was the same every day: passing by in the morning, there was always the delicate image of a beautiful woman in the morning sunlight, and at dusk, passing by in the shadows of the setting sun, the same figure was there, leaning against the railing. The same two bewitching eyes shone down like lightning, seeming to fix upon his own person. Freeman began to realize she was watching him in particular, and every day as he passed by, would regularly deliver her a glance toward the sundeck. From then on, the light of those two pair of eyes—one gazing warmly down, one glancing excitedly

up—never failed to meet twice a day. It was as if they had concluded a secret pact.

Before long it actually seemed as if they had known one another for years. When Freeman passed by, it became standard practice for him to tip his hat toward the sundeck, and from the sundeck a happy laugh would answer. The flow of their feelings could find expression only in this wordless exchange. Only their four eyes could convey their thoughts. The impulsive hand of Heaven had brought them together.

One day in his comings and goings, Freeman happened to walk through the Chinese park. Striding in and taking a look around, he saw an exquisitely beautiful Chinese girl walking smoothly and gently toward him. He thought he recognized her lovely face. And indeed, it was none other than the girl who leaned on the railing every day and favored him with glances. Marshall Freeman removed his hat, took one step forward, and eagerly blurted out the word "Miss . . ." The girl's cheeks flushed and two dimples appeared; she lightly brushed her hand past the side of her head and smiled. The two of them then sat down on a bench at the side of the walk and fell into earnest and intimate conversation.

The girl could handle English surprisingly well. Her words flowed, as water from a vase, with perfect ease. She originally was from Panyu in Guangdong Province, and her name was Hua Guifang. She had gone to missionary schools since she was little, which accounted for the splendid condition of her English. Her father had been killed by foreigners during the trouble in Peking in 1900. Her mother, grief-stricken, had herself fallen ill and died shortly thereafter. What a pity! This poor little orphan girl was left all alone in the world to fend for herself. Luckily she had an uncle to take care of her. He brought her to Shanghai and, using some inheritances they had, was able to secure a fine large house in a peaceful location. There they lived together, passing the months and years in calm repose. The only problem was that she had grown up now, and had not married. The human being is a sentimental creature, and there could be no denying her infatuation with youth.

The two of them chatted for a good while, and with perfect ease. They seemed like old friends. Not until the last glow of the day had faded from the west, and the new moon had risen in the east, did they manage, with the greatest of reluctance, to clasp hands and say good-bye. Before they separated, those two pairs of eyes met repeatedly in direct exchange.

The next day when Marshall Freeman emerged from the consular offices and walked to the Chinese park, he did not raise his head toward the sundeck. Instead he proceeded directly to the gate and entered it. The shining knight from outside had become the honored guest of within. From that time on he made it a point to enter the park every day. Now strolling arm in arm, now standing together beneath the flowers, the two of them had soon fallen irrevocably, head-over-heels in love.

One day he rode in his horse carriage to the girl's house. The carriage stopped in front of the garden, and he rushed inside, sitting down in an easy chair which had been placed inside an elegant little room. As he removed a letter from his pocket and began to read it, he raised his voice to call, "Guifang! Guifang! Where are you?" In a twinkling, the gentle footsteps of the young beauty came from behind a painted screen. In her dainty hands she held a bouquet of voluptuously brilliant red hibiscus flowers. Her face and the flowers each mirrored the other's luster. Her alluring eyes glanced quickly toward Marshall Freeman, and in a tender voice she murmured, "Ah! You've come! I was just in the back garden picking a few hibiscuses to put into this jade vase to brighten up the room. I'm only sorry to have kept you waiting so long."

"I just arrived," answered Freeman, and for a moment went on reading his letter. Guifang went over to a table to take care of the flowers. Suddenly Freeman spoke up again. "Guifang, guess what. Our Foreign Office is calling me back to England." When Guifang heard this the hibiscus flowers in her hand fell like a vermillion rain helter-skelter to the floor. Her eyes fixed themselves on Freeman and she asked in amazement, "What? You're going to leave? Go away from Shanghai?"

"That's right," said Freeman. "I have to go back to London, Guifang . . . London . . . Guifang . . ." His voice trailed off. Bending her willowy waist, Guifang silently stooped to retrieve the flowers from the floor. Glistening tears welled up in her eyes and nearly overflowed. Freeman stole a glance at her. "Guifang, come here," he said. Guifang hurriedly took the hibiscus flowers and walked over to sit beside Freeman. Her slender fingers played gently through his hair.

Freeman spoke softly. "When I go, why don't you come with me?" As he said it he took a hibiscus blossom from Guifang's hand and pinned it to her collar. But seeming not to notice, Guifang's brow wrinkled into a worried frown.

"It just isn't possible," she said. "I cannot go with you."

"But how can I leave you?" asked Freeman.

"And how could I wish to leave *you*?" Guifang sadly answered. "I would love to go with you, and be together everywhere. But I do not, alas, have this freedom. I have to obey the word of my uncle."

"But you're almost my wife by now," said Freeman.

"You must come with me. Besides, you're grown up now, and ought to be entirely free. Why must you listen to your uncle?"

Guifang sighed. "You don't know about our Chinese customs. They're very different from yours in England. Here women are not free at any time in their lives. In addition to that, both my parents died suddenly, and luckily I had an uncle to take care of me and keep me from wandering loose in the world. I was like a little bird and he like a great tree in whose branches I found many years of protection. Now that the little bird has grown its feathers, do you think it can simply be rid of the big tree, spread its wings and fly away?"

Freeman sat in silence for several moments, then spoke. "Guifang, other than you, there is no one else in my heart. You are a most adorable and tender woman. I want to be with you my whole life, till our hair turns white together. My love, when we go back to London we can have so many happy days!"

Guifang leaned away ever so slightly, looked at Freeman, and sadly replied, "My uncle will never permit it. He will never permit it."

"Guifang, you mustn't refuse this request of mine," said Freeman. "Do you mean to say the half year of our love now counts for nothing?"

Guifang hid her face. "You must pity me, and forgive me. I am beholden to my uncle."

"All right, what you mean to say is that you really don't love me?" said Freeman, angering.

"My love," said Guifang, removing her hands from her face, "how could I not love you? Oh how I wish we could always be together, wherever in Heaven or Earth that might be, never parting no matter what. If I could only dig out this heart of mine and let you see it! Please, you must never say that kind of thing again! It tears my heart to pieces."

By now it was already dark. The moonlight shone in like a stream of mercury on this woebegone young couple, who sat in silence with tears in their eyes. After some time Freeman finally rose and said, "Dear one, our love will never die. Try to rest a bit, and don't feel so painfully sad. I must go now; let's see how things seem tomorrow." As he said it he put his arms around her willowy waist and ever so sweetly kissed her cherry-red lips. He then left the house and wound his way along a path through the flower garden back to his carriage. Outside the gate he looked back one more time and waved his hand. Guifang bowed in return and called out, "See you tomorrow. See you tomorrow."

After Freeman had left, Guifang stood preoccupied for several moments, then quietly turned and stepped inside. Three minutes later a man of about fifty years walked slowly through the flower garden and into the house. He had a greying head of hair and a few tufts of a grey moustache. As soon as Guifang saw him she called out, "Uncle! You're back!" She hastily poured a cup of tea and offered it to him in her two hands.

Her uncle glanced at her and said, "Did that foreigner come today?"

"Yes," replied Guifang, "Freeman has already been here."

"Does he treat you well?" asked the uncle.

Guifang lowered her head and blushed profusely. "He treats me very well, Uncle," she replied.

Her uncle sipped his tea and heaved a sigh. "I ran into him just now, and for the first time got a clear look at his face.

I must tell you a story.

"Seven or eight years ago there was a wealthy merchant from Panyu in Guangdong who, accompanied by his wife and daughter and an elder brother, went into business at Peking. He was doing very well. Who would have known that the Boxer bandits would cause trouble? Killing foreigners left and right, bringing the great city of Peking to a boiling point of confusion? Before long, the foreign countries sent troops to Peking, and there is no telling how many good, innocent people died in their line of fire. A pity it was that that wealthy merchant also could not escape this ill fortune. One day, when he was passing in front of the British Legation with his brother, he was shot to death by a foreigner with a pistol. Fortunately, his brother was quick and slipped away. . ."

"Uncle!" Guifang urgently broke in, "Aren't you talking about yourself and my father?"

"I am indeed," replied the uncle. "And although I slipped away at the time, I got a very good look at that foreigner's features. I swore on the spot that in the future I would find this enemy and avenge my brother. Haven't you also clenched your teeth in hatred whenever I've spoken of this foreigner in the past?"

"Yes, I have," answered Guifang, "and if I ever meet this enemy, I am ready to plunge a knife into his chest to balance this irrevocable account."

Her uncle smiled. "My dear," he said, "things are looking good. The Lord of Heaven has probably taken pity seeing us here, and so has caused that enemy to fall into our hands—to fall, in fact, right into your hands."

"Uncle! What do you mean by that?!" asked Guifang, greatly startled.

"Guifang," said the uncle, "today I have found the man who killed your father."

"Really?" cried Guifang excitedly.

"Yes. And now our hidden desire of ten years' standing can be fulfilled at a single stroke. The enemy is none other than that foreign sweetheart of yours."

The words shocked Guifang. She reeled backwards a step. "What? How can he be my enemy?"

"No doubt about it, " said her uncle. "Your sweetheart is your enemy."

"It can't be true! He is a warm and charitable person. How could he ever kill a person?"

The uncle leaned forward and stared at his niece. He spoke angrily. "Well, then, I suppose you're forgetting about your father for the sake of a foreigner? And forgetting about the oath of revenge you once took? Forgetting about your father's tragic end?"

"How dare I forget?" Guifang's voice trembled.

"Your father in his grave would be pleased that you have not forgotten," her uncle said. "And now I must say one more thing to you: Marshall Freeman is the villain who killed your father, so tomorrow you must put him to death to fulfill your duty as a daughter."

Guifang listened without a word. One saw only a twist of her lithe body as she flew like a swallow to kneel before her uncle. She raised her ashen face and cried mournfully, "Uncle! Oh, Uncle! How could I do it?! How could I kill Marshall Freeman?"

"Guifang," the uncle solemnly replied, "you must remember your father did not have a big family, but had only you. If you do not avenge his death, who will? If you want to be a filial daughter, you must put his soul at ease. How can you cast aside your father's revenge for the sake of some childish infatuation?"

As he spoke, the uncle searched in his vest for a medicine bottle, which he handed to his niece. "Just put a few drops of this in his tea. He will pass away in a deep sleep, without the least bit of suffering. It will be much less painful than your father's death."

Guifang extended her two arms toward her uncle, beseeching him. "How can I be such an assassin? We have been so deeply in love these days, and he has never directed the slightest harsh word or deed toward me. Tender in every way, considerate beyond all else—and if the slightest unhappiness ever showed on my face, he was right there with a soft voice to comfort me. Uncle, I really love him. We may not be married, but our love is even deeper and richer than married people's. For the past half year he has been as close to me as the pupils of my eyes and the blood of my heart. My first thought upon rising in the morning is of Marshall, my beloved. My last thought upon retiring at night is likewise always of Marshall. And now you want me to kill him. Uncle! How can a little girl like me be as cold and fierce as that? He is my sweetheart, and my husband of the future. Uncle, you must take pity on me."

Her uncle stood up, trembling with rage. Grasping Guifang's arm, he shouted, "Don't forget you're Chinese, little girl! You must obey your elders like it or not. Tomorrow you must send him to his death!" Having spoken, he released her arm.

Guifang stared in disbelief. Her head was spinning and her heart breaking. After a moment she slowly raised her head and spoke. "Uncle," she said, "is it possible you mistook him? Perhaps he is not really the villain who killed my father?"

"The image of that face," her uncle answered, "has been deeply engraved in my memory for seven or eight years now. How could I mistake it? I began suspecting the connection a month or two ago. Then tonight, with the moonlight so bright, I got an extremely clear look at him. There is no doubt he's the one. If you don't believe it, tomorrow you can draw him into conversation and find out for yourself. If he is *not* the one who killed your father, then of course I have nothing more to say. But if he really is the one, you must pay attention to your duties as a daughter."

"If it turns out he killed my father," said Guifang, "then I naturally have no choice but to avenge my father. But then, my filial duty will be completed, and I may follow him along the same road."

"My child, listen to me," said the uncle. "He may die but you may not. He must walk the road to death alone. You may not accompany him. Your father would certainly not approve of your dying. You are a filial daughter, and you must be thoughtful of your father's departed spirit. Tomorrow at six in the evening I will be waiting for you in the park. As soon as he's dead, come look for me. I will bless you before Heaven and ensure your success. Good night." Her uncle left the room as he spoke.

Guifang lay on the floor and covered her face. There she sobbed softly until dawn, by which time her tears had run dry and her heart was in shreds. She lived through the next day only with the greatest difficulty, shedding goodness knows how many more tears.

At five o'clock Marshall Freeman arrived in high spirits. When he saw his favorite kneeling on the floor, covering her face and apparently in tears, he rushed over and took her in his arms. As they moved to a couch, he caressed her and tenderly enquired, "Precious one, what is wrong? Tell me! What is it?"

Guifang sat rigidly without responding. She softly tilted her head to rest on Freeman's shoulder. Teardrops streamed down her cheeks. Freeman was perplexed. He couldn't imagine what to think. All he could do was to keep kissing her neck and collar. After a moment Guifang finally parted her sweet lips to speak. "My dear one," she said, "we have loved one another all together six months now. Have I made you happy?"

Freeman laughed. "Of course you have, dear one, of course you have! Before I met you I did not know what love was. From the time I saw you, I began to fall gradually deeper and deeper in love, and by now I feel myself to be the most fortunate person in the world. Every day when the consular offices close, I can come to this heavenly place, link arms with my love, pour out my heart, and enjoy a warm and tender reception." As he spoke he held up Guifang's face in his hands. Then he went on. "My Guifang, you are my one and only love in the whole world. Do you love me, too?"

"We Chinese girls do not know of such things as to 'love' or not," she answered, "so I cannot really say whether I love you or not. All I know is that in the daytime my thoughts always turn to you, and at night you always appear in my dreams; when you hold me in your arms and keep calling 'My Guifang, my love,' I feel indescribably happy. All this, dear one, probably amounts to saying I love you." Freeman continued kissing her silken black hair, but said nothing. He was extremely satisfied.

After a few moments Guifang suddenly asked him, "Were you still at home in England seven or eight years ago?"

"No," said Freeman, "I was already in China then, working as a clerk at the British Legation in Peking."

"That was around 1900," said Guifang, "when the Boxer bandits rose up in China and opposed themselves to you foreigners. The whole splendid and brilliant city of Peking was reduced to tatters and rubble. Were you frightened then?"

"I was only a bit afraid," Freeman explained. "At the time I was young and arrogant, and I hated those Boxers to the marrow of my bones. One day when I was busy in the Legation there came a great din from outside the door. There was a cry that the Boxers had come to attack the Legation. I was uncontrollably angry, grabbed a pistol, leaped out the door, and fired several shots in a row. I did manage to scare off the Boxers. But, when we inspected the damage, not one Boxer had died. It appeared that none had even been injured. But several innocent bystanders had been. There was a man who looked like a merchant of about 40 whom I had killed. To this day I am still tormented by the memory."

Guifang heaved a sigh. "You really did kill that merchant?"

"It was just the hastiness of a moment," said Freeman. "By now there's no point in speaking further of it."

Guifang's head was resting on Freeman's knee. She pulled from her collar the hibiscus flower which had been pinned there, plucked it apart petal by petal, and threw the remains on the floor. She was silent for a long time, then rose and said, "Please wait a moment. I will go make a cup of coffee for you."

She took several steps, then suddenly stood still. She returned to Freeman's side and said, "Please tell me again that you love me, that you never want to leave me. Please, dear one, take me in your arms and say 'My Guifang, my love.' "

Freeman was still unaware of what was going on. He just pulled her towards himself, kissed her all over, and said, "Dear one, my love, what is troubling you? Of course I love you with all my heart. I care for absolutely no one else. Don't cry. Wipe

your tears and go make that coffee." And so saying, he kissed her once on the lips.

Guifang walked as far as the painted screen, then quickly turned once more and came back to kneel before the couch. "Sir," she said in a mournful voice, "whatever may happen to you, you must always forgive me, and always think of my feelings for you. I will always love you. I am willing even to sacrifice my life in this world for you. If you should go to the ends of the earth, I will follow you to the ends of the earth. I would never let you go by yourself, lonely and without a companion." Covering her pretty face with her hands, she knelt there perfectly motionless.

Freeman was most surprised to see her this way. But he still did not understand. He could only imagine it was because of the previous day's talk about returning to England. Feeling depressed at this, he once again held Guifang's face in his hands, smiled, kissed her, and said, "Dear one, all of this is a simple matter. Of course I will bring you along wherever I go. I may lose every one of my possessions, but I will never spend a single day out of sight of my Guifang." Guifang stood several moments in a daze next to the couch, then moved daintily across the room to disappear behind the screen.

Before long she returned with a tea tray. Hesitating a moment, she then held out a cup of coffee for Freeman, her hand trembling. "Dear sir, a cup of coffee for you," she said.

"Thank you, my love," answered Freeman with a smile. Raising the cup to his lips, he drank until it was dry. When he was finished he fell with a thud back onto the couch, as the cup fell to the floor and shattered. Guifang stood staring at her sweetheart with tear-filled eyes. Then she slowly stretched her neck down to give him one final kiss. Kneeling on the floor, her utterly despondent voice cried out in spine-chilling lament, "Dear sir! Till we meet again!"

(From *The Saturday Magazine*, No. 3, June 20, 1914)

People Who Insult People

By Ye Sheng-tao

translated by Perry Link

In recent issues, Shanghai newspapers have been carrying an advertisement which grieves me deeply, and I imagine there must be a lot of people who feel as I do. I almost couldn't believe my eyes at this advertisement, but there it was—unmistakably written in big, clear characters. It read: "I'd rather not take a concubine / Than to miss out on reading *The Saturday Magazine*." Below this was a list of *The Saturday Magazine*'s current contents. Every time they run an ad, they open it with a ditty which is enough to leave one sick at heart and full of pity—this time it was just particularly bad, that's

all. I wonder if they're going to think of something even worse in the future.

This really is an insult—a wide-ranging insult. They insult themselves, insult literature, and what's worse, insult others! I have never berated them before; but now, with this latest move, I have no choice but to berate them. No kind of game-playing has ever been as debased as this; even when playing games one should keep things on a fairly high plane and be sincere! But now we have people who write catchwords like this—and many people in society who absorb them—so that the same type of lines appear each week in the newspapers. This not only leaves the future of literature uncertain and worrisome; it actually leaves the whole advancement of the Chinese nation uncertain and worrisome.

Yet we hold the following as an item of faith: only literature has the power to serve as the tie which binds together the best in the human spirit, which unites countless small and weak consciousnesses together into one great consciousness. It can expose the darkness, usher in light, and lead people to abandon their mean and shallow side in favor of more honorable and profound tendencies. How can we let its future fall subject to uncertainty and worry?

There are really very few people in China who have contact with literary art. Our hope naturally must be to find a way gradually to increase their numbers. But even among this minority which does have contact with literary art, people lack the power of discrimination, and cannot understand the true nature of the things which appeal to them. Here our hope naturally must be to provide them the power of discrimination, that they may realize the nature of literary art. But can the current new literature movement extend its influence to those who have never been in contact with literary art? And can it make those who have taken the wrong path discern their own true and proper tendencies? We have no choice but to postulate an answer of "yes" to these questions. Leaving aside those who have never been in contact with literary art, some of those who have taken the wrong path have developed a weakness for doing so, and of course will continue in their ways. Good and proper material is also extremely scarce, and extremely weak in its impact, while bad and absurd writing grabs the opportunity to rise with continuing demand. Good and proper works really are too few: aside from a few magazines and collections of reprinted works, what else is there?

When we see the kind of advertisement I have described above, we must not be merely grieved. We should be all the more industrious. Naturally, we must first fix our sights upon the people who have had contact with literature. Their tastes have gone awry, and they haven't realized it; it has become a habit with them to mistake wrong for right; and they often don't want anything to do with our so-called real literature. We must break down this barrier before anything else. Accordingly, we should examine and consider what points we might adopt from them; and only then proceed with writing stories. This is not to say we should grope blindly or stoop to their level, but just, as the saying goes, "provide judicious guidance according to the circumstances"—which in fact will be stinging satire and proper correction. When they have experienced the new literature, and have found it to be not unappealing, they will experience it more and more, their feelings will gradually change without their noticing it, and they will embark upon the new road. It is extremely important that we now pay attention to these factors. And the number of people working in literature must be increased as much as possible. Only then will we be able to enlarge the scope of the literary realm and supply ordinary readers with their literary fare.

I believe that the day will come when the kind of advertisement I have described above will completely disappear. How soon that time comes will depend upon the degree to which we exert ourselves.

(From *The Literary Thrice-Monthly*, No. 5, June 20, 1921)

A Literature of Blood and Tears

By Zheng Zhen-duo

translated by Perry Link

Don't we now need a literature of blood and a literature of tears more than works which are "stately and graceful" or which "sing to the wind and moan to the moon"? To be sure, "stately and graceful" and "moan to the moon" works can comfort our troubled souls and frustrated spirits with the beauty of nature. But in this world overgrown with thorns, full of tragedy, where rifles bark and cannons fire, I'm afraid our disturbed souls and frustrated spirits are not things which can be so easily comforted. And how are we to put up with the comforting? Satan's arrows day by day are shooting down our brethren, and the god of war intones his war cry ceaselessly. The gunfire at Wuchang, rifle muzzles on the passenger coaches at the Xiaogan railway station, the bloodstains outside the Xinhua gate ... have we forgotten? Even a heartless person would find it hard to forget! Even people with blood frozen solid would find it hard to forget! Shall we be "stately and graceful"? I'm afraid that's impossible!

Yet there actually are those who can somehow manage it: they rattle on about pure art, plagiarize a few bits of new terminology, and continually turn out vernacular Mandarin Duck and Butterfly style love stories and sentimental poems. Or they call for drawing close to nature, and pile up words about the clouds, the moon, the tree shadows, the gleaming mountains. Their "imperturbability" goes beyond even that of Confucius and Mencius. Fires of the revolution, burn, burn! Fire of youth, go ahead and burn! The disturbed souls have boiled over, and the frustrated spirits have burst at the seams. Brothers! Are we really unperturbed? Remember! Remember! What we need is a literature of blood and a literature of tears, not those cold-blooded products which are "stately and elegant" or "sing to the wind and moan to the moon."

(From *The Literary Thrice-Monthly*, no. 6, June 30, 1921)

Introduction to Ye Sheng-tao's "On the Bridge"

Fiction in 20th century China has had a turbulent course, marked by the brief or discontinuous careers of prominent authors. Some became famous, then wrote little new because the times had passed them by (Zeng Pu) or they seemed to lose interest (Yu Da-fu); they died of overwork (Lu Xun), were executed (Rou Shi) or compelled to stop by illness (Zhang Tian-yi). The profession was poorly paid and often politically dangerous. It was difficult, even with the determination to proceed in the face of enormous swift changes in China's social order, to feel that from one decade to the next one still understood and still had something to say.

Ye Shao-jun (1894-   ), also known since the '30s as Ye Sheng-tao, is unusual for the length of his creative career, which spanned the three decades that led to the founding of the People's Republic in 1949. Educator, essayist, author of one novel and initiator of children's literature in China, his preferred genre was the dominant one of the May Fourth period—the vernacular short story. The volume and the quality of his pieces (there are approximately 100) establish him as a major author, specifically of the '20s and '30s when most of his stories appeared.

Until late 1927, six themes pervade his work: the bourgeois family, the status of women, relations between children and society, the role of the educator, alienation of labour, and the experience of isolation. Though rural life is occasionally and powerfully observed, the majority of protagonists are intellectuals or urban dwellers, often people of modern views, and the world presented in the fiction is largely in relation to their experience. The earlier stories give sympathetic treatment to their views: of the nuclear family as a form of personal liberation and sincere feeling; of nature as a solace for suffering; of the child, symbol of a presocial self, as the hope of humane individual growth unwarped by society; and of education, which is to realize the hope, as the means of peaceful reform of society. These ideals presume a separation of the private and the social spheres. The inadequacy of the conception is clearest in the fate of women: here, the social formation of the individual is seen most directly and brutally, and the pressure to internalize even oppressive social values in order to remain human is almost inescapable.

Between his first two collections of short stories (1922, 1923) and his second two (1925, 1926), Ye Shao-jun's position has shifted. Domestic themes are eclipsed by social; the focus shifts, for example, from the child to the educator. The gap between self and society is now depicted as a socially conditioned *process* ultimately destructive of the personality. The new emphasis is realized in a more sophisticated art: protagonists are more fully and distinctively characterized while society, now shown in terms of struggle rather than the mere juxtaposition of classes, takes on a more complex and differentiated appearance.

With "Ye" (Night) in late 1927, the theme of political struggle becomes paramount. Whether it takes the form of revolution or (in the '30s) of patriotic resistance, the class nature of the goals is never obscured. In addition, a small group of stories focuses directly on the capitalist social order. The familiar themes of family and woman's status get little attention. The significant settings are more often neighborhoods and streets, and a striking use of crowd scenes becomes increasingly common.

The immense distance covered in the corpus of Ye Shao-jun's stories, from the May Fourth Movement to the resistance against Japan, represents the evolution of a Marxist perspective in the midst of fading bourgeois ideals, and of an art adequate to express the new vision of experience. The generally richer and artistically superior quality of the later work is already apparent in the 1925 collection, *Xianxia* (Under the Line), which contains "Qiaoshang" (On the Bridge). This story, from 1923, is an example of the author's transition to the more complex vision; he retains and develops the portrayal of inner life and is already a master of setting that reveals social and psychological conflicts simultaneously. This translation is of the text in *Xianxia* (Shanghai: Commercial Press, 1935)

Donald Holoch

On the Bridge

by Ye Sheng-tao

translated by Donald Holoch

The fan, revolving, made a commotion like a humming mass of bees. The hiss occasionally heard was a waiter in white jacket uncapping a bottle of soda. A record started to play: Maestro Tan, of course, in "The Outlaw's Horse," or Maestro Liu singing "Emperor Beheaded," which were meant for the customers' pleasure; it was natural to cater to their tastes.

The room was the white of snow. A canvas-like awning, unrolled to keep the scorching sun off the street window, and the fan turning so busily gave the entering customers sudden relief for the eyes and the impression that the worst heat of summer was over. Elegantly simple chairs and tables were like marshalled forces; flowers in the vases trembled unceasingly, and the tall glasses reflected a dazzling light.

Quite a few customers were seated in booths: white and black and light red and pale blue dresses; and soft or hard broad-brimmed or high-crowned straw hats, and the exposed but fully powdered arms and the fluffy white feather fans were all quietly slowly swaying in place. Holding a spoon of ice cream in the mouth or sipping liquid through a straw, never glancing aside, they had a certain air of respectability. They spoke softly and laughed with reserve so that nothing would destroy the peace in the room.

Near the wall by the window two men had just taken seats. When the waiter walked over with an expression of readiness, lean Zu-qing, who had taken the best seat, doffed his straw hat and stroking his hair casually said, "Red bean ice, two glasses."

The waiter turned and left.

"We haven't finished talking yet," said Xin-bo, the man in the other seat; his interest was aroused. He had a small round face, the eyes seemed especially small, the eyebrows were light, and the nose was slightly flat which gave the center of his face a comical look; his lips were thin, an indication of skill in argument as they say.

He moved his chair, got a bit closer to his friend and said, "There's just no way! Bian the Fifth is afraid if he gets into the limelight he'll never get out; 'Noble' Nann would love to try, but the public isn't prepared for...."

"I wish you'd use plain language." There was a stern glint in Zu-qing's eye as he contemptuously cut him off. "Where do we get all the time to memorize the rank and order of what bunch, and who goes by what nickname!"

"That's what they're all called, you get used to it without realizing," Xin-bo said by way of excuse.

"What nonsense!" Zu-qing turned his head, withdrawing his gaze from his friend's face. "Even if you didn't call them Fourth, Fifth, Sixth and didn't use their disgusting nicknames, bringing them up as you do isn't reasonable either."

Xin-bo felt slightly uneasy and, wiping his temples with a handkerchief, gingerly said, "Why . . ."

"Such an attitude as yours practically concedes that their behavior is as it should be, that there's no other basic consideration. But let me give you an analogy: We're watching a bunch of robbers break and enter our homes, they grab whatever is there and attack the members of our families. Yet we're on the sidelines discussing how the short robber won't be able to lift the safe and how that tall one already has three bundles on his back. Isn't that the height of stupidity and

21

senselessness? But that's exactly what your attitude is!"

After a pause he went on, "Actually a good many people have such an attitude! What I hate most is those pudding-like newspapers full of articles on the guests 'Taiyuan' received, the activities of so-and-so the Fourth, where Messrs. Pan and Lu went to contact what faction, and that sort of news. Certainly these are all facts, but when they come up there must be at least a glimmer of hostility, a spirit of condemning what's low and contemptible. To put it another way, I mean. . . ."

The waiter bearing two glasses of crushed ice on a small lacquer tray approached the booth of the two men, set the glasses on the table and withdrew with the trace of a bow.

Each man picked up a glistening spoon and stirred the ice chips floating near the top of his glass. Zu-qing continued, "To put it another way, I mean those who speak shouldn't adopt a spectator's view: we should reject them entirely, we should have methods of dealing with them." He began to sip the iced drink as if he had no attention for anything else.

Xin-bo too sipped his drink in silence, then said in self-defense, "Perhaps they can't be rejected. You yourself conceded they are facts, yet you want to reject them. Depart from the facts, and how is it possible even to talk, much less get any practical result?" He forced a smile to conceal that this was meant as a rebuttal.

"Fact doesn't mean sensible! Fact doesn't mean unopposable! The present disease is that these facts can only be seen, there's nothing but talk about these facts."

"Naturally we hope for gradual improvement but present conditions are the necessary basis for it," said Xin-bo, taking the edge off his words.

"'Let the river cleanse itself,' right?" Zu-qing gave a depressed smile and showed, by the lift of his head, that he'd brook no opposition. "Was there ever soapy water could clean out a black dye vat? Did preservative ever make a rotten peach look fresh again? Gradual improvement on the basis of present conditions, why that's strictly a pipe-dream for idiots."

"What about teaching, then, like your profession of teaching?"

"Oh, maybe there's some point to that," Zu-qing replied with displeasure, intent on spooning up the ice and chewing it.

He was thinking, "Even that is too late in a crisis; besides, it's not yet possible to give a verdict on whether teaching can be worthy of the name.—To talk it over with him is fruitless, there's no point in another dreary conversation: why not change the subject." So he said pleasantly, "Why don't we go to the park and sit for a while?"

All that Xin-bo had to say was about to sprout stem and leaf and blossom out when without warning the tender shoots were firmly stamped back by his friend, and there wasn't a hint of any growth; he had a tremendous sense of being stifled or of having lost something. His friend was now inviting him to come to the park and sit for a while, but it held no interest for him and he excused himself, "I have another appointment. We'll stroll through the park some other day."

"Well, then it's goodbye." Zu-qing took out some money and placed it on the table. They walked out of the soda shop into a sudden glare and heat so fierce it felt as if his whole body were distending. Few people were on the street, along which spread an infinite fiery carpet. When a streetcar came along, he watched his short friend hastily waddle off to board it and be submerged in the crowd of passengers.

He thought the park would be no fun; that fruitless vista of animated mannikins in Chinese gowns affectedly swaying by would be sheer boredom. "So home then," and he hopped a streetcar running north.

The streetcar was packed. There was no place for him to sit so he stood with his hand in an overhead leather strap. The odor of pomade from women's hair, the odor of powder unique to Japanese women, the sweat of a fat person, panting of an old one, humming of an opera fan, every kind of noise and stench that filled the car made it seem more cramped than its actual dimensions. He was highly impatient and looked at his fellow passengers in anger.

It was like any other day, of course; what were the faces but glazed, wooden, unreflective, craving some sleep, distinguished only by age and complexion. Every time he took the streetcar he pondered the faces: "You proprietors of these faces, what ideas are going through your heads? Are you aware that in the world there's yourself? Are you aware that beyond yourself there's a world?" Then he answered himself, "They

have no ideas; they're completely unaware; it's as if they're sleeping a sleep where even dreams are blurred." His sympathy was promptly roused: "Pitiable sleeping people! This isn't the proper course for you. Wake up, wake up, all you need to hear is a good loud shout, I'll give one and wake you."

His thoughts having traced the old route and come now to this point, the anger in his look turned to gentleness and his overbearing expression softened. To the passenger pressed tightly up against his back, he humbly yielded a little.

As they passed along a stretch of trees, the sound of cicadas could be heard above the streetcar noise. The many villas, no two alike, standing among the trees, red rooftiles like fish scales, simple white buildings like farmhouses, and swaying flower bushes, rapidly splashing fountains, could all be glimpsed through rifts in the foliage. Now and then proprietors, men of elegant pleasures, were seen strolling under the flowers or, hand on her fully exposed arm, tête-à-tête with a woman.

Watching from the streetcar window, he felt his eyes were more refreshed; but he had other thoughts on his mind beyond savoring the scenery. As the groves raced by and receded he became more immersed in his thoughts, nearly forgetting he was on the car.

Outside the window a great crowd in an uproar obstructed his vision and the streetcar pulled up to its stop. Everyone on it was looking through the windows. A few, with some pushing, hopped off to take a look. Most of the crowd had the appearance of workers, and all were yelling in alarm. The noise was too great to make out distinctly what it was they were shouting. Apparently there was something in their midst which they had encircled, leaving a gap the space of three or four people; those near the center were bent forward looking down, the many standing on the fringes were all concentrating on the center. A fire of a sun shining generously upon them, their worn and dirty black cotton shirts were thoroughly drenched, and on the chests and backs of those stripped to the waist, sweat converged into streaks of water like the course of rivers on a map.

In dismay he thought, "Here's another incident. It can't possibly be anything enjoyable; they might even be up to killing each other off."

Some busybody asked the spectators near the streetcar, "Friends, what's happening here?"

And this is what one man replied: "A bricklayer fell from a three-storey building. They were carrying him to the hospital. They got this far and he breathed his last."

"It's a sin, a sin," exclaimed several women on the car involuntarily clicking their tongues. The male passengers started talking about how in construction of tall modern buildings one or two workmen who were fated to die would run into such bad luck. And one man expounded on the meaning, saying otherwise what would anchor such a tall building in place. It depended on living human souls and blood to anchor it. Once this view was expressed quite a few nodded in approval of it as a novel but valid observation.

The ticketseller, having got the whole story straight and satisfied his usual curiosity, blew the whistle and signaled to start. The crowd and the green trees were already receding when several people caught up and hopped aboard.

"Scary!" a middle-aged man who had just boarded said to himself. "Blood is running out his anus, all his insides were crushed by the fall."

"Where is the three-storey building that he fell from?" a fat man now chose to inquire. Afraid the noise of the car would muffle the other man's reply and make it hard to hear, he drew his massive body a bit closer; in the crowded car everyone inevitably felt the effects of this.

The other man pointed backwards: "It's in that stretch of trees over there, a villa built by the Bian family they say, and there's still work to be done on it. This poor guy was putting the final touches on the balcony, I don't know how he could have fallen."

"Ah, a rich man's villa, a poor man's life!" With this sudden awareness the fat man nodded his large round head and began to ponder.

"They've been building that villa for months and months already," said an old woman with a burst of envy; one could tell from her tone she loved talking about anything and everything. "I recall going by in February, plenty of workmen had put up wood shacks to stay in. Those workmen ate a big pot of rice and drank a big bucket of tea, enough to show that the owner of that villa sure is some millionaire. The best thing in the world is money, people with money can do anything, raise mountains on flat land, build villas in the wilds. Right?" she asked the crowd in general, apparently convinced the crowd couldn't say no.

Listening to the conversation of the crowd, Zu-qing thought, "So it was *his* villa the man was working on. Intentional or not, that bunch always ruined other men's lives!" He became tense, as he always did on the average day when he met something disgusting, then he thought of the lovely pistol at home in the drawer of his desk.

After the downpour there was a pleasant coolness in the courtyard; rattan leaves growing up the walls had been washed a lovely fresh green. As he was staring out the window, he heard someone knock and softly ask, "Zu-qing, are you in?"

The voice was familiar. Without a second thought he knew it was Xiru, answered and promptly opened.

Xiru was wearing a brand new summer long gown of light cotton, but it was quite wrinkled both front and back. He had let his hair grow long and combed it straight back; since he had used no oil it was a rumpled mass. Nor was there anything special about his face except for his sunken eyes and the dark circles around them indicative of a frail constitution. He hadn't much beard, only a few wisps approximately half an inch long on his upper lip. He came in and nodded but said nothing, simply sat in an armchair and looked at a landscape on the wall.

"What's up? Haven't seen you for days, what have you been doing?" Zu-qing also sat down. "Been reading? Painting anything?"

"I haven't done a thing," said Xiru listlessly. "I'm home all day long just sleeping, hearing the long-drawn-out sound of cicadas."

"You're always like this. To my way of thinking such an attitude is useless. Haven't I told you that time and time again?" Zu-qing spoke in earnest.

"I know it too. I want to find some meaning in all things, but in the end the answer is always negative: 'There is no meaning at all.' For sure I haven't fallen short of them, in fact they have disappointed me. I'm afraid of becoming a decadent in my outlook, but they're making me, I can't avoid becoming decadent!"

"And I'm afraid for you, if you do become a decadent. But to judge from my own outlook, I don't think I would ever take this path of yours. From your perspective one might say it's because I can't see through the ultimate veil. However I feel I really don't want to see through that ultimate veil."

Xiru smiled sarcastically; in a while, coldly, he said, "Exactly as you're urging me now, suppose I really did listen to you and changed my former outlook and action, just try to imagine it, what, after all, would it mean to you? And what, after all, would it mean to me? Wouldn't it be the same as if it hadn't happened?—You'd still be the person you are, I'd still be the person I am."

"This is getting metaphysical," Zu-qing gave him a steady look, a severe expression on his thin face. "To a person like me, unable and unwilling to see through the ultimate veil, it is not the same at all. If you were to listen to me, it would give me the satisfaction of progressing a step, expanding the circle, during my lifetime; while you, turning from passive to active, of course would also be oriented toward progress and expansion. Isn't that obviously different from nothing having happened?"

Xiru smiled skeptically. He thought that here was nothing to argue, they differed in what they felt, that was all; other people couldn't force their beliefs upon him any more than he could force his beliefs on anyone else.

"You must realize," Zu-qing went on in a tutorial mode, "I don't always feel happy either, without a trace of heartache, but I'm certainly not decadent. When I don't know where to turn and it looks like my life is a bottle with all the air pumped out, when I encounter some inhuman act and everyone has his hands folded dozing on the sidelines, then I start getting a heartache. That heartache is as unbearable as an arrow in me. Still I don't adopt the poet's style: incessantly drinking hard liquor to dull the spirit, to forget the pain in my heart. The only cure I have for it is that I act! to make the bottle fill up; I shout! to make the dozing men leap up; I go first! to make those coming behind run with a will. I feel *this* is the way to pluck out the arrow. So I . . ."

Xiru examined Zu-qing's face and thought how the air of utter seriousness, the modulated voice were those of an orator from his rostrum. By association, speeches came to mind, namely a primary school literature class, where one time it was "China's undoing is the spread of lethal opium," and next time "China's undoing is the failure of civic conscience," any old nonsense to suit the topic. Then he recalled the mass of foolish listeners, mouths agape, biting their tongues, eyes fixed straight ahead so as not to miss a good look at any gold that might flow from the speaker's mouth. Then he recalled a thunderous burst of applause and couldn't resist clapping derisively.

Zu-qing found this odd and checked his argument to ask, "What are you doing?"

"Nothing. I saw how lovely the rainbow is so I clapped my hands." Xiru was looking through the window at the sky. Painted on the clear pure blue was a half-circle rainbow like the arch of a bridge.

Zu-qing couldn't help his despondent mood, like that of antiquity's lone loyal ministers. He spoke with anxiety, "You're sick of listening to me? You think what I say hasn't the least bit of value?"

"Please don't misunderstand, I don't have any such unpleasant ideas. It's not that I'm sick of listening to you, to

tell the truth, at bottom what I'm sick of is listening to myself; and it's not that what you say hasn't the least bit of value, in fact at bottom I don't understand what value is supposed to be. If you can see that, you know this won't harm our friendship." He rose and looked off in silence at the horizon.

"It won't harm our friendship," Zu-qing declared as well. But he was thinking to himself, "The power of speech is so uncertain! Who is there to speak to—and what is there to say! My only course is be true to my credo and never speak again. But that's not any cause for heartache, I still have reliable authority here! I'll act, I'll shout, I'll go first, with a solid grip on this authority of mine. . . ."

There was an undulating sound, one couldn't tell from what direction, of several cicadas in the trees, far different from the pressing cry during the heat of the day. Neither person said a word.

Thinking of it often, Zu-qing considered this the one thing both necessary and possible for him to do. Convinced that discussion with anyone was quite pointless, he certainly wasn't going to discuss it. When school started after the summer he went back to teaching; he wasn't one to treat the work at hand casually but wanted a drop of flavor from it, so his teaching was devoted.

One morning, the day's paper having arrived, he was leafing through the pages. In the local news column he noticed an item which made his heart skip a beat. The gist of the news item was: "Work has just been completed on Bian the Fifth's new villa. It contains expansive lawns, cool raised pavilions, and man-made waterfalls and streams in a notably tasteful arrangement. An open house and tour is planned for Saturday when guests and friends will view the grounds. There will be a dance that evening. Since yesterday Bian the Fifth with his wife and concubine have been making preparations to entertain their guests on that date."

He thought, "So he's here!—Even he will do. It's not that I particularly hate him. Among that bunch I'll deal with whoever qualifies for punishment and gets close to me."

He had drifted off but was suddenly assailed by doubts: "Can this be done? Isn't it a sin for one man to destroy another? To take it further, am I fit for this? Am I somehow not good enough?"

"Like being haunted!" He lay down the paper in his hand and smiled scornfully, still thinking. "Didn't I think it out definitely long ago? When we destroy flies, destroy mosquitoes, why don't we ask whether or not it's a sin? And the question of fitness, if I'm not fit, then who is? How could it be people who take the chance to get something out of it for themselves? How could it be people who make a living out of *this*? They're definitely unfit to do this, they can only huddle in corners till someone works out a world ready-made and then they emerge to enjoy it in peace and comfort."

Chewing his lower lip in thought, he nodded slightly, showing a certain determination. "No more thinking, it's settled this way," and he began to prepare the day's classes as though a moment ago he'd had nothing on his mind.

That afternoon Xin-bo came looking for him.

Xin-bo mentioned in passing that he would go to the Bian's open house on Saturday; squinting his small eyes he said, "Bian the Fif . . .", suddenly winced and switched to, "His secretary, Mr. Wang, knows me and invited me, so I'll get to look around at the arrangement inside."

"I'll look around too, alright?" Zu-qing asked hopefully.

"Of course it's alright. I'll introduce you to Mr. Wang, and then you'll be equally welcome."

"We'll go together." Zu-qing was extremely happy.

On that Saturday, Zu-qing held his morning classes, then with Xin-bo visited the Bian villa, not leaving until the dance was over. He had a sharp image of the owner's face: notably broad chin, a short clipped mustache, very thick brows, a sparkling light in his eyes; even fatter than in the photographs frequently carried in the papers, as well as more crafty. He tested himself: he concentrated and the face appeared with full clarity in his mind; if he encountered it anywhere, he would instantly know the name of the owner of the face.

"No one knows." Treading the fall evening moonlight, he savored the thought: "Mother doesn't know, kid brother doesn't know, my colleagues don't know and neither do the students; if the chance comes my way I'll do what I hope single-handed.—It doesn't amount to much actually, there's no real need for people to know. When we read a book or write a letter at home, do we make it a point to let people know? This is merely on the level of reading books and writing letters, when you want to, you just do it; it's nothing very rare and nothing to marvel at, so of course you keep quiet."

No one was out on the still street, patrolmen on duty were not in sight, and the rickshaws waiting for their riders at dusk had all left. Moonlight shone on the roadside trees, transforming the leaves, enveloping them in an indescribable radiance as if in a thin ivory-colored veil. The intermittent sound of crickets was like an antiphonal lovesong sung by man and woman across the vast luminous night.

"If he came along at this moment," he stopped in his tracks, looked all around, "how easy it would be. With no commotion, no need to panic others, I could do the thing I intend to do."

He resumed his walk, but as he watched the shortened shadow of himself on the ground, a set of images from thirteen years back appeared in his mind.

He was only sixteen or so at the time, attending middle school. Slogans of nationwide military training were everywhere, gym periods were devoted to platoon drill. The weapons they used weren't bad, Mauser five-round repeaters, which the principal had somehow drawn from the Army Supply Office. But there wasn't a single bullet. When the drillmaster shouted "Ready, aim," and they all raised their weapons, he always had the hollow sensation that this was only a child's game; in merely pulling a trigger with the right index finger and producing a slight abrupt "pop," what was there to savor!

One morning in early winter, the local people opened their doors to see a white band on the arm of each patrolman and a white flag hanging in front of the police station. They asked each other what it was supposed to mean, and the bright ones answered, "This is known as Restoration!"[1] At that everyone was perplexed, feeling that Restoration was like an evil spirit: who could tell what it was going to do. Besides, a little caution was always a good thing, so they shut their big doors again。

It showed that the area was a bit unstable. That's why Merchant Corpsmen patrolled the streets and markets fully armed to guard against any surprises.

By then the school had suspended classes. An excited student shouted, "We should do our part too! We can form a Student Corps!" Everyone figured it was a truth that needed no discussion and assembled on the sportsfield with their weapons. They drilled more energetically than usual; they also went through the streets on patrol. But right away they felt dissatisfied—they had no heavy cartridge clips on their belts.

There was ample reason why, during a period of instability in the area, those under arms should also have bullets. In that vein the Student Corps petitioned Commander and Governor and such and were promptly authorized to carry five rounds each. They were delighted, coming out of the Army Supply Office, at the sight of the five dandy cartridges on their belts and felt ten times as bold.

In a few days they all felt there was nothing to savor in having five cartridges on their belts; they must fire some real shots to be satisfied. So they got the idea of target practice. That was when Zu-qing unexpectedly discovered his talent. All five of his shots hit home, spotting the cast iron target with depressions, from the back they looked just like a number of teats. Some of his classmates scored a hit, some even scored two or three, but there was no one like him on target with all five shots. Everyone sincerely praised his triumph, and he felt it *was* something to be proud of.

Later on he bought a fowling piece. On free days with bright clear weather he would go hunting in some woods half a dozen kilometers from home. He seemed always in practice. When the gun barked, the prey cried and fell; a shot was rarely wasted. No need for sighting; his hands raising the gun with ease, he would spontaneously find the perfect aim. He himself didn't understand how he did it.

This spring a demobilized officer anxious to pay off gambling debts, holding the object he now had hidden in his desk drawer, asked if he wouldn't like to buy it cheap. He thought there might well be a need for the thing during this period and bought it.

At the recollection, his pace became more brisk. "A person like that is no more work than shooting a bird, that's how it can be dealt with, a very commonplace event!" He now seemed to see numberless people all of whom were qualified to be dealt with by him; people not so badly deluded eventually knew enough to watch their step, solely out of fear at first, but then sincerely reforming, some as though they'd been reborn. He couldn't help an approving smile at his own shadow.

It was not yet 10 p.m. There were already quite a few passengers on the waiting northbound express; the first bell had sounded. About 500 meters from the station was a bridge. There was no moon tonight, the river was fearfully black; the glow of a single lamp near the right-hand railing put a limited stretch of murky light on the water. Far beyond the left-hand railing two or three thatch-cabined boats were moored as one could infer from lamplight the size of beans and the audible crying of a child in a cabin.

Just left of the north abutment was a teahouse. The

1. Zu-qing is recalling the year 1911. The word "restoration" was used then for the revolution which established a bourgeois republic: the idea was that China was restored to indigenous rule after overthrowing the alien Manchu dynasty. By the time this story was written, the bourgeois revolution was generally felt to have been a failure. (tr.)

entrance to the teahouse was in a small alley parallel to the river. Most of those who came here for tea were railroad workers, carters, rickshaw men and such. They had no sense of what elegance might mean, but simply pulled up their sleeves, spoke in loud voices, but loose with laughter. By now they were going full tilt; a solid uproar met the ear. Once in a while men in long gowns also came here for tea; and travellers on their way to the station, if they still had time, would often step in to relax over a pot of tea. The owner had reserved a section facing the river for finer seating, where there were such things as rattan chairs and foreign posters which the rest of the place lacked, and where the price of tea was distinctly higher. In the twilight of a single kerosene lamp, everything in the room now seemed enveloped in illusion. The sole customer was seated near the riverside. There was no one else. It was Zu-qing.

Watching from the window, Zu-qing could see pedestrians and traffic on the bridge; he could also watch a stretch of winding road south of the bridge, a patrolman pacing the street, telephone poles along the road, and sidewalk trees. Head leaning on one hand, he had the normal air of a bored customer, but he never took his eyes off the stretch of road south of the bridge. Lying on the table was an oblong camera case, just the thing that travellers normally carry.

He was becoming slightly annoyed; it felt as if his whole body were constricted. With unblinking eyes that seemed rooted there he watched the twists and turns of the road to see what traffic was coming. There were rickshaws coming, and automobiles, and carriages, but not what he was waiting to see. They came rapidly closer, went serenely over the bridge and passed into the distance.

From the station came repeated abrupt blasts of the whistle.

"Has he gone past already? Or has he changed the date of his trip? Or does fate control it, purposely not letting me do this tiny little job?" He felt some misgivings, and the trace of a hollow sensation.

"Corrupt idea!" he berated himself mentally. "How can fate control me! It's up to me to make a success of it, for my own pleasure—there isn't a chance of failure, it's as dangerous as a smoothly laid out lawn."

He imagined, in the houses along the road and in all the places submerged invisible in the boundless darkness, innumerable people, listless, drowsy, perhaps already sound asleep. "Little do you know that I'm about to shock you awake and make you rub your eyes and take a second look at what kind of world this is!"

A sudden flash in his eyes and an indescribable feeling of wild joy and terror flooded his chest. It took nearly ten seconds before he could think, "A pair of headlights with those special green beams! Those rolling sparkling wheels! That extraordinary great white horse! If it isn't him!" He was no longer aware of other things, neither bridge nor road, telephone poles nor sidewalk trees existed at all; here came the carriage growing rapidly larger until it seemed a broad lofty wall totally blocking his field of vision.

His practiced hand opened the camera case and took out the object within.

The carriage was now at the southern abutment, the only vehicle for the moment.

His hawklike vision penetrated the carriage window just as it got the lamplight, precisely the dark silhouette of that thoroughly familiar person!

In what seemed an almost insanely rapid motion his right hand extended through the window, he readily found the perfect aim, there was a solid "bang" . . .

July 28, 1923

Introduction to Guo Mo-ruo's "Revolution and Literature"

Guo Mo-ruo, the author of the following article, is today a leading member of the Chinese establishment. Since Liberation he has held an almost innumerable number of different influential positions in the cultural field, the most important being that of president of the Academia Sinica, the Chinese Academy of Sciences, a post he still holds. He has also been honored with the vice-chairmanship of the Standing Committee of the National People's Congress and has acted as one of the four vice-premiers under Premier Zhou En-lai (Chou En-lai). In 1926, when the present article was written, however, Guo Mo-ruo was a much more controversial personality in the field of Chinese culture and politics.

Born in 1892 in southwest Sichuan (Szechuan), Guo Mo-ruo, with the original name of Guo Kai-zhen, grew up in a wealthy merchant-landlord family. Because of the position and wealth of his family he got a thorough traditional education in the classics starting at an early age. Later on, in late 1913, he followed the example of many other young Chinese intellectuals of the time and went to Japan in order to get a "modern" university training of a more Western type as was available in that country. He chose to study medicine, but as his natural artistic inclinations simultaneously found inspiration in the discovery of Western literature, especially its Romantic variants, he soon became intensively involved in more literary pursuits.

Thus the famous literary group *Chuangzaoshe* (Creation Society) was established in 1921 by Chinese students in Japan partly at the initiative of Guo Mo-ruo, and from the start he was considered a leader of the group. Soon Guo and his friends found themselves engaged in sometimes quite bitter feuds with other literary groups. In the beginning they propagated a view of literature which was deeply influenced by European Romanticism and idealist literature and philosophy. They worshipped genius and art as autonomous phenomena with intrinsic value. However, increasingly concerned about the social and political situation prevailing in China and influenced by their contact with Marxist philosophy, they gradually changed their position towards a revolutionary or "prole-tarian" standpoint. During the latter part of the twenties the Creation Society became a main channel for the propagation of an engagé literature of social consciousness and clear class stand. By that time, however, Guo Mo-ruo had already left his editorial and literary work in Shanghai and was participating more directly in the revolutionary efforts to transform China.

When Guo Mo-ruo wrote the article "Revolution and Literature" he had been in Guangzhou (Canton) a few weeks as the new dean of the Department of Literature of Zhongshan University. This was in the final year of the First United Front between the Communists and the Guomindang (KMT) and the political atmosphere of Guangzhou was dominated by a spirit of revolutionary optimism in anticipation of the launching of the Northern Expedition. Guo was going to participate in this offensive as a leading member of different political departments of the revolutionary forces.

This situation and these feelings are clearly reflected in the straightforward and uncompromising revolutionary message of "Revolution and Literature." First published in the Creation Society organ, *Chuangzao Yuekan,* I, 3, 1926, the argumentation and theoretical position of the article undoubtedly derive from Guo's increasingly intensive study of Marxist theory during the two years previous to this. However, the mechanical character of the argumentation reveals that Guo had not yet managed to assimilate fully the dynamic nature of Marxist dialectics. Guo's postulation of an "eternal progress" of revolution furthermore seems to have more in common with traditional Chinese theories of historical development than with classic Marxist theory with its enunciation of communist society as the ultimate stage of historical development. Finally the preoccupation with such unmaterialistic things as great literary men, genius and psychology betrays Guo the Romantic behind Guo the Marxist. Thus this article can be said to be an example of both the achievement and the difficulties of ideological reorientation for Chinese intellectuals of the twenties.

Lars Ellström

Revolution and Literature

By Guo Mo-ruo

translated by Lars Ellström

Our time is a revolutionary epoch, and we are people preoccupied with literary work. How the literature we create relates to the epoch we live in, what demands this epoch makes upon us, what attitude we adopt to this epoch; these questions I intend to discuss here.

Let us first discuss the relation between revolution and literature.

We can immediately imagine that to put revolution and literature in the same category will be met by two diametrically opposite opinions.

Some people say: revolution and literature are as incompatible as ice and burning charcoal; they simply cannot be linked together. Those who advocate this opinion can

furthermore be divided into two factions: the one faction consists of the so-called literary men, the other faction consists of the so-called revolutionaries.

The so-called literary men, especially our Chinese so-called literary men, are a different kind of human beings who live in a different kind of world. They live poetically with their heads in the clouds, and they never ask a thing about mundane affairs. When tranquility descends upon the world, they might possibly sing praises for a while unto its peacefulness, but as soon as revolution approaches their lives are immediately threatened. Though they had been rather indifferent to the revolution and were able to adopt a kind of condescending attitude to it, they now, on the contrary, must suddenly begin to curse it with all their might. We can see examples of this behavior everywhere, whether the writers under consideration are traditional ones or modern ones. In their opinion literature and revolution can never stand together.

And perhaps they cannot, in fact, co-exist. The man of letters tries with all his might to stand above the revolution, to curse it, and the revolutionary in his turn tries with all his might to belittle literature, to disown it. We often hear it said by those engaged in actual revolutionary work: "Literature! What could such a thing as literature ever contribute to our revolutionary cause? It is only a pastime for simple-minded young girls, it is merely a forbidden fruit which decadent youth long to devour when they sit in the lecture hall and get bored listening to their lessons. Those who occupy themselves with literature aren't worth two cents!"

The literary man curses the revolution with all his might, and the revolutionary curses literature as hard as he can. Though the standpoints of these two kinds of people are not the same, still they agree in the opinion that literature and revolution never can co-exist.

This point of view, namely that it is quite impossible for literature and revolution to co-exist, both in theory and in actual fact, is extremely widespread. But there is the converse argument which contradicts this in the most extreme way by insisting that literature and revolution are inextricably linked together in a unity. According to this view, literature is a forerunner of the revolution, and a revolutionary epoch will necessarily be accompanied by a golden age of literature. This kind of opinion is also often heard.

Let us first of all look to history for confirmation of this opinion. There appeared, for example, quite a few literary men before the French revolution of 1789, men like Voltaire and Rousseau. They were epoch-making personalities and many critics and historians of the French revolution said that they were aroused by them. And the situation for the Russian revolution of 1917 was, to take another example, the same. Before the Russian revolution had succeeded, there appeared I do not know how many outstanding writers in Russia. Naturally, one cannot say that there did not exist some among them who were against the revolution, but those who bravely acted as the vanguard of the revolution and did not take a back seat to Voltaire and Rousseau were also certainly innumerable.

Let us now turn our attention to China. For example the *Feng* and *Ya* odes of the Zhou period [Chou Dynasty, ca. 1000-400 B.C.] and the *Li Sao* of Qu Zi [Ch'ü Yuan, ca. 340-280 B.C.] are all immortal literary works produced in revolutionary periods. Furthermore, the writings in which loyal and heroic officials poured out their innermost feelings at the time of each dynastic change and which are remembered and discussed right up to the present, indeed these writings may be said to be numerous beyond all counting.

Seen thus it is not only quite possible for literature and revolution to co-exist, but they furthermore relate to each other as cause and effect and there is the possibility of complete agreement between them. One cannot, of course, say that those who advocate this kind of viewpoint completely lack evidence.

So, how are we then to reach a better understanding of these two different opinions?

We are faced with two different opinions in answer to one and the same question, and these two opinions are both based on facts and are quite reasonable. In which way can we resolve this problem?

This problem seems very difficult to solve, but we only need to discuss the essential causes of revolution and the nature of literature for a while, and it will then not be difficult to arrive at an appropriate solution.

Revolution is not something that is of a fixed nature. The revolution of each epoch is imbued with the spirit of that epoch, however the form of revolution is always one and the same. The revolution of any period is inevitably an all-out resistance of the oppressed class of that period against the oppressing class. Although the division in classes is not the same, and although the objective of the resistance is not the same, the form in which it is expressed is however always the same.

Consequently we can understand that there exists at least a contradiction between two classes whenever a period of revolution appears in a society. When there is a contradiction between two classes, then the one will uphold the power it has possessed until then, and the other will overthrow it. At such a time each class will of course have its own spokesmen, and what you say depends on what class you are loyal to. If, for example, you are loyal to the oppressing class, then you will of course oppose the revolution; if you are loyal to the oppressed class, then you will of course praise the revolution. If you oppose the revolution, then the literature you write or appreciate will naturally be literature which opposes the revolution, literature which advocates the cause of the oppressing class. This kind of literature obviously cannot co-exist with the revolution, and it must likewise be belittled and disowned by the revolutionary. If you praise the revolution, then the literature you write or appreciate is, of course, revolutionary literature, literature which advocates the cause of the oppressed class. It goes without saying that this kind of literature will act as a forerunner to revolution and will, of course, bring forth a golden age of literature in the revolutionary period.

Thus we can understand that the general term "literature" comprises two categories: one is revolutionary literature, the other is counter-revolutionary literature.

Now when we have derived the two categories of literature, then all the confusions of abstract terminology can be erased without a trace, and our attitude towards literature can thus also be determined. Literature should not be opposed in general, nor should it be praised in general. On this point each of us must be absolutely clear and precise in recognizing one's own standpoint, whether one is creating literature or doing literary research. Each kind of literature of each historical period has its eulogists and its opponents, but now let us step back for the moment to a detached perspective. When we take a good hard look and apply our critical faculties to literature, what kind of literature is it that will actually be worthy of praise? And what kind of literature should in fact be opposed? In order to solve this question, it is first necessary for us to inquire into the fundamentals of social organization and the forms of social development.

Literature is a product of society. It cannot exist in direct opposition to the foundation of society, nor can it develop in contradiction to the evolution of society. Consequently we can formulate a principle: any and all literature congruent with the foundation of society is literature which may have value in its existence, moreover literature which is in accordance with the evolution of society may be living and progressive literature.

What are in fact the fundamentals of social organization? I dare to believe that our human society is established in order to seek the greatest happiness for the greatest number. If, however, the greatest happiness is monopolized by a minority, then the majority of people have no way to reach happiness in their social lives, and such a society shall certainly disintegrate. In a society of such character, the majority of unfortunate people will inevitably rise up to overthrow the minority which has appropriated all blessings to themselves, attempting to create instead a new society structured upon this principle [of greatest good for the greatest number]. This is precisely the phenomenon of revolution in said society.

The social phenomenon of revolution has never once ceased since the system of private property first appeared. Social wealth has gradually been monopolized in the hands of a minority, and each revolution has therefore forcefully sought to realize its equal distribution and to create an opportunity for the majority of people to attain equality. Thus the character of social development is dialectic. This means that when a certain system, A, has lost the power to control society, then another system, B or not-A, will appear and replace it. Then the B, or not-A, system will gradually develop over a long period and blend with the A system, so that a third system, C, will be brought forth. Also this system will gradually lose the power to control society and another system, D or not-C, will necessarily occur and replace it. Thus one system will always replace another in eternal progress, always based upon the search for a happy life for the majority of people. Consequently, on the basis of social progress we can derive a conclusion, i.e., everything which is new is always good, and everything which is revolutionary will always be in accord with the demands of mankind, in accord with the fundamentals of social organization.

Accordingly we can say that all revolutionary literature is literature which should be praised, and that all counter-revolutionary literature is literature which should be opposed. As for the literature which should be opposed we can essentially refuse to recognize its [right to] existence, or we can simply come right out and declare it non-literature. Generally speaking, literature produced in a stagnating society is counter-revolutionary, and at the same time it is completely worthless. This is exactly the reason why our stilted 'eight-legged' Chinese essays and poetry in the examination styles are completely worthless.

From this we can deduce yet another principle: what is literature is always revolutionary, and there is only one kind of true literature—revolutionary literature. Thus true literature is always the vanguard of the revolution, and in the revolutionary period there will always appear a golden age of literature.

Therefore, when I discuss the relationship between literature and revolution, I constantly affirm that literature and revolution are inextricably linked together, they definitely do not stand apart.

Literature and revolution are bound together in a unity in which they do certainly stand together.

What is the reason for this?

The reason is that literature is the forerunner of revolution and that there always will appear a golden age of literature in the revolutionary period.

Then how is that literature the forerunner of revolution, and why will there appear a golden age of literature in the revolutionary period? This is the next question to be taken up in our discussion.

One general point of view is that literature is the work of genius and thus can move society. This kind of proposition is too mystic, and I dare not agree with it. It is truly very difficult to put our finger on what genius actually is. Let us not allow this point [about what is genius] to cause us to digress into irrelevancies but simply leave it to be used by some as a pretext for flattery and by others as a tool of invective. If we are to solve this question we must find some other approach which is not so mystic but more scientific.

The temperament of each human being is different. Formerly scientists divided them roughly into four categories: one is the *choleric* type, one the *melancholic*, one is the *sanguinic* type and one is the *phlegmatic* type. The melancholic type is very sensitive and subtle in his reactions and fluctuations in his emotions are both very accentuated and long-lasting. A person of this type often has artistic inclinations. Because his emotions fluctuate strongly and persistently, he is only well suited to emotional and meditative activity. When a society is about to be transformed, he has already felt the cruelty of the oppressing class very intensely due to the susceptibility of his sensitivity, even though people with other kinds of temperament have yet to fully discern it. It is when the melancholic type has yelled out [his intense feelings] that the people with other kinds of temperament cannot help but respond. The reason why literature can be the forerunner of revolution is, I think, just this. The writer is certainly not a person endowed by heaven with miraculous talents which enable him to move society. The writer is merely a somewhat special kind of human being whose soul is particularly sensitive.

The reason why literature can flourish in a revolutionary period can also be explained with evidence from psychology.

We know that it is in the nature of literature to begin and end within the emotions. The writer expresses his own feelings, and his intention—whether conscious or unconscious—is always to incite the same emotions in the heart of the reader. Thus the stronger and more universal the feelings of the writer are, the stronger and more universal will be the influence of his work. This kind of work is, naturally, a good work. A large number of good works in a given period is indicative of a flourishing of literature at the time. In a revolutionary period the feelings of hope and anticipation for a revolution are a collective emotion of the strongest and most universal nature. It is through the expression of this kind of feelings that literature is created, and as the sources of these feelings are inexhaustible and the means of their expression manifold, therefore a revolutionary epoch always entails a golden age of literature.

Furthermore, a revolutionary period is a time which easily brings forth tragedies since until the revolution is successful, resistance by the oppressed class against their oppressors may result in a defeat. Whether class resistance is represented by an individual or breaks out in violent collective action, the story of this kind of individual or collective defeat becomes tragedy when embodied in literary form. As tragedy is the highest form of literary works, and since a revolutionary period will easily bring forth tragedies, this is a second reason why a revolutionary period will always be accompanied by a golden age of literature.

I have given above some indication of the relationship between revolution and literature. One very important question still remains to be discussed here, that is: What exactly is the kind of literature that is to be termed revolutionary literature? Or to put it in other words: What will the content of revolutionary literature turn out to be in fact? In discussing this question, I do not think it is possible to limit oneself to only one historical period. In the process of social evolution, each historical epoch has advanced through continuing revolution. Each historical epoch has its own spirit, and when the spirit of the epoch changes, then the content of revolutionary literature changes with it. Here we may derive the following mathematical formula:

Revolutionary literature = F (the spirit of the epoch)

which can be expressed in a simpler way, thus:

Literature = F (Revolution)

This means, expressed in words, that literature is a function [hánshù or "algebraic function"] of revolution. The content of literature changes in accordance with the meaning of the revolution; when the meaning of the revolution changes, then literature changes as a result. Revolution is here the independent variable and literature is the dependent variable, both of them are x, y or z, both of them are indeterminate. What is revolutionary in one historical period becomes counter-revolutionary in the next period. Consequently, though the term revolutionary literature is fixed, the content of revolutionary literature is, however, never fixed.

Let us now turn our attention to the theories of European art and literature to demonstrate the developmental progress of revolutionary literature.

The origin of European artistic and literary ideas was Greece. Greek humanism was introduced into Rome and became popular as the hedonism of the aristocracy. Before Pope Gregory I ascended to the [papal] throne in A.D. 590, the Roman emperors and their aristocracy ruled despotically and lived licentiously so that the living conditions became unbearable for the ordinary masses of people, thereby giving rise to a tendency of cynicism and disdain for this world. In response to this the asceticism of Christianity emerged. Thus the revolution of that time was a revolution of the second estate [sic] of priests against the first estate [sic] of the nobility, and its expression in literature was the revolution of the literature of religious asceticism against the literature of aristocratic hedonism. So at that time the literature of religious asceticism was revolutionary literature.

Gradually religion prospered and little by little the second estate of priests and the first estate of nobility moved closer to one another and banded together for treacherous purposes so that asceticism and hedonism joined in debauchery and generated formalism. The clearest expression of formalism in literature is so-called classicism. The resistance at this time against the united front of the first and second classes came from the common people living in the cities (the bourgeoisie) of the oppressed third estate. At that time the ordinary city-people had lost their individual freedom and they were choked under two kinds of oppression. Therefore, simultaneously the thinking of individualism and liberalism arose in response, giving rise in turn to the artistic renaissance in Italy and bursting into violent action in the great French revolution of 1789. The expression of this in the literature of this time was the struggle between Romanticism and formalism. The literature of Romanticism was a literature which had the deepest reverence for freedom and individuality. On the one hand it resisted religion while on the other resisting the power of the monarchy. The great writers of the Italian renaissance, England's Shakespeare and Milton, France's Voltaire and Rousseau, Germany's Goethe and Schiller—all these writers can be called great representatives of this literary school. The spirit of this literary school is individualism and liberalism and its manifestation is the literature of Romanticism, and it is thus the revolutionary literature of the 17th and 18th centuries.

However, after the ascent of the third estate, capitalism with individualism and liberalism as its very core, gradually turned ruthless and forced society to bring forth a new oppressed class, the fourth class of the proletarians. In present-day Europe the period of struggle between the fourth and third classes has already arrived. Romantic literature has now become counterrevolutionary literature, and though naturalism, which has existed for some time, is a literature that has risen in opposition to Romanticism, it still has not completely cast off the garb of individualism and liberalism. The ebbtide of naturalism and of other currents following in the wake of Romanticism such as symbolism and aestheticism are nothing but the literature of a transitional period. They have not still awakened to a full realization of the meaning of class struggle, and they merely waver along unsteadily between the extremes. However what is emerging in Europe nowadays is a socialist art and literature characterized by a spirit of complete sympathy with the proletariat and of a realist form that completely rejects Romanticism. This kind of literature is the newest and most progressive revolutionary literature.

When we trace the trends in the development of European artistic and literary ideas in this way, we can see that revolutionary literature in historical practice does indeed change with the spirit of the time. The revolutionary literature of a certain historical period is attacked as reactionary by the revolutionary literature of the following period, which in its turn is overturned by the revolutionary literature of a third period. Thus the development progresses until the present time, and the content and form of the literature we demand becomes quite obvious. All literature which sympathizes with the proletariat and at the same time opposes Romanticism is revolutionary literature. But revolutionary literature certainly does not have to describe and praise revolution, nor should it only superficially decorate itself with grenades, guns and eager exhortations to action, etc. The ideals of the proletariat must look to the revolutionary writer for their elucidation, the distress of the proletariat must turn to the revolutionary writer for its depiction. This is what we are now demanding of true revolutionary literature.

And now some words about our situation. We live in the world of today, in China of today. What kind of content should the literature which we demand have?

I think that our demands and the demands of the world have reached the same level. Capitalism develops step by step, and it will soon reach full maturity as it gradually is transformed from a national to an international system. It is exactly the internationalization of capitalism that we presently meet in the oppression of imperialism which we are straining to overthrow. In consequence of the occurrence of the internationalization of capitalism there is the internationalization of class struggle, and therefore our demand to overthrow imperialism is simultaneously a tribute to socialism.

Of course, at present we have much national revolutionary work besides this work of resisting imperialism, but in my opinion our internal national revolutionary work is also an effort that is contributing to the external world revolution. The warlords here in China have, for example, partly been generated by imperialism, their armaments are the merchandise of imperialism, their armies are filled with soldiers who have been forced into their service after imperialism destroyed China's indigenous handicrafts and turned these ordinary people into vagrants. Consequently, if we want to completely overthrow the warlords, it is absolutely necessary also to completely overthrow imperialism. Thus our national revolution is simultaneously also part of the world revolution. From the economic point of view the significance of our national revolution is also part of the international class struggle. The reality of this class struggle (it should be noted that this is a reality and not some personal opinion!) is something that cannot be blotted out. The majority of the masses of people here in China have reached the state of the proletariat. It is basically impossible for anyone who sympathizes with the masses of the people and the national revolution cannot but resist imperialism. Those who do not sympathize with the masses of the people and the national revolution not to warlords, bureaucrats, compradores and evil gentry, etc., can ultimately unite with imperialism in order to oppress us (indeed they have already taken this step). So, is not our revolution fundamentally a struggle against the propertied classes with the proletariat as the main force? Thus the demands of our nation or people in the final analysis are completely one with the demands of the proletariat under the capitalistic state system. We demand liberation from economic oppression, we demand the right to live as human beings, we demand equal distribution, and therefore we must unequivocally dispose of individualism and liberalism and we must also adopt an attitude of all-out resistance against counter-revolutionary Romantic literature.

Youth! Youth! These are the circumstances we live in, these are the times we live in, and if you are not writers—well enough—but if you are fully determined to become writers, then you must hurry to pull taut your nerves and hurry to grasp the spirit of the times. I hope you will become writers of the revolution and not the laggards of our historical period. And this is certainly not out of consideration just for you but out of consideration for the masses of the people in general. Under the present system it is impossible to attain complete individual freedom. Do not believe that you will achieve some kind of romantic spirit by drinking a couple of cups of wine, nor that you are some kind of genius because you have written some crooked verses. You must invigorate your lives, you must control the mainstream of literature! You should go to the soldiers, to the people, to the factories, into the whirpool of the revolution. You must understand that the literature which is demanded by our historical period is socialist realism literature which sympathizes with the proletariat, and that the demands of China are already one with the demands of the world. The times call on us: Let us exert ourselves, let us advance bravely and swiftly!

April 13, 1926

Introduction to Cheng Fang-wu's *"From a Literary Revolution to a Revolutionary Literature"*

The New Culture Movement and the accompanying Literary Revolution (both embraced by the oft-used term, "May Fourth Movement") constituted the focal point of all the socio-political-cultural conflicts and contradictions which had been building up in China since the late nineteenth century. In the resulting charged atmosphere of intellectual intensity, a great many forces vied for influence, if not supremacy. Every imaginable ideology—both Chinese and foreign—found converts and proselytizers in the Chinese political and cultural scenes, and serious intellectual disputes often broke out into full-fledged name-calling and propaganda wars.

Perhaps the most vociferous and spirited battle cries in the literary sector were raised by the highly self-righteous and irreverent writers and critics of the Creation Society (Chuangzaoshe), founded in 1921 by such prominent figures as Guo Mo-ruo, Yu Da-fu, and Cheng Fang-wu. Primarily concerned with "art for art's sake" aestheticism and European romanticism, they nonetheless found ample time to devote to the attempt to enhance their own position with their main constituency, the "newly-awakened" (i.e., politically conscious) Chinese youth, by engaging in vituperative flailing at all other literary groups.

Cheng Fang-wu, along with Guo Mo-ruo the chief theoretician of the Creation Society, was a primary participant in the literary battles and was one of the most persistent critics of other writers and theoreticians. His conversion to Marxism in 1925 only caused him to redouble his attacks on his cultural and political enemies, which at times included such giants as Lu Xun and Mao Dun.

Nevertheless, Cheng Fang-wu was most definitely in the vanguard of the progressive forces who were re-evaluating the Literary Revolution and who began calling for a qualitative change in both the form (colloquial language, approximating the actual speech of the worker-peasant masses) and content (revolutionary, taking the masses as the target) of the newly-reformed Chinese literature. He was not the first to come to this position, but he was among the most influential, and his essays helped spark a great debate over revolutionary literature in the period 1928-1932.

The present essay, first published in 1928 in the Creation Society's journal, *Creation Monthly (Chuangzao Yuekan)*, at once sums up the history of the Literary Society, criticizes many well-known and highly respected individuals and groups within the literary world, and sounds the call for the uniting of all revolutionary elements in the struggle against world capitalism and imperialism—in all of their economic, political, and cultural forms. The author repeatedly sets forth the concept that literary movements are inseparable from social ones and that there is no discussing one without the other. Hence, the essay ranges over a far broader area than purely literary concerns.

The essay, from a stylistic point of view, is not particularly well written: there is a profusion of neologisms and foreign borrowings, several unclear terms and hastily applied logic, and the outline format does not always flow. Nonetheless, the piece undoubtedly was not intended to represent creative writing style, nor has it been chosen by the translator for that purpose. The great and lasting value, rather, lies in both its reflection of the contemporary literary scene and also the stimulating effect it had on general readers and other Chinese writers and critics alike. In this respect, it stands as an historical landmark in the development of modern Chinese literature.

The translator would like to call attention to the fact that all words and phrases in the translation appearing within parentheses and in quotes are to be found in the same form in the original text. Anything enclosed in brackets has been added by the translator.

Michael Gotz

From a Literary Revolution to a Revolutionary Literature

By Cheng Fang-wu

translated by Michael Gotz

I. The Social Basis of the Literary Revolution

Every social phenomenon must have a social basis from which it arises. So, wherein lies the social basis of our Literary Revolution of the past ten years? According to my investigation, it should be as follows:

A. The 1911 Revolution, the failure of the democratic revolution against feudal power, along with the rapidly advancing oppression of imperialism, caused a portion of the so-called intellectual class that had already been in touch with world currents to engage wholeheartedly in the thought enlightenment movement (the so-called New Culture Movement).

B. This kind of campaign for enlightened, democratic thinking necessarily demanded a new medium of expression (the Vernacular Literature Movement).

However, the leisure class intelligentsia of the time lacked both a thorough knowledge of the age, as well as a thorough understanding of its thought. Moreover, the majority were literary people, so their achievements were limited to superficial enlightenment, and their greatest efforts were primarily in the area of the new literature. Consequently, the New Culture Movement more or less became identical with the New Literature Movement, and it was overshadowed by the

literary movement almost to the point of disappearing without a trace. In fact, in terms of visible achievement, only a few slight and indistinct rays of light of the literature remain.

II. The Historical Significance of the Literary Revolution

Historical development invariably proceeds by the dialectical method *(dialektische Methode)*. As a result of a change in the economic base, the mode of human life and all ideology change accordingly. Consequently, the old way of life and old ideology are sublated *(auf[geho]ben)* as new ones emerge.

The invasion of the torrent of modern capitalism has long since destroyed the foundations of our old economic system. During the European War [World War I] there sprang up in China a modernized capitalist class as well as a group of petty-bourgeois intelligentsia. The revolution in the form of ideology that is literature gradually became inevitable, and the key to the solution of it all lay in the antithetical relationship between the literary and the spoken language.

The literature of the ancient period and the spoken language of the time did not have separate and distinct

34

principles. Later, the combined result of the refining of the written language, the stubborn adherence to tradition, and the special creation of rare and useless terms (Emperor Qin Shihuang's special term for "I, imperial we" [a pronoun which can only be used by an emperor], etc.), caused the literary and spoken languages gradually to separate and become mutually distinct. However, the elements of the spoken language and their influence outside of the sphere of classical literature could not be wiped out.

Translations of Buddhist canons into Chinese, largely because of their catechistic format and wide dissemination, plainly caused the colloquial style to constitute itself into a significant school. Later, following the development of the vernacular lyric metre [ci] and dramatic verse [qu] and the flourishing of vernacular fiction, the effecting of a "qualitative change" here lacked only a slight "quantitative change." On the other hand, the classical written style, as it gradually developed to the point of exhaustion, came to shackle the expression of new content; it could but idly await the pealing bell which would announce the hour in which it, the classical written style, would be sublated forever.

Ultimately, the slight quantity [needed to effect the aforementioned "qualitative change"] arrived, via foreign literature and the new thought, and the shackles were broken. Newly developed content sought new forms by which to soar to freshly opened realms.

III. The Course of the Literary Revolution

It is not necessary to relate here at length the historical facts of the Literary Revolution. I will limit myself to briefly summarizing its general course, as well as comparing it with the New Culture Movement. Because theoretically speaking the former is a division of the latter, they have many common tendencies.

The first task of the New Culture Movement was the negation of the old thought; the second task was the introduction of the new. But neither stage produced the required results. This is because the people engaged in these two tasks were not complete in their negation of the old thought; even less did they bear the responsibility of introducing the new. We need go no farther than mention the so-called National Learning Movement, which emerged but a short time after the [New Culture] Movement had been launched. Hu Shi and his ilk, having yelled out just a few shouts, fled back to their old nest as if they had exerted themselves to a state of exhaustion. Once there, they voraciously drank from the broken old wine bottle [of classical learning], thinking to imbibe thereby a dose of vitality. The rest of the half-dead monsters and ghosts kept pace with their confused shouting. We need only look at the half-baked translations made by Zhang Dong-sun and others of the Study Clique and the Cooperative Study Society; we need only read Liang Shu-ming's queer work, *Eastern and Western Civilizations and Their Philosophies*.

Most unfortunate, however, is that these "famous personages" totally lacked comprehension of their times, totally lacked understanding of their readers, and totally lacked clarity as to the goods they were peddling. This is why the New Culture Movement in no more than three or four years seemed to die peacefully of old age. They did not realize that the awakened youth of the period had already refused

their anesthetic herbs; they really ought to have carried their medicine baskets to the stable capitalist countries and gone begging for food!

The literature movement, during its initial period, on the whole had the same tendency as the New Culture Movement. Hu Shi and his set were never able to discard their old cadence; the Literary Research Society's translations pretty much matched those of the Cooperative Study Society. Standing opposite to the "National Learning Movement" was the "Modern Punctuation" group; in fact, they were merely punctuating chaotically.

After 1921, creative writers endeavored to support the Literary Revolution movement and prevent it from likewise following the New Culture Movement to an early demise. By that time, the Creation Society already had ascended that stage and was engaged in unremitting struggle with the wretched environment. Its writers, via their spirit of defiance, via their fresh work style, within four or five years had nurtured in the literary world a spirit of independent creation, greatly stimulating the general youth population. The Society steered the course of the Literary Revolution, taking the lead in moving forward; they swept away all false literary criticism, and they drove out a good many clumsy, inferior translations. They made the most complete negation of the old thought and the old literature; with genuine zeal and critical attitude they fought for the whole literary movement.

There are those who say that the Creation Society's characteristic features were romanticism and sentimentalism; this is merely a partial observation. My own analysis is that the Creation Society represented the revolutionary petty-bourgeois intelligentsia. Romanticism and sentimentalism are qualities peculiar to the petty bourgeoisie, but in terms of their significance vis-à-vis the bourgeoisie, these qualities still can be considered revolutionary.

It was this endeavor within the creative sphere which saved our entire Literary Revolution movement. The Creation Society, through its spirit of defiance, ardent zeal, critical attitude, and unceasing effort, on the one hand gave encouragement and comfort to awakened youth, and on the other hand unceasingly worked to perfect our vernacular form. Due to the inspiration of the Creation Society, the intelligentsia of the entire country never failed to continue its struggle; the great fire of the Literary Revolution is burning to this day; the New Culture Movement fortunately has preserved this one field of endeavor.

IV. The Present Stage of the Literary Revolution

To what stage, after all, has our Literary Revolution now advanced?

A.   The present mainstay of our literary movement: Mainstay—one section of the intellectual class.
B.   The present actual situation of our literary movement:
Content—petty-bourgeois ideology;
Medium—vernacular style, although differing quite a bit from actual speech;
Form—fiction and poetry comprise the bulk, very little drama.

The results of practical analysis are thus, and in theory they should also be thus. All of this originated from the basic nature of the petty bourgeoisie.

The Creation Society always has been extremely diligent in the perfection of our vernacular form; its writers do not forget for a single minute their work in this area. In fact, owing to great effort in this area, their success has not been inconsiderable. Formerly, they had three guidelines:

A. strive to use correct grammar;
B. strive to adopt common idioms, create an increased vocabulary;
C. experiment in the use of complicated syntax.

When it came time to apply these three principles, they never dreamed that their writing would depart so far from actual speech!

Turning away from literature per se, but within literature's sphere of influence, there are several kinds of phenomena worth noting:

1) every large bookstore at present still sells textbooks written in the classical style;
2) many textbooks written in the vernacular style contain quite a few unclear passages;
3) modern punctuation is still in the process of becoming prevalent, and as before there is chaotic punctuating.

As regards the investigation of the present stage of the Literary Revolution, a word must be said about a special phenomenon in Beijing. This is the little game being played by the Zhou Zuo-ren clique, centered around the *Thread of Words* magazine. Their motto is "taste." I have previously stated elsewhere that what they take pride in is "leisure, again leisure, and a third time leisure"; they represent the leisured capitalist class, and the petty bourgeoisie who are "sleeping inside a drum." They have transcended the age. They have already lived this way for several years; perhaps if Beijing's foul and murky fog is not someday blasted through by a million tons of smokeless gunpowder, they will muddle through in this way forever.

V. The Future Progress of the Literary Revolution

Does the foregoing historical·investigation enable us to determine the future progress of the Literary Revolution?

No, this we decidedly cannot do.

Literature, in the total organization of society, constitutes one part of the superstructure. We cannot comprehend each individual part when separated from the whole; we must take up the entire social structure to investigate the part that is literature. Only then can we acquire a true understanding.

If we want to research the future progress of the literary movement, it is necessary to understand clearly the current stage of our social development; if we want to understand clearly the current stage of our social development, it is necessary to engage in complete and rational criticism of modern capitalist society (critique of the economic, political, and ideological processes), grasping firmly the method of dialectical materialism, understanding the inevitable development of history.

We can set it forth simply as follows:

Capitalism has already developed to its final stage (imperialism); the reformation of all human society is now at hand. We, who are under the double oppression of capitalism and feudal power, are already dragging our lame feet in starting our national revolution, while our literary movement—one line of demarcation of the total liberation movement—still searches wide-eyed and in broad daylight for the remnants of a bygone and illusory dream.

We have fallen far behind the times. We have as our mainstay a class which is soon to be sublated [*aufgehoben*], using its ideology as our content. In thus creating a "middle-of-the-road" vernacular writing style, which is "neither ass nor horse," we have given free scope to the wretched qualities of the petty bourgeoisie.

If we still would bear the responsibility of revolutionary intelligentsia, we must negate ourselves once more (the negation of negation), we must endeavor to acquire class consciousness, we must make our medium approach the spoken language of the worker and peasant masses, we must take the worker-peasant masses as our target.

In other words, our literature movement henceforth should constitute a step forward and take the one step—from a Literary Revolution to a Revolutionary Literature!

VI. Revolutionary Intelligentsia Unite!

Capitalism already has reached its final hour; the world has formed into two warring camps: one side is the isolated citadel of fascism, capitalism's lingering poison; the other side is the united war front of all the world's worker-peasant masses. Each and every cell is organizing for combat, and the literary workers ought to take charge of a sector. Forward! Have you not heard the stirring battle cry?

No one is allowed to stand in the middle. You must come to this side, or go over there!

Do not merely follow, much less fall further behind; consciously participate in the historical process of social change!

Strive to obtain an understanding of dialectical materialism, make an effort to grasp the dialectical materialist method; it will give you correct guidance, show you invincible tactics.

Overcome your own petty-bourgeois qualities; turn your back on the class which is soon to be sublated. Start walking toward the ragged mass of workers and peasants!

Persevere in your work with a clear consciousness; banish the spreading evil of capitalist ideology and its influence from among the masses. Cultivate the masses: unceasingly give them courage, maintain their confidence! Do not forget—you are standing in a sector of the battle front!

Describe with true zeal what you see and hear on the battlefield, the acute sorrow and anger of the worker-peasant masses, heroic behavior, the joy of victory! By so doing, you can ensure final victory, you will achieve outstanding merit, and you will not be ashamed to call yourself a warrior.

Revolutionary intelligentsia unite! Don't worry about losing your chains!

From Guling to Tokyo

By Mao Dun

translated by Yu-shih Chen

Introduction to Mao Dun's *"From Guling to Tokyo"*

"From Guling to Tokyo," written by Mao Dun in July 1928 in Tokyo, was published in *Short Story Monthly,* XIX, 10 (October 28, Shanghai). Many issues concerning revolution and literature are raised in this article, especially those that deeply involve intellectuals and writers who are either themselves revolutionaries or are devoted to the revolutionary cause. Among these issues, there are the questions of subject matter, audience and class orientation in revolutionary literature. Mao Dun examines some of these questions at close range and measures the distance between their ideal goals and current reality. His position was challenged by Qian Xing-cun (Ch'ien Hsing-ts'un, also known as Ah Ying), a radical leftist of the Sun Society, in an article called "Mao Dun and Reality." "From Guling to Tokyo," together with Qian's article and another article written by Mao Dun in May 1929, "On Reading *Ni Huan-zhi,"* are key documents showing two different attitudes taken by intellectuals and writers toward the issue of revolution and literature in modern China.

— *Yu-shih Chen*

I

An English critic once said something like this: Zola went to gather social experience for the sake of writing fiction, while Tolstoy came to writing fiction after he had experienced much about life.

The starting points of these two masters are so different, and yet their works were alike in being world-shaking. At the very least, Zola's attitude toward life can be said to be "detached," just the opposite of Tolstoy's ardent love for life; but their works are alike in being a critique and a reflection of real life. I love Zola, I also love Tolstoy; I had enthusiastically, although ineffectually and with much misunderstanding and opposition, beat the drum for Zola's naturalism, yet when I came to attempt writing fiction myself, my approach was closer to Tolstoy's. Of course I am not so arrogant as to put myself in the same class with Tolstoy; moreover, there is not the slightest resemblance between my life and my thought and those of this great Russian writer; all I am trying to say is this: although people regard me as a disciple of naturalism (this despite the fact that I have not talked about naturalism for a long time), I did not begin my life of creative writing by following the rules of naturalism. On the contrary, I genuinely lived and had my part in the most complex drama in China at a time of great turmoil, eventually becoming personally aware of the sadness of disillusionment and of life's contradictions. In a depressed mood, in loneliness and isolation, yet still in the grip of the stubborn will to live, I began to do creative writing. I had decided to exhaust the little that remained of my vital force in order to send out one small beam of light into a new area of this confused and grey life. It was not for the sake of writing fiction that I went out to experience life.

During the past six or seven years people have quite naturally regarded me as a worker in the field of literature, a disciple of naturalism; but let me confess sincerely: I do not really have that kind of undivided loyalty toward literature. In those days, my profession demanded that I be occupied with literature, but the deep interest in my heart as well as the company of many other friends (bless the souls of these friends) brought me close to social movements. I did not concentrate on either of the two areas; in those days I had no intention of writing fiction, even less the intention of becoming a literary critic.

II

In the summer of 1927, I stayed at Guling to recuperate from an illness; five or six of us had gone there together originally, but later on they left the mountain, one after the other, some going further back into the mountains to visit scenic sites, leaving behind my sick self to be attacked by insomnia every night. Listening in the quietness to the rattling of the windows in the mountain wind, my head aching, I read M. Maeterlinck's collection of essays, "The Buried Temple," and spent the short summer nights thus without ever shutting my eyes. During the day, I sometimes translated fiction, but I often looked up several acquaintances who had remained at Guling or had just come to have a chat. Among them was a Miss Yun in "the second stage of T.B." For this Miss Yun "the second stage of T.B." was very important; not because the "disease" had actually damaged her health, but rather because the dark shadow of the "disease" had created in Miss Yun a wavering state of mind which alternated between pessimism and excitement. She also spoke of her own life experience, which to my ear sounded like a medieval romance—not that it was not ideal but rather too ideal. It produced in me an interest to study this "melancholy and bedridden" Miss Yun, as people called her. She said that her life could be written into a novel. That was unquestionably true. But I must be explicit here that Miss Yun does not appear in the three novels, *Disillusionment, Vacillation,* and *Pursuit,* which I have written; perhaps there are persons with her type of character, but she herself is not in them. Because many people have for a long time been guessing which woman character in these novels is Miss Yun, I felt I had to make it quite explicit here, but it is all so annoying!

The idea of writing a novel did, however, emerge when I was up at Guling. When I returned to Shanghai at the end of August, my wife fell sick. While at her bedside I wrote the first half of *Disillusionment.* Then my wife recovered. I shut myself up on the third floor and completed *Disillusionment* and the two works following it, *Vacillation* and *Pursuit.* Altogether for ten months I did not once go out of the house; especially when I was writing *Disillusionment* and *Vacillation,* virtually no friends came to visit; during that period, except for four or five members of the family, I was completely isolated from the world. I used the ambience of "reminiscence" to write *Disillusionment* and *Vacillation;* I was only concerned with one thing: not allowing my own subjectivity to intrude upon them. I tried to make the feelings and responses of the characters in *Disillusionment* and *Vacillation* appropriate to the objective conditions at the time.

III

When I was writing *Disillusionment* and had already roughed out the outline of *Vacillation* and *Pursuit,* two ideas were active in my mind: the first was to write a novel of over two hundred thousand words, the second was to write three novelettes of about seventy thousand words each. I had long since decided to write about the three stages which modern youth has gone through in the revolutionary tide: (1) the excitement on the eve of revolution and the disillusionment when one has come face to face with the revolution; (2) the vacillation at the height of revolutionary struggle; (3) the unwillingness to withstand loneliness and the attempt to make yet a final pursuit. It is feasible to put the three stages all in one piece; but it is also possible to divide them into three pieces. Because I did not have enough confidence in my ability as a creative writer I decided to write three separate pieces; but I still intended to use in the second piece the same characters as in the first, thus making the third piece separate and yet simultaneously a sequel to the other two. This plan was abandoned when I began to write *Vacillation;* because the period of time covered by the second half of *Disillusionment* overlapped with the period covered by *Vacillation,* I was therefore obliged to create new characters. As a result, only Shi Jun and Li Ke who appear in *Disillusionment* as secondary characters reappear in *Vacillation* in a somewhat more important light.

It would probably have been better had I made a detailed plan right from the beginning in order to have the same characters appear in all three pieces, as well as to link events together so that the three pieces could be regarded simultaneously as three independent works and an integrated whole. I am deeply aware of this defect in their structure. Even within each single piece, the structural looseness is also evident. I have taken the greatest of care in delineating the characters; among them, the several quite exceptional women [characters] in these works have naturally attracted a great deal of attention. Some people believe that they are "modeled" on so-and-so; others feel that such types of women do not actually exist, that they are purely a matter of the author's imagination. I have no wish to offer any defense or argument with regard to this question. The reader may judge the matter for himself. Moreover, even though there are quite a number of women in the three pieces, *Disillusionment, Vacillation,* and *Pursuit,* there are only two types which I have taken pains to describe: Miss Jing and Mrs. Fang belong to the one type; Miss Hui, Sun Wu-yang and Zhang Qiu-liu belong to the other type. It is quite natural that Miss Jing and Mrs. Fang should win the sympathy of most people (perhaps some would blame them for not being complete), Miss Hui, Sun Wu-yang and Zhang Qiu-liu are not revolutionary women, but neither are they merely superficial and licentious women. If the reader does not consider them lovable or worthy of sympathy, it is the failure of the author's technique of characterization.

IV

Disillusionment was written from the middle of September to the end of October 1927, *Vacillation* was written from the beginning of November to the beginning of December, *Pursuit* from April to June 1928. The period from *Disillusionment* to *Pursuit,* therefore, coincided with a troublesome time in China, and the author naturally had many stirrings of emotion and could not help but let them show through. I also know that if I were more daring in words like a person of heroic stature, there would probably be more people praising me; but I have never been good at making a public display of my feelings, be they heroic or otherwise. When I remind myself that it is already a pitiful, cowardly thing to be able only to closet myself in a room to do some writing, to go ahead and shamelessly spout out tough words would be quite out of the question. I am beginning to feel that hiding in a room to write brave words on paper is laughable. I have no objection to other people doing this in hopes of deceiving the world and stealing some fame, trying to get people to say "he is a revolutionary after all," but I myself am totally unwilling to do so. I can only, therefore, tell the truth: I *am* rather disillusioned, I *am* pessimistic, I *am* depressed, and I express these feelings in the three novelettes without the slightest disguise. I confess honestly: *Disillusionment* and *Vacillation* do not express my own thoughts, they are descriptions of objective situations; *Pursuit* does, however, include the thoughts and feelings present in me during the period when the novelette was written.

The basic tone of *Pursuit* is extremely pessimistic; the large and small goals pursued by the characters in the book are, without exception, thwarted. I even went so far as to describe the failure of a cynic's attempted suicide—the most minimal kind of pursuit. I admit that this basic tone of extreme pessimism is my own, although the dissatisfaction with the existing situation, the frustration and the searching for a way out on the part of the young people in the book are objective reality. If one says that this shows how my thoughts are backward, then I do not understand why blindly crashing like flies against a window pane should not also be considered backward. Likewise, I will admit to the charge that I am only negative and do not give my characters a way out; but I myself cannot believe that making oneself into a gramophone shouting "This is the way out, come this way!" has any value or can leave one with an easy conscience. It is precisely because I do not wish to stifle my conscience and say things I do not believe, and because I am also not a great genius who can discover a trustworthy way and point it out to everybody, that I cannot make the characters in my novelette find a way out. People say that this is because I vacillate in my ideas. I also do not wish to argue or protest this. To my mind I have not in fact vacillated. From the beginning I have never approved of what many people have for the last year or so emphatically called "the way out." Hasn't it now already been proved clearly that this way out has become almost a "dead end"?

Hence, *Disillusionment* and the other two works are only portraits of the times. I rendered these portrayals faithfully and to the best of my abilities. However, to call them revolutionary novels would put me to great shame because I was unable to point to anything constructive in these works—a so-called "way out" or whatever.

Because my portrayals are emphatically profiles and because the reader himself is subjective, I have, as a consequence, heard and read quite a number of different opinions. Against some of these opinions, I cannot help putting forth a few words in protest. Let me also put them down on paper.

V

Let me begin with *Disillusionment.* Some people say that this work describes the conflict between love and revolution, some other people say that it tells of the vacillation toward revolution of the petty bourgeoisie. I say sincerely now: neither of the two characterizations agrees with my original intention. I am very simple, I still retain the habit of always sticking to the title of the piece, a habit acquired while writing compositions in middle school; since the title is *Disillusionment,* the central point of the narration is therefore also disillusionment. The main character, Miss Jing, is of course a woman from the petty bourgeois class, her reason directs her toward the light and toward the "wish to be revolutionary," while her emotion makes her despondent every time she encounters any obstacle; but neither can her despondency last very long, the feeling of loneliness after a depression leads her to search for the light again, this is again followed by disillusionment; she pursues continuously and becomes disillusioned continuously. While in middle school she was enthusiastic about social movements; later she became disillusioned and used concentration on her school work as a refuge. But she could not stand loneliness and finally fell into a love affair, which unexpectedly led to an even quicker disillusionment and she escaped into a hospital. Gradually in the hospital she recovered from the wound of her disillusionment with love, her reason directed her again to continue her pursuit, this time wishing to devote herself to revolution. There are many aspects of revolutionary work, but Miss Jing experienced disillusionment everywhere; at first she wanted to do political work, she got a chance to do it but experienced disillusionment; she took part in the women's movement, she also worked at the general headquarters of the workers' union, all these led to disillusionment. Finally she escaped into a hospital in the rear wishing to do a solid and down-to-earth job, but really it was evasion and retirement. But she was not able to persist in being retired and lonely, her instinct for pursuit and groping revived again and once more she walked into love. But the result of this love was disillusionment again: the man she loved, Captain Qiang, eventually had to go to the front, the future was a bleak greyness.

Disillusionment was written down in just such a simple manner. I did not wish to ridicule the petty bourgeoisie, nor to use Miss Jing as representative of the petty bourgeoisie; I just wrote about a general feeling of disillusionment toward the revolution between the summer and autumn of 1927. Before that time, people generally had maintained their illusions about the revolution, but at that time disillusionment set in; before the revolution came, there had been much longing and anticipation; when it was about to come, how exciting it was, seemingly tomorrow would bring us utopia, but tomorrow had come and gone, day after tomorrow had also gone, the happiness over all those ideals had turned out to be used-up tickets while new pains were added on bit by bit; it was then that everyone sighed to himself: "Ah, this is how it is!" Thus came the disillusionment. This was universal, all those who had sincerely and eagerly looked forward toward the revolution experienced just such a disillusionment at that time; not only the petty bourgeoisie, but also many poor and suffering workers and peasants. This was disillusionment, not vacillation! After disillusionment, one may become negative, or become more positive, but there is no vacillation. The disillusioned see through whatever phony thing they are confronted by and kick it away; after that, they may stop bothering with such things entirely and look for another course to pursue. Only those who still cling to that thing but cannot see through it suffer from vacillation. Therefore, in *Disillusionment* I was only writing about "disillusionment"; during the revolution [of 1927] Miss Jing also felt the same disillusionment that was generally experienced by all, and it was not vacillation!

Similarly, it is vacillation that is described in *Vacillation*, it is the vacillation experienced by participants in revolutionary activities when the revolutionary struggle is fierce. There is not a single main character in this novelette; to consider Hu Guo-guang the main character and take this novelette as an attack on opportunists comes to me as a complete surprise. When I was writing this novelette, the word opportunism never once crossed my mind. The period covered by *Vacillation* represented the most momentous stage in the history of the Chinese revolution, the vacillation of revolutionary ideas and revolutionary policies—from the leftist tendency to the emergence of even infantile leftism, from coping with infantile leftism to the ascendancy of rightist thoughts, and finally the great reaction. Nor was this vacillation subjective. It had its objective background. In *Vacillation* I could only depict the situation by resorting to profile sketching. Those who are not familiar with the political circumstances in Hubei at that time naturally will not know what I am talking about in the novelette, especially if they do not understand in which county the little county seat in *Vacillation* is located. The characters are naturally fictitious, the events are also not entirely real; but several of the important episodes in the story are based on news dispatches which I had obtained but could not publish at the time. There were many opportunists like Hu Guo-guang; they were more leftist than anybody, many of the highly unpopular cases of left infantilism were actually their work. I portrayed a Hu Guo-guang because this was also a phenomenon of "vacillation," but I did not concentrate my attention on him, nor did I have the slightest intention of attacking opportunism. Of course this is not to say there is no need to attack opportunism, but at that time all that I wished to do was write about "vacillation." I could have written about a greater and more vicious profiteer, but a little county can only produce somebody like Hu Guo-guang. Even such an insignificant town already contained horrifying cruelty: women [radicals] who had cut their hair short, once captured, had their breasts pierced by iron wire, were paraded through the streets, and eventually clubbed to death. The impact of fiction has always been its ability to use a part to hint at the whole, it is neither like a newspaper which must report everything heard, nor like history which must not leave out any great villain. That is why there is only one Hu Guo-guang in *Vacillation*. I think that only one is already more than enough.

Fang Luo-lan is not the main character of the piece, but my original intention was to make him a representative figure in *Vacillation*. He differs from his wife. Mrs. Fang does not know how to deal with the disturbances in the current situation, she is confused and lost, and she perceives that the turbulent new situation is pregnant with contradictions, so that she feels somewhat disillusioned and depressed. She has

completely failed to enter into the new situation and the new era, she cannot be said to be either vacillating or not. Fang Luo-lan is the opposite. He and his wife are alike in not seeing clearly the nature of the era, but since he has assumed the role of an important figure in the Party organization, he has no choice but to spend his time in confronting problems, so that his thoughts and actions are seen to vacillate a great deal. And not only in Party affairs and the mass movement, but also in love. At present we can still paint a frontal view of the political attitude of a character, we do not have to, like Turgenev, use love to hint at it; but since one purpose is to describe how Fang Luo-lan, the representative character in *Vacillation*, vacillates in every way, the love episode between him and Sun Wu-yang is probably not something casual. Moreover, if one remembers that *Vacillation* is about "vacillation" and Fang Luo-lan is its representative, and that Hu Guo-guang has no more significance than should belong to one subordinate character amidst the phenomena, then it is probably no defect that Hu Guo-guang does not appear again at the end of this piece.

This was my original intention for *Disillusionment* and *Vacillation*: I proceeded according to this idea, took constant care not to deviate from the main themes, and all the time took heed that every action in the pieces was oriented in a common direction, all being part of an organic structure that brought about the general goal; if the reader gets a totally different impression, then the author's descriptive powers have failed.

VI

Pursuit is just being serialized, I have not yet heard any comments. But according to friends who have seen the first two chapters, it is oppressively gloomy and depressing. They all care for me, they all hope that I can produce some spectacular masterpiece, and they are not happy that I should come out with such a sentimental and melancholy air. I am grateful to them for their deep affection. But at the same time I am still going to hold fast to my own opinion, I myself love this piece very much, not because it is well written, but because it expresses a period of depression in my life. As I have said before, the time span covering the writing of *Pursuit* was from April to June of this year, nearly three months; *Pursuit* is not any longer than *Vacillation*, but it took twice as much time to write, two solid months, not counting the days spent on other interruptions. I could not proceed very quickly because I was undergoing a period of spiritual depression at that time; in an instant my mind would dash back and forth between several conflicting ideas, my emotions would suddenly ascend to burning heights, and just as suddenly drop to icy coldness. This was because I met several old friends and learned about a number of heart-piercing events from them; those who can stand unyielding in the face of strong forces can still be made to despair and go mad over the perverse acts of those dear to them. These events may come to light in the future. This imbued my work with a pessimistic color and brought about the interweaving of both sorrowful and rousing strains in it. *Pursuit* is just such a wild and disorderly mixture. My moods which went up and down like waves are revealed between the lines, from the first page to the last.

There is no central character in this work either. There are four types of characters in the book: Wang Zhong-zhao is one type, Zhang Man-qing is another type, Shi Xun is another, and Zhang Qiu-liu and Cao Zhi-fang are yet another. They were all unwilling to spend their days unthinkingly and without purpose, they all wanted to have something to pursue, but in the end they all failed; even Shi Xun's goal of committing suicide failed. I feel very apologetic to have written such a depressing novelette. What I had to say went from bad to worse. But please forgive me, I really could not push this away. I could only let it be written down as it is, a sort of memorial. But I did decide to have a change of environment in order to revive my spirits.

I have already done this, I hope I can be strong and keep my spirits up. I believe I definitely can, I see in front of me one of the goddesses of fate from Northern Europe augustly urging and guiding me forward! Her spirit of ceaseless struggle will draw me forward!

VII

Finally, I would like to state some of my opinions about the literary scene in our country. Perhaps this will not put off the reader too much.

Since the beginning of this year, frustrated young people have begun to read more and more works of literature; the call for "revolutionary literature" has also emerged in the literary arena. Revolutionary literature is, of course, a broad term, so that now things have been carried a step further with the direct declaration that the new literature of tomorrow should be proletarian literature. But what is proletarian literature? Apparently there has not yet been a definitive introduction or discussion. There are two reasons for this: first, it is inconvenient [politically dangerous] to say what it is; second, it is difficult to say what it is. It is a shame that I have not read carefully all the new literary periodicals from our country; I can only work from what I have heard from friends' conversations. Apparently the following viewpoints are held and have been stated by friends who promote revolutionary literature: (1) opposition to the indulgence in leisure and individualism of the petty bourgeoisie; (2) collectivism; (3) the spirit of revolt; (4) a tendency toward new realism in the matter of techniques. (Although I have not yet seen works which approximate new realism.)

There is nothing wrong with these proposals. But when they are manifested in actual literary work, the results invariably fall far short of expectations. If we consider all the works written in this vein during the past half year, although they have been well received by some people, there are more who can only shake their heads. Why do they shake their heads? Is it because they are petty bourgeois? If there are those who insist on using this accusation to block all avenues to self-criticism, that's all right with me. But if one is still able to feel that taking that tack is tantamount to self-deception, then one needs to engage humbly in self-criticism. I dare to state in all seriousness that many of the people who shake their heads at the current "new literature" are in fact sincerely in favor of revolutionary literature. They do not have petty bourgeois indolence or stubbornness, as many of you imagine. Although they approach the "new literature" with high hopes and expectations, yet they wind up disappointedly shaking their heads for the simple reason that the "new literature" exposes itself as unable to shake off the shackles of "slogan

literature." Here we come upon a problem: does "slogan literature" have value as art? (Notice that in this context "literature" is meant in a broad sense, as the word "literature" in "socialist literature.") Instead of arguing in a vacuum, let us consider the case of a foreign country for comparison. From 1918 to 1922, the Russian futurists produced a large body of "slogan literature" and told the Soviet Russian proletariat that these works were produced for it, but the proletariat was not grateful, the peasants did not even attempt to disguise their distaste for these writers, they welcomed instead Pasternak and Pilnyak, who smelled somewhat putrid to the futurists. The masses of Soviet Russia were not alone in this, the leaders in Moscow such as Bukharin, Lunacharsky and Trotsky also felt that "slogan literature" had become unbearably tedious. Why? Was it because the futurist "slogan literature" still lacked "revolutionary passion"? Of course not. The important point is that what people look for when reading literature is not merely "revolutionary sentiment."

If our "new literature" did not get into the blind alley of "slogan literature" intentionally, it has at the very least stumbled into it unintentionally. Whether there is revolutionary passion or not, if writers ignore the fundamental nature of literature, or if they look upon literature as a tool of propaganda in the narrow sense, or if they, while being free from the aforesaid negligence or prejudice, still lack cultivation in literary art, they will unconsciously get themselves trapped in this same blind alley. But our revolutionary literary critics had apparently never anticipated this possibility. As a result, we encounter the following distressing phenomenon: works that are supposed to be the most revolutionary are the very ones which make those who are by no means against revolutionary art and literature shake their heads and sigh. This helps to explain why the "new literature" got some attention at first but was in the end met by shaking heads. The blame cannot be placed entirely on everyone else's not being revolutionary. And this is a fact; we should have the courage to acknowledge this fact, acknowledge the reasons for this failure, and acknowledge the necessity for improvement!

Thus far I have spoken about the nature of revolutionary art and literature. Next there is an objective question, namely the envisaged audience of revolutionary art and literature of the future. You may think this question of mine terribly strange. But this is not at all a strange question but rather one that requires careful study. Literature or art which has a new form and a new spirit, yet lacks a corresponding body of readers, will necessarily wither away or remain an oddity in history, it cannot be something which was produced by the spirit that pushes the times forward. Who are the envisaged readers of our revolutionary art and literature? Some people would probably say: the oppressed toiling masses. Yes, I very much wish and hope that the oppressed toiling masses *could* be the envisaged readers of revolutionary literature. But what is the actual situation? Please forgive me for again having to say something disagreeable. The fact of the matter is, when you shout to the laboring masses, "This is written for you," the toiling masses not only are completely unable to read the work themselves, but even if it is read aloud to them, they still will not be able to understand it. They have their own "reading matter" which they whole-heartedly enjoy, things like narrative songs, folk tunes and drum songs which you regard as poisoned. Shall it be said that one should strive even harder to produce some new material for them? Well and good. But the fact remains that they still cannot understand your language, your too Europeanized or too classicized colloquial language. If the first task is to render the material understandable when heard, the only solution is to write fiction and drama in local dialects. But unfortunately "dialect literature" is extremely hard work, which at present has not even been attempted yet. Therefore, it comes down to the fact that your new literature "written for the toiling masses" is only read by the "nontoiling" petty bourgeois intellectuals. Your work is intended for X, but those who accept your work can only be Y; this is really a most distressing and contradictory phenomenon! Perhaps some people will say: "This is not too bad; better than having nobody to read it." But we should not indulge ourselves in this kind of rationalization. If it is X whom you expressly wish to awaken and whose revolutionary sentiment you wish to raise, yet at the same time the work you have written for this purpose clearly cannot reach X, this is at best a wasteful misapplication of effort and energy. I am not saying that the writing of this type of literature should be stopped, but I have always felt that we should also have some works which are written for the readers we actually have today. It is the height of dogmatism to claim that petty bourgeois people are all nonrevolutionary, and hence, it is just a waste of effort to address them. Whether or not China's revolution can ultimately do without the petty bourgeoisie is a problem that requires very careful study. I for one feel that the future of China's revolution cannot leave out the petty bourgeoisie completely. If this is regarded as a backward way of thinking, I do not wish to argue too much; future history will supply a fair verdict. It is on this account that I consider the "new literary work" to have neglected the petty bourgeoisie far too much in its choice of subject matter. The present trend is more or less as follows: if you are writing a story to expose the suffering of the toiling masses of workers and peasants, then everybody will praise you as a revolutionary writer no matter what; however, if you are describing the hard lot of the petty bourgeoisie, then you will automatically incur the charge of being counter-revolutionary. This is a very unreasonable situation! Do petty bourgeois people nowadays not suffer? Are they not oppressed? If they do suffer and are oppressed, then why should the revolutionary writers look upon them as outcasts from civilization not worthy of soiling your sacred brush tip? Some people would probably reply that "revolutionary literature" *does* also describe the many sufferings of petty bourgeois youth; but I wish to retort: has there been any work that portrays the sufferings experienced by small businessmen, middle and small peasants, declining educated families, etc.? None, absolutely none! Can it not be said that it is a most strange phenomenon that in China where almost sixty percent of the country consists of the petty bourgeoisie, there is no work in the realm of literature that represents the petty bourgeoisie! This seems to have proven that all along our writers have only busied themselves in chasing after the new tides in world literature almost in the matter of Dongshi knitting her brows [in a vain attempt to imitate the legendary beauty Xishi (Hsishih), noted for her charming way of frowning], and apparently have never once considered the problem as to what principal material exists right here at home.

We should admit that although during the last six or seven years the "new literature" movement has produced a body of writings, it has not yet penetrated the masses; the works remain reading material for young students. On account of the fact that the "new literature" has not taken root within the terrain of the broad masses, it has not been able to grow into a force propelling society forward for the last six or seven years. The present "revolutionary literature" has an even smaller territory and has therefore become the reading material of only a part of the young students, even further removed from the masses. The underlying reason is that the new literature has forgotten to depict its natural reading public. What you have portrayed is all too distant from their [the petty bourgeoisie's] real life, and the language you use is not their language. They cannot understand you. Yet you turn around and blame them for reading only senseless trash such as *Shigong An, Shuang Zhu Feng,* etc. You insist on saying that their thinking is too old-fashioned and hence hopeless; isn't this subjective misconception of yours carrying things a bit too far? If you could enter into their lives, understand their thoughts and feelings, and give expression in writing to their sufferings and enjoyments with language both colloquial and not too Europeanized, then they would take pleasure in reading you even if your facts were infused with a great deal of the new thinking. They may take you to task but they will enjoy reading you and will not disregard you as they do now with their heads turned the other way. Therefore, for the sake of the future development of "new literature," or, putting it in braver terms, the future development of "revolutionary literature," the first important step now is to get it out from among the young students and have it enter into and get a firm footing amid the mass of the petty bourgeoisie. In order to achieve this, we must first switch the subject matter over to the life of small businessmen, the middle and small peasants, etc. Not too many new terms, no Europeanized sentence structure, no preaching-type propagandizing of the new thinking; let us have only portrayals which simply and forcefully grasp the core of petty bourgeois life!

This leads to another problem, that of the technique of literary representation. With respect to this point of technique some people advocate new realism. From an advertisement I have seen, I know of an article in the July issue of the periodical *Sun* which includes a detailed discussion on "The Path of New Realism." But I have not seen the whole article and therefore do not know exactly what is being proposed. I myself, for more than two years, have not read any literary magazine published in the West and do not know what the recent developments of new realism are. I can only speak on the basis of what I knew four or five years ago. (I then wrote some introductory notes on the subject in *Short Story Monthly,* probably in a column on literary news from overseas in 1924; the title was "New Realism in Russia.") New realism arose in response to the force of actual circumstance; at that time in Russia the internal strife with the White party had just ended, there was an extreme shortage of paper, the space reserved for literary sections in periodicals and newspapers was exceedingly limited; moreover, life at that time was tense and rapidly changing: all of which made loose and discursive style inexpedient. As a result, there naturally emerged a style which was appropriate to the spiritual rhythm and the practical difficulties in question, a style that condenses the sentences and paragraphs of literary works, leaving out unnecessary physical and psychological descriptions to achieve the effect of being brief and forceful, tense, and provocative. Because economy of words was a primary consideration, as in the case of telegramming, the style was first jokingly called the "telegram style," it later on developed into new realism. By now we have already had translations of this type of writing, for example, Semyonov's *Hunger* [Alexandrovich Semyonov, 1893-1943]. Although that was a retranslation and had lost much of its original spirit, we can still discern the general form of the original.

Thus, new realism did not come about by accident, nor was its emphasis on succinctness the result of an intention to preach to the proletariat. It is, nonetheless, already beyond dispute that it is a new form in terms of literary technique. We are now attempting to transplant it. How should this be done? This is a problem that yet awaits experimentation. But there are two points which can be considered at the outset. First, the problem of syntax. With the written vernacular language [*baihuawen*] today it is very difficult to make it terse, is it not? Any attempt at simplification would lead it back into the classical style. This is probably an experience many people have had themselves. Second, we have the problem of the society's living language and the nature of that language. That is to say, whether the language spoken in real life by the social class we wish to describe is itself repetitive and drawn out or brief and terse. I feel that small businessmen are used to speaking in a repetitive and drawn out manner. One can almost say that this is true of the whole petty bourgeoisie. Therefore, it is an open question whether terse descriptions would create difficulties for their understanding. And as for tense spiritual rhythm, we obviously do not have any now.

The traditional Chinese folk literature which is understood by the petty bourgeoisie is again, on the whole, slow and repetitive. Take, for example, "story-telling." If you have been to a story-telling assembly, you must know that the "story-teller" who is best received by the urban petty bourgeois audience is one who is capable of describing, for instance, the dismounting of Zhang Fei from a horse in such elaborate and complex detail that his descriptions would last one or two hours.

Therefore, in order to bring our new literature to the ranks of the urban petty bourgeoisie, our descriptive technique has to undergo some reform, but whether such reform is

necessarily "on the road to new realism" will have to await various and sundry experiments.

To give some opinions of my own: it seems that our literary technique has at least first to satisfy several negative conditions—don't be too Europeanized, don't use too much new jargon, not too much symbolic color, and not too directly and evangelically propagate the new ideology. Although I believe in the above, my past work nevertheless suffered from such failings, and, needless to say, it is only read by the intellectuals.

VIII

I have already said a lot, now let me give a brief conclusion. I believe that our new literature and art need to address a broad audience, that we must extend it from young students to the petty bourgeois city dwellers, that we must articulate their sufferings, and that we must stimulate their enthusiasm.

In order to bring new literature to the ranks of the urban petty bourgeoisie, to replace *Shigong An, Shuang Zhu Feng*, etc., our new literature must cut a new path insofar as its technique is concerned; be it new realism or new something else, the most important thing is to enable the audience to understand it and not be bored.

The tone of being pessimistic and depressed should be totally done away with, but we can also certainly dispense with the rabid shouting of slogans, we must be equipped with a reawakened spirit, firmly and bravely fixing our gaze on reality, and march forward in big steps, yet never letting ourselves fall victim to rashness or impatience.

I have myself decided to try to follow this road; the pessimism and gloominess in *Pursuit* have been completely blown away by the ocean breezes, the brave goddess of fate of Northern Europe is now my spiritual guide. But I also know as a matter of course the feebleness of my own ability. I do not have the great talent needed to propel the literary world to a new base. I can only act on my own conviction and do my utmost. By the same token, I can only state openly my own opinion and wait for general discussion. I hope that those who travel the same road in literature and are capable of self-reflection will join together to strive for a common goal.

July 16, 1928
Tokyo

Introduction to Qu Qiu-bai's "Who's 'We'?" and "The Question of Popular Literature and Art"

Qu Qiu-bai (also Ch'ü Ch'iu-pai, 1899-1935) is most often remembered as the person who led the Chinese Communist Party during the difficult months which followed the disastrous counter-revolutionary victories of mid-1927. It is often forgotten, however, that he was the first significant Marxist literary critic and theoretician to appear on the Chinese scene.[1] Steeped in China's vast traditional and modern cultural history, the studious Qu, in fact, regarded himself primarily as a literary figure. The diversity and originality of his voluminous creative writings, polemical essays, theoretical works, and translations place him second only to his close friend and admirer, Lu Xun (Lu Hsün), as the most outstanding cultural revolutionary of his time. Consequently, the task of selecting two short, yet typical, essays by Qu has not been easy.

The two works translated below were written in the early 1930s, unquestionably the most brilliant period of Qu's literary career. At the time, Qu Qiu-bai was the leader of the Shanghai League of Leftwing Writers, a most impressive coalition of revolutionary writers who were grappling, in one way or another, with the problem of the relationship between literature and revolution. Working underground, and trying to keep himself, his wife Yang Zhi-hua and daughter one step ahead of the KMT secret police, Qu made an extensive review of the history of the revolutionary literary movement in order to explain what he believed to be the most serious problem confronting League members—the isolation of revolutionary writers from the masses. The dynamic left-wing literary movement, Qu insisted, had never attained a mass base. The two essays translated here are extraordinarily interesting because they clearly reflect two of the most significant conclusions reached by Qu in this complex period: first, that the "Europeanized" May Fourth literary and cultural revolution should be viewed as a failure rather than as an unqualified success story, and secondly, the revolutionary literary movement should be thoroughly restructured along popular lines if it hoped to ever make contact with the masses of illiterate and semi-literate Chinese. Indeed, these two themes—his critique of the May Fourth generation of revolutionary intellectuals and his theory of revolutionary popular literature and art—constitute two of Qu's most original and enduring contributions to Chinese Marxist literary thought.

The first selection, "Who's 'We'?", written appropriately on the thirteenth anniversary of the celebrated 1919 May Fourth Incident, has been included in most anthologies of Qu's writings.[2] Although the essay is brief, the direct and critical approach taken by Qu sets this piece apart from the more muted public exchanges ordinarily made among close revolutionary comrades. Of course the point Qu makes in this and other essays is that Europeanized revolutionary intellectuals remained captives of the abortive May Fourth bourgeois-democratic literary movement. Instead of actively promoting the spread of modern culture and literacy among the masses, China's modern literary movement—including its "proletarian" and revolutionary wings—had become increasingly elitist and exclusive. Consequently, revolutionary writers remained isolated from the masses, and the movement as a whole lacked a mass base.

The second selection, "The Question of Popular Literature and Art," which appeared in the June 10, 1932 issue of the League publication *Literature Monthly* (Wenxue Yuebao), is more systematic and complex.[3] It is not merely an appeal to writers to "popularize" their works. Instead it represents a fairly elaborate conception of how a variety of China's modern cultural and literary problems might be confronted in a revolutionary environment. There can be no question, for instance, that Qu's intense interest in China's traditional non-literate forms is related to his rejection of the extreme cultural iconoclasm which had prevailed in Chinese intellectual circles since 1915. By rejecting traditional popular forms for a few exclusive Western forms, China's revolutionary writers had cut themselves off from the people. And the nationalist overtones of Qu's remarks suggest that his concerns were not merely practical. A staunch anti-imperialist on the cultural as well as political front, it is apparent that Qu himself found the new stress on the art forms of the people to be culturally and psychologically satisfying. Similarly, his populist appeals for revolutionary writers to "go to the people to learn" represents an unmistakable assault on the social isolation of the "Europeanized" generation.

In the last analysis, it is Qu's vision of a "Proletarian May Fourth Movement" which best characterizes his view of the problems and possibilities of China's revolutionary literary movement. As a "stage" of development in the cultural realm, it bears some resemblance to the "New Democratic" stage in the political, social, and economic realms discussed by Mao Tse-tung nearly a decade later. Both recognize the failure of "old" (or European) bourgeois-democratic revolution in China. For Qu, the completion of the bourgeois-democratic cultural revolution is linked to the emergence of a distinctively socialist cultural movement in a single "Proletarian May Fourth." While the proletariat would exercise leadership for the duration of this period (owing to the failings of the bourgeoisie), the Europeanized writers were to be particularly active in the first and more bourgeois-democratic phase by popularizing their work and making direct contact with the people. But even during the first phase, the seeds were to be sown for a socialist cultural movement which would involve the direct participation of the masses in the cultural movement and the promotion of a genuinely popular literature and art based, in part, on artistic forms familiar to the people.

Aside from providing us with a glimpse of certain concrete proposals put forward by Qu in the difficult years of the early 1930s, these two selections are interesting because they reflect some of the important, and perhaps characteristically Chinese, assumptions about art and revolution held by Qu—assumptions which set his work apart from the tradition of Plekhanov and other Western Marxist literary critics. For example, one detects, even in these brief translations, the unusual amount of importance Qu attached to the role of the superstructure in society, and to the role of culture and art in particular. In Qu's view, one of the most effective methods employed by the ruling class to perpetuate its domination of Chinese society was its use of popular culture. The people, he points out, "are still in the Middle Ages in their cultural life," and are bombarded constantly by the very stuff of feudal consciousness. His attempts to have literary intellectuals confront this problem suggest that he strongly believed that a dramatic revolutionary breakthrough in the cultural area was both possible and necessary. In fact, it is apparent that Qu views a radical shift in human consciousness (or ideology) as a precondition for genuine popular support of the revolution and the complete liberation of society.

Finally, it is also interesting to note that neither of these pieces makes reference to Soviet practice or Soviet literary canon. In short, these are creative works born of a penetrating knowledge of *Chinese* conditions and problems, and not shaped by the imperatives of foreign dogma. In fact, the problems to which Qu addressed himself—namely the impact of "Europeanization" on revolutionary literary intellectuals and the role of popular culture among the illiterate and semi-literate masses—continues to be raised throughout the Third World today.[4]

In January 1934, a year and a half after he wrote these essays, Qu travelled to the Jiangxi Soviet where, as Mao Ze-dong's Commissar of Education, he attempted to implement many of the policies sketched out below. Suffering from chronic tuberculosis, Qu was advised to stay behind when the Long March set out in mid-October 1935. Attempting to make his way back to the coastal region, Qu was apprehended by the KMT in March, and executed by firing squad in mid-June at the age of thirty-six. Until the mid-1960s Qu was viewed in Chinese Marxist circles as a revolutionary martyr and ranked just below Lu Xun as the most important cultural revolutionary and literary thinker of the 20th century. In the early stages of the Cultural Revolution, however, at a time when the standing of many revolutionary martyrs was being reappraised, Qu was repeatedly criticized and condemned as a "renegade" by some Red Guard groups. Attacks on Qu were confined, however, to criticisms of his unsuccessful political career and charges that many of his activities while in prison, including the writing of a gloomy memoir, were acts of betrayal. Significantly, his literary views were not subjected to criticism—probably because they approximate so closely the literary policies and attitudes advanced by Maoists during the Cultural Revolution itself.

Paul G. Pickowicz

Who's "We"?

By Qu Qiu-bai

translated by Paul G. Pickowicz

Zheng Bo-qi's[5] essay "The Essence of Popularization" is the leading article of the recent debate on revolutionary popular literature and art.[6] Of course revolutionary and proletarian literature should be popularized—this is contested by no one. The slogan of "popularization" was raised at the very outset of the proletarian literary movement (the March 1930 edition of *Popular Literature and Art* [2:3], entitled "A Special Issue on the New Vogue in Literature," carried the proceedings of a conference on the popularization of literature and art in addition to the essays of a number of people, all of which debated the so-called "questions about the popularization of literature and art"). But from the outset the slogan of "popularization" has been so much empty talk; from the outset there has been no *practical resolution* of the real problems of implementing popularization. Why have mistakes of this sort been made? Because, aside from empty talk, nothing has been accomplished in the last few years! Of course, the most significant reason is that the proletarian literary movement has not yet gone beyond the stage of "research societies"; it is still an intellectual clique, and not a mass movement. These revolutionary intellectuals—the petty bourgeoisie—have still not resolved to go among the ranks of the working class. They still view themselves as teachers of the people, and dare not "go to the people to learn." Consequently, in word they advocate "popularization," but in fact they oppose "popularization" and obstruct "popularization." Zheng Bo-qi's essay reflects precisely this sort of intellectual attitude, thus it permits us to recognize an even more formidable obstacle to "popularization"—the fact that the majority of revolutionary writers and "literary youth" stand *outside* the people, intent on positioning themselves *above* the people and instructing the people.

Zheng Bo-qi asks, "Is our method mistaken? No. Are our slogans too lofty? No. Is our written language too difficult? No. . . . Yet a majority of the people are not influenced by us."

When Zheng Bo-qi says *"we,"* to whom is he referring?! His use of the term "we" places it in opposition to the "people." His "we" stands beyond the people. In essence he does not feel that this "we" is simply one group among the "people." Consequently he cannot recognize his own errors, nor can he reject his status as a member of the "intellectual class." In precisely what areas is he mistaken? First, he claims that "our" written language certainly is not too difficult. That statement is obviously wrong. At present the written language used in most creative works is exceedingly difficult; not only is it difficult for the masses to understand, but it is a language hard for all readers to understand. This written language is the so-called vernacular language [*baihua*] of the May Fourth Period.[7] More specifically, it is a half-classical language which, when read aloud, does not resemble in the least the speech of living people, thus it is a half-dead language. Therefore, the question is hardly whether it is difficult, but rather whether the language used is or is not Chinese—the speech of living Chinese people, the speech of China's masses. Basically, Bo-qi does not understand this problem. Therefore, he basically fails to understand the need to thoroughly complete the literary revolution. Secondly, he claims that "our" slogans are not too lofty. Actually this statement is not too bad. But he should have gone one step further and said: in fact the slogans are too low! The fundamental problem of revolutionary literature and art concerns the use of artistic forms to convey revolutionary political slogans—it is not a question of the political slogans themselves being too high or too low. On the contrary, when these political slogans are reflected in literary and artistic works, they are sometimes distorted and *even lowered* as a result of vagueness and wavering. The people demand that revolutionary literature and art spell out practical problems in some detail—to move from the political realm directly to everyday life and family life. But current revolutionary literature and art has been unable to satisfy this demand of the people. Therefore, it should be said that "our" slogans are too low. Third, he claims that "our" method definitely is not mistaken. This too constitutes adherence to an erroneous notion. The movement for popularization launched in the past two and a half years has accomplished absolutely nothing, yet they still claim that their method is not mistaken! Speaking only of the past six months, this movement has continued to suffer from mistaken methods in many places.

The movement for the popularization of literature and art must be a movement of the laboring people themselves, and it must be led by the proletariat. We certainly must lead the people, but in a way that will permit them to produce revolutionary literature and art themselves, and in a way that will result in a struggle against the impact of "Lin Shu"[8] among the people, that is, a movement against knight-errant fiction[9] and all other kinds of reactionary literature and art. The tasks of the *people's literary revolution* are the following: to do away with May Fourth style semi-classical language and to do away with the dead vernacular language of traditional fiction. This is the only correct path. Revolutionary popular literature and art should make use of the vernacular language spoken by Chinese today (the simplest, most genuine vernacular language), it should create reading material for the vast masses, reach out to the districts in which the poor live, constantly criticize all reactionary popular literature and art, fiercely advance the struggle in opposition to reactionary merchant-gentry consciousness, develop worker-peasant-soldier correspondence movements, and foster working class writers.... Of course there will be many difficulties and a long period of hard struggle will be required.

But what are the difficulties recognized by Zheng Bo-qi? What methods does he suggest should be used in overcoming these difficulties? Here is what he says:

> The primary type of difficulty has to do with the masses themselves, and it concerns whether the people are sufficiently prepared to comprehend our views. A second type of difficulty has to do with us writers, and it concerns

whether we writers are sufficiently understanding of and sympathetic toward the daily life of the people. There is really only one way to overcome these difficulties ... writers' lives must be popularized.

Of course, the popularization of writer's lives is a most central question.[10] But words of this sort were uttered as early as three and four years ago, yet, as usual, nothing has come of it. At present this kind of talk represents nothing but empty generalities, thus it is not a response to the question at hand. What is required now is a much more concrete and detailed resolution of the problem of popularization of lives. I have already written an essay on this general problem.[11] At present what I want to draw our closest attention to is Zheng Bo-qi's remark that "the primary type of difficulty has to do with the masses themselves"! It seems that the level of the people is "too low," that fundamentally they are unable to understand revolution and fail to understand revolutionary literature and art and proletarian literature and art. In actuality, however, perhaps it is the people who have a more profound understanding of revolution than do writers, that the people themselves are quite capable of waging revolutionary struggle. In fact, it is because writers do not understand revolution that they are unwilling to go to the people to learn about matters related to both artistic form and language and are unwilling to recognize the difficult nature of their own written language. Consequently, proletarian literature and art "as usual is unable to make an impression on the majority of people." The writers are unwilling to go among the people and are unwilling to work together with the people to create a new literature and art. On the contrary, they call upon the people to "adequately prepare" themselves first, so that later they might have the good fortune to be admitted into the "Temple of Art"!

Zheng Bo-qi's essay sheds light on the posture assumed by our intellectuals—a posture which not only separates them from the people, but also compels them to look askance at the people. *The source of this malady must be completely uprooted,* otherwise the development of popularized literature and art will be obstructed in a very serious way.

Of course, among the hundreds of millions of laboring Chinese, and even among the industrial proletariat, there are many people who continue to be subjected to the restraints and deceptions of the enslaving education of the landlord-capitalist class—reactionary popular literature and art are precisely a tool of this enslaving education. Therefore, the sentiments expressed in this literature are definitely not those of each and every worker or peasant. But precisely because of this, the proletarian vanguard must use all weapons, including *literary and artistic weapons,* to assault reactionary thought. If the writers of proletarian literature and art continue to insist that the people are not "prepared," while at the same time insisting that their own written language, methods, and slogans are not mistaken, then there is nothing that can be done but to wait for the level of the masses to be raised. Objectively speaking, this "wait-ism" mentality contributes to the perpetuation of the influence of reactionary thought among the people.

"Recognizing one's errors is the first step toward overcoming and correcting them"—I hope the comrades doing proletarian literature and art and revolutionary literature and art will discuss this problem in a detailed and concrete fashion.

May 4, 1932

The Question of Popular Literature and Art

By Qu Qiu-bai

translated by Paul G. Pickowicz

What Is the Problem?

In China the laboring people are still in the Middle Ages in their cultural life. Popular literary and artistic forms such as storytelling, romantic adventure, ditties, cinematic peep-shows, comic books, and outdoor theatre are used by China's merchant-gentry class as tools to impose their enslaving education on the laboring people. In both written and oral form the origins of all this reactionary popular literature and art lie several centuries in the past; in a most subtle fashion it penetrated deeply among the people and became a part of their daily lives. Consequently, their knowledge of life and their observations of social phenomena—in a word, the cosmology and view of humankind held by the laboring masses—have been derived, for the most part, from this corpus of reactionary popular literature and art. Naturally reactionary

popular literature and art of this sort give full expression to the prevailing feudal consciousness of the time. In it we see the flesh devouring principle of *li* (Confucian doctrine of propriety) flash its teeth and brandish its claws, we witness the terror of Hell, prostrations before Grand Magistrates, fantasies of Knighthood-errant and magic swordsmen, the propaganda of popularized Eastern culturalism, and evil, indecent, and cruel attitudes towards women ... as usual everything is shrouded over in a fog, and there is *no representation whatever* of the birth and growth of revolutionary class consciousness or the emergence of a determination to resist. Recently during the Manchurian and Shanghai Incidents[12] the counter-revolutionary bourgeoisie made use of these same tools to obstruct increasingly revolutionary expressions of understanding on the part of the masses.

The May Fourth New Culture Movement was a waste of time with regard to the people! May Fourth new classical literature[13] (the *so-called* vernacular or *baihua* literature) and the early revolutionary and proletarian literature, which clearly arose from this May Fourth foundation, simply provided the Europeanized gentry[14] with yet another sumptuous banquet to satisfy their new tastes while the laboring people were still starving. How did this come about? Because under the prevailing class system, feudal remnants in China are particularly evident in cultural life. In the past the gentry used the classical language and it had a system of writing; the common people used the vernacular language and they simply had no system of writing, thus the only things they were able to use were the dregs of the gentry's writing system. Now, one portion of the gentry class has been Europeanized and it has created a Europeanized new classical language, but, as usual, the common people once again are left with the dregs of the gentry's writing system. Thus, the inability of the common people of today to understand the so-called new artistic works is no different from the inability of common people in earlier days to understand the written language of ancient poetry and literature. In a word, there is no common language linking the new style gentry to the common people. As a consequence, therefore, regardless of how good the contents of revolutionary literature might be, these works will have no relation whatsoever to the people so long as they continue to be written in the language of the gentry. In short, the May Fourth New Culture Movement has had almost no impact on the masses. Among the masses, for example, anti-Confucianism is a lesson derived directly from a practical revolutionary struggle to which the literary struggle has not contributed in the least.

Currently, therefore, the problem definitely is not a simple matter of popularizing literature and art;[15] it is a question of *creating a revolutionary popular literature and art.* What is needed is a *literary renaissance movement led by the proletariat, a cultural revolution and a literary revolution led by the proletariat, a "proletarian May Fourth Movement."* Of course, from time to time this movement will have an anti-bourgeois thrust, but in the present stage this movement obviously will be performing an essentially bourgeois-democratic task.

This is where the problem lies!

Up to the present time the revolutionary struggle on the literary and artistic front has been limited to opposing the influence of the various reactionary groups upon the Europeanized intellectual youth; the struggle to go among the laboring people to oppose all forms of reactionary landlord-capitalist literature and art has hardly begun. Proletarian revolutionary ideas point to the need to win over the laboring people, to assault and wipe out the influence of the landlord-capitalist class; in literary and artistic matters this necessarily requires an ardent struggle for a new cultural revolution. Accordingly it will be necessary to do research on what the people are reading these days, on what sort of views the people have of life and society, on the type of material the people can understand or are accustomed to reading, and finally on the type of literary and artistic works the people will need as they struggle in this society. In sum, this means it will be necessary to use the language of the laboring people themselves, to keep in mind the actual life of the laboring people while responding to all problems, and to create a revolutionary popular literature and art. In the process of doing this, the literary revolution of the working people will be completed and a literary language (*wenxue di yuyan*) of the working people will be created.

In short, *the problem of revolutionary popular literature and art concerns nothing less than the movement for both a cultural revolution and a literary revolution led by the proletariat.*[16] The tendency to ignore this bourgeois-democratic task in the past explains why, on the one hand, there has been so much hollow chatter in the revolutionary literary world about popular literature and art and the popularization of [elite] literature and art, while, on the other hand, there has been no effective struggle.

What Sort of Speech Should Be Used When Writing?

After the May Fourth Movement, appeals for "literary revolution" were replaced by appeals for "revolutionary literature," and this represented a step forward in the struggle.[17] But it was precisely in the revolutionary literary camp that the tendency to ignore the continuation and final completion of the literary revolution was most noticeable. Consequently it became a common practice to thoroughly disregard the customs of spoken Chinese, and to make widespread use of classical Chinese grammar, European grammar and Japanese grammar, and to write in a so-called vernacular language that in fact cannot be read aloud, for when read aloud it cannot be understood by the listener. Without question there were some famous writers who were capable of writing in a genuinely vernacular language. But, since 1925 no one has pointed out the need to continually stress the question of literary revolution. All the creative writings and essays of the "new literature," and especially translations, make carefree use of the new-style classical writing (the so-called vernacular), but as yet this work has not received the slightest bit of criticism. Of course, it is unnecessary to point out that landlord-capitalist literature is like this, but so too is revolutionary literature. The reactionary groups are able to exploit this weakness among the revolutionary rank and file, and, thereby, strike a blow at the development of revolutionary literature. There is no difference between this mistake and the sort of errors made in leading revolutionary political organs which, objectively speaking, assist the forces of counter-revolution, and cause a widening of the distance separating them from the broad masses.[18]

Thus, in the first place, the problem of popular literature and art involves the need to begin work by thoroughly completing the literary revolution. Although the matter of what spoken language to use in writing popular literature and art is not the most important question, its resolution is a precondition for asking all the other questions. Just as English workers are unable to read fiction written in medieval English or Latin, so too are Chinese workers unable to read the various written works which use ancient Chinese and Europeanized grammar.

Today the situation regarding the written Chinese language is this: a variety of dissimilar systems are being used simultaneously—first there is the ancient classical language (used now in sending "four-six" style telegrams),[19] second is the classical style of Liang Qi-chao[20] (used in legal and official papers, etc.), third is the so-called vernacular language of the May Fourth period, and fourth is the vernacular used in traditional fiction. We are aware that the Chinese ideographs themselves are a most damnable legacy, but, in addition to this confusion, a variety of different grammars have been thrown in. Under these circumstances how are the more than 300,000,000 Han people going to be able to acquire literacy?![21] It has virtually been decided that this task is impossible. To understand a copy of *Shen Bao*[22] requires a minimum of five years' study! It is precisely this state of affairs that serves to sustain the landlord-capitalist class. To revolutionize the written language is unquestionably a bourgeois-democratic task, but China's bourgeoisie is unable to complete this task—indeed, it has already opposed a deepening of the literary revolution. They took advantage (perhaps unconsciously) of the early May Fourth movement for literary renaissance by creating a new classical vernacular, and then bestowed this new classical gift upon their own Europeanized sons for their enjoyment. As usual, the laboring people were left with the dregs of merchant-gentry language—the vernacular of traditional fiction found in the tunes sung by the fortune teller.

Nevertheless, when compared to May Fourth new classical, the vernacular used in traditional fiction has a number of things to recommend it.

The written language of May Fourth new classical is composed of a mixture of classical Chinese, European, and Japanese grammar along with the vernacular speech of both ancient and modern times, thus it is basically a written language which cannot be read aloud. But the vernacular used in traditional fiction is ancient vernacular, and it regulated the influx of classical grammar relatively well. It was the language spoken by the people of the Ming dynasty, and although we can tell when it is read aloud that it is not the language spoken by modern Chinese people, it is, after all, the speech of traditional drama and definitely can be read aloud. For this reason the vernacular used in traditional fiction is relatively close to the people, and the people are accustomed to reading it. When compared to all the other so-called Chinese languages, this variety of vernacular has one important special feature—it has developed from the oral literature of the people (the common speech of the Sung and Yuan dynasties). Reactionary popular literature and art take this characteristic into account, thereby strengthening its hold on the literary and artistic life of the laboring people. If revolutionary literature and art do not fight this, then they are simply handing the people over to literature and art of this sort.

Therefore the new literary revolution must not only continue to clean out the remnants of the classical language and overthrow the *so-called* vernacular or new classical, but it must also *firmly oppose the vernacular used in traditional fiction*, because, in fact, it is a dead language. To oppose a dead language of this sort means that we must *all* make use of the modern vernacular spoken by living Chinese when we write, especially the language spoken by the proletariat. And the proletariat cannot be compared to the rural peasantry. The language of "rural folks" is primitive and obscure.[23] But in the major cities, which have drawn people from all parts of China, and in the modern factories, the proletariat's language has already evolved, in fact, into a Chinese street vernacular [*putonghua*]—not to be confused with the so-called national language [*guoyu*] of the officials! It contains aspects of a variety of local dialects while having eliminated the obscure localisms of these dialects, and it has been receptive to foreign phraseology. Thus it is creating a new technical language for modern scientific, artistic, and political usage. But, on the other hand, it is clearly not the same as the new classical language of the intellectuals. New classical has *invented* a considerable amount of new phraseology and it has stolen European and Japanese grammar, thereby not only failing to take into account the customary features of grammar found in *classical* texts, but actually violating the customs of all Chinese grammar. As it developed and grew, street vernacular was also infused with foreign phraseology and even some foreign syntax, but it was placed on the foundation of the customary grammar of spoken Chinese. In sum, each written work should adopt the following standard: "it can be understood when read aloud." Then there can be no question about its being the language of living people.

As for revolutionary popular literature and art, it is especially important that it begin by making use of the *most simple* proletarian street vernacular. On the surface of things, it will appear at the outset to be modeled on the vernacular of traditional fiction. But on no account should this be construed as a policy of surrender. It is a matter of the proletarian vanguard leading *all* the laboring people in the task of creating a new and rich *modern Chinese literature*. At times it will be necessary to use the various local dialects in writing, and in the future perhaps a special literature for Guangdong, Fujian and other places will be constructed.

What Should Be Written?

What sort of things should revolutionary popular literature and art write? For the purposes of discussion, let us divide the question into two parts.

First there is the question of form.[24] At the outset, the following must be explained clearly: the revolutionary vanguard should not separate itself from the mass rank and file or engage single-handedly in "heroic and magnanimous activities." To insist that new content must necessarily be expressed in new forms, and to insist that the level of the people be raised in order that they might appreciate art rather than lowering the standard of art to the level of the people is to speak with the arrogance of a "great writer"! Revolutionary popular literature and art must begin by utilizing the strong points of traditional forms—things the people are accustomed to reading or viewing such as fiction, lyrics or drama— gradually adding new ingredients and cultivating new habits among the people, so that by working together with the people the level of art will be raised. With regard to form, there are two points to be made for traditional popular literature and art: one is its relationship to the oral literary heritage, and second is its simple and plain manner of narration and exposition. Revolutionary popular literature and art should heed these two points. Fiction of the storytelling variety can reach the illiterate, and this is exceedingly important for revolutionary literature and art. It represents sensible and straightforward narration—in contrast to the "mindless and confusing" writing method of the new literature and art—and it is the easiest thing for the people of today to understand.

Revolutionary popular literature and art, therefore, should make use of forms such as storytelling and boatman's songs. Naturally we should be ready to introduce new forms which can be readily accepted by the people. For example, it might be possible to compile current events fiction by inserting some spoken dialogue into popular folk music, or to use pure venacular to create a new short story form. And the possibilities for handling drama in new ways are even greater. After practical work begins, our experience will teach us many new methods and the people themselves will be able to create new forms. To totally rely on traditional forms is to walk down the path of surrender.

Second, there is the matter of content. At present the primary work slogan for revolutionary popular literature and art and for the proletarian literary movement in general should be: *"Tear off all masks and put the heroes of revolutionary war on display."* But of special importance is the need to have a clear perception of precisely where the consciousness of the enemies of the revolution has made its impact among the people. This is a cardinal task in the revolutionary struggle on the literary and artistic front. If the enemy's strength cannot be calculated, then naturally there can be no fight. Because there was no assessment of the actual situation during the early period of revolutionary literature, only posters and slogans were yelled out. This is not attacking the enemy, nor is it assaulting reactionary consciousness, it's just yelling. To be assembled on the battlefield shouting in triumph with all eyes fixed on flags fluttering in the heavens, rather than pointing the guns of the revolutionary army in the direction of the enemy, may appear to be very "bold," but in fact it is not the same as doing battle! For this reason there are those among us who oppose ripping masks from the faces of the enemy, that is, they are not in favor of us writing about the landlord-capitalist class and the petty bourgeoisie.[25] At present it must be profoundly understood that it is the task of the revolutionary literary movement to clearly perceive what means the enemy uses *in each and every crisis* to mislead the people, to clearly perceive what sort of reactionary consciousness is inflicted upon the *daily lives* of the people, and to rip off every variety of mask. Our work must reflect the *actual revolutionary struggle* by presenting revolutionary heroism, particularly the heroism of the people. This will require exposing reactionary consciousness and the timid wavering of the petty bourgeoisie, thereby bringing to light the influence of this consciousness upon the struggle of the people, and thus assisting in the growth and development of revolutionary class consciousness.

Revolutionary popular literature and art, therefore, can have a variety of dissimilar source material. In order to reflect quickly the revolutionary struggles and political crises of a given moment there can be "instant" and "rough" popular literature and art of the reportage variety. Perhaps works of this sort have no artistic value; perhaps they will be nothing more than new, popularized current events essays. But art will be created in the process of the agitation-propaganda struggle. Content can be drawn from traditional source material, giving rise to a "New Yue Fei" or a "New Water Margin."[26] It can be "romantic adventures" or revolutionary struggles such as "The Taiping Revolution," "The Canton Commune," or "Zhu De and Mao Ze-dong Atop Jinggang Mountain." It can be translations of international revolutionary literature. It can be work which exposes capitalist-imperialist aggression on the part of the Big Powers. It can be a new form of "social gossip," because if reactionary popular literature and art can make use of things such as the trial of Yan Shui-sheng, the love affair between Huang and Lu, and the Shu Jing murder trial,[27] then revolutionary popular literature and art should also describe the family life of the laboring people and the question of love, while describing the landlord-capitalist class for everyone to see. This last point is worthy of everyone's attention, because, up to the present time, revolutionary literature and art has been deficient in accomplishing the special tasks of this literary and artistic struggle.

What Lies Ahead?

The future of revolutionary popular literature and art will depend on its ability to become a strong and powerful enemy of reactionary popular literature and art and to become the true successor of "non-popular revolutionary literature and art."

The struggle to create a revolutionary popular literature and art will be long and hard. It will necessitate linking up with the broad masses, tapping vast public potentialities, and establishing a cadre for the literary and artistic movement of the laboring people (it is important that it be led by workers). At first the cadres should be concerned with oral literature, but in time they certainly will become involved in written literature. All these things will require a long and difficult period of organized and systematic work.

The situation at present is this: popular literature and art and non-popular literature and art exist side by side. This is because the remnants of the feudal system—particularly in the area of cultural relations—still retain a dominant position: the gentry class and the people have no common language. Whoever ignores this fact will be unable to adopt an appropriate line of struggle, and consequently will either abandon the tasks of the new cultural revolution or be deluded into thinking that it will be possible to thoroughly rely upon the Europeanized intellectual youth to engage in a liberal program of *"instructing"* the people in the matter of cultural revolution.

At present we must popularize non-popular revolutionary literature and art while simultaneously carrying forward the struggle against the influence of all reactionary Europeanized literature and art among the masses of petty bourgeois intellectual youth. We must also see to it that a *revolutionary popular literature and art arises from the people,* and working with people insure that the level of art is raised, and that the difference between popular literature and art and non-popular literature and art is erased. To accomplish this it will be necessary to get rid of non-popular literature and art which uses the new classical language while building a "modern Chinese literature" of high artistic quality, but one which the people are able to use.

Rewritten on March 5, 1932[28]

Notes

1. For a more detailed discussion of Qu's intellectual development see the following: Paul G. Pickowicz, "Ch'ü Ch'iu-pai and the Origins of Marxist Literary Criticism in China," Unpublished Ph.D. dissertation, University of Wisconsin, Madison, 1973, or Paul G. Pickowicz, "Ch'ü Ch'iu-pai: Die Verbindung von Politik und Kunst in der chinesischen Revolution," in Peter J. Opitz (ed.), *Die Sohne des*

Drachen (Munich: Paul List Verlag, 1974), pp. 292-321.

2. For the full text see Qu Qiu-bai, *Qu Qiu-bai Wenji* (Collected Literary Works of Qu Qiu-bai), 4 vols., Peking: Renmin wenxue chu-ban she, 1953-54, vol. 2, pp. 875-78. The Chinese title is " 'Women' shi shei?"

3. For the full text see *Qu Qiu-bai Wenji*, vol. 2, pp. 884-893. The Chinese title is "Dazhong wenyi di wenti."

4. For a discussion of the present-day import of these problems in China see Paul G. Pickowicz, "Modern China's Artistic and Cultural Life," *The Holy Cross Quarterly*, Vol. 7, Nos. 1-4, 1975, pp. 108-116.

5. Zheng Bo-qi (1895-) was a leading member of the Creation Society and later a member of the Executive Committee of the League of Left-Wing Writers. In this essay Qu refers to Zheng as He Da-bai, a pseudonym used by Zheng in the 1930s.

6. It is important to elaborate on what Qu means by his use of various cultural terms. For example, "dazhonghua" means "to popularize." This term is normally used by Qu when he is referring to the need for revolutionary literary intellectuals to rewrite their works in a more vernacular form. "Dazhong wenyi" is, of course, the general term for "popular literature and art." "Fan dazhong wenyi" or "reactionary popular literature and art" refers to both traditional and modern commercial popular art which Qu views as feudal or enslaving. "Geming dazhong wenyi" or "revolutionary popular literature and art" is obviously what Qu is hoping will emerge from the literary debates of the early 1930s. It includes *both* "popularized" writings done by literary intellectuals and non-literate art done by the people themselves—that is, traditional popular forms infused with new, revolutionary content. In Qu's view, the rise of truly "geming dazhong wenyi" will involve the decline of "fei-dazhong pulo wenyi" or "non-popular proletarian literature and art," the literature of the "Europeanized" generation.

7. Qu is denying here that the vernacular or *baihua* so closely identified with the May Fourth literary revolution was genuinely vernacular.

8. Lin Shu (1852-1924) became well known in the late 19th century for his translations of sentimental and romantic Western novels into classical Chinese. See Leo Ou-fan Lee, *The Romantic Generation of Modern Chinese Writers*, Cambridge: Harvard University Press, 1973, pp. 41-57.

9. "Wuxia xiaoshuo" or knight-errant fiction as well as other forms of traditional fantasy and adventure literature are discussed more fully in the next essay translated here.

10. The Chinese term used here (zuojia shenghuo di dazhonghua) is difficult to translate smoothly. As Qu uses the term it means the populist process of intellectuals merging with the masses.

11. Qu is probably referring here to an earlier and more lengthy piece he wrote in October 1931 entitled "Pulo dazhong wenyi di xianshi wenti" (The Real Questions of Proletarian Popular Literature and Art). See *Qu Qiu-bai Wenji*, vol. 2, pp. 853-874.

12. This refers to Japan's seizure of three northeastern provinces (September 1931) and Japan's attack on and bombing of Shanghai (February 1932).

13. "New classical" (*xin wenyan*) is used to satirize May Fourth "vernacular."

14. "Ou-hua" is also used sarcastically to refer to radical iconoclasts among revolutionary May Fourth writers.

15. "Popularizing," of course, means popularizing elite, May Fourth, Europeanized revolutionary literature and art.

16. Here is a clear statement of the need, in the Chinese case, for the bourgeois-democratic revolution to be led not by the bourgeoisie, but by the proletariat—elements representing the proletariat or having proletarian consciousness.

17. Qu is referring here to attempts made during the Great Revolution of the 1925-27 period to shift the orientation of the literary movement from literary revolution (*wenxue keming*) to revolutionary literature (*keming wenxue*). It was during this period that many Chinese writers became radicalized politically, although they were still using Western literary forms.

18. This is an extremely interesting, if oblique, reference to Qu's disenchantment with the Wang Ming leadership group which dominated the CCP in the early 1930s. It was precisely their dogmatism and subjectivism which helped widen the gap between the party and the urban masses in this period. Qu himself was expelled from the Politburo of the Central Committee by the Wang Ming group in early 1931.

19. Apparently the "siliu dianbao" was an extremely concise and stylized method of sending telegrams in the early Republican period—a form which alternated between lines of four and six characters.

20. Liang Qi-chao was a brilliant reform thinker of the late Qing period. For an outstanding study of his intellectual development see Joseph Levenson, *Liang Ch'i-ch'ao and the Mind of Modern China*.

21. By using the ethnic/racial term "Han" here, Qu is suggesting that the literacy problem is a Chinese problem. There is no need to impose the Han language and script (and its problems) on minority groups in China.

22. *Shen Bao* was a major Shanghai newspaper in this period.

23. This remark reflects more than the anti-rural bias of Western Marxism which influenced Qu until perhaps the last year in his life. His point is, of course, that local peasant dialects are not sufficiently modern for use as a national language.

24. In Qu's view the question of form is different from the question of "language"—form refers to the vehicle of artistic expression or the method of exposition.

25. This is a specific reference to the "romantic" Marxist writers who criticized Mao Dun and others for writing about the petty-bourgeoisie in the late 1920s and early 1930s.

26. Yue Fei, a Sung Dynasty general, is the hero of a variety of traditional popular novels including *Jingzhong Shuo Yue* and *Shuo Yue Quan Zhuan*. He has been called the "military person's Confucius." *Water Margin* (Shuihu Zhuan) is one of the most famous of all traditional novels.

27. This is a specific reference to the popularity of that genre of sensationalist literature known as the Mandarin Duck and Butterfly School (*yuanyang hudie pai*). What is particularly noteworthy about this passage is Qu's explicit appeal for the use of the despised "Butterfly" forms by left-wing writers.

28. Quite by accident I have come across what I believe to be the rough draft of this essay. It is contained in Ding Yi (ed.), *Dazhong Wenyi Lunji* (Essays on Popular Literature and Art), Peking: Beijing Shifan Daxue Chubanbu, 1951, pp. 141-145. The article is undated and entitled "Dazhong wenyi di wenti—chugao pianduan" (The Question of Popular Literature and Art—Draft Fragments).

Introduction to Ding Ling's "A Day"

Ding Ling (Ting Ling), a woman writer purged from the Chinese Communist Party (CCP) in 1957, was born in rural Hunan in 1906 into a family of some wealth and an intellectual tradition. She became aware of the need to change China's political and social order at an early age and much of her adolescence and early adulthood was devoted to that end. She took part in demonstrations for women's rights. She participated in the national salvation activities following the May Fourth Incident. She worked to improve the lot of workers through education. She also struggled to achieve more education and independence for herself.

During the course of several difficult years, however, her orientation seemed to change. She became less sanguine about the prospects for changing society and more self-centered. She "hibernated" (one of her own terms) in Peking and even advised her common-law husband, Hu Ye-pin, against leaving a promising writing career and going to Wuhan in 1927 to seek a position in the new governmental bureaucracy.

In that same year, 1927, Ding Ling herself began writing. The reasons were mostly personal. As she said later, she needed a way to express her frustration with society and relieve her loneliness. In keeping with her outlook at this time, her first stories were highly individualistic in nature—psychological examinations of young women trying to cope with the complexities of their own lives.

Gradually, however, Ding Ling became active in the communist revolutionary movement. Hu Ye-pin was an influence in this direction. Friends, leftist critics, and developments in the socio-political situation also played a part in this development. As she moved toward the left, her fiction changed, too. Finally, of course, she became a CCP member and achieved recognition as a prominent revolutionary writer.

"A Day" was written in the midst of this process of change. Published in 1930, almost two years before she joined the CCP, it is as much an examination of the ills plaguing Chinese society in general as it is a description of the heroine's individual psychology. Yet, in keeping with the author's own uncertainty at this time, it offers no hope for curing those ills. Exhortation to adopt revolutionary goals and to work actively for their realization is conspicuously absent—the flippant quote by Wei-li of the first part of Sun Yat-sen's statement, "The revolution has not yet been completed. Comrades, we must continue to work hard," notwithstanding.

Actually, "A Day" addresses itself to a "pre-revolutionary" problem, namely, what should be the response of intellectuals to a society riddled through with injustice and misery. First of all, they should be concerned about the problem. This Yi-sai is. Her heart goes out to the "nightsoil" (human excrement used for fertilizer) collectors. She thinks that if she went among them she could improve their lives and make them realize that they are men. She has also been interested in changing the attitudes and ideas of her maid. Unfortunately, however, these concerns do not find expression in action, as they should if anything constructive is to be accomplished. Yi-sai is unable to break out of her own class isolation and establish an understanding relationship with the workers she wishes to help. There is, therefore, little else for her to do but fall asleep and await the repetition of this ugly depressing cycle.

Gary Bjorge

52

A Day

By Ding Ling

translated by Gary Bjorge

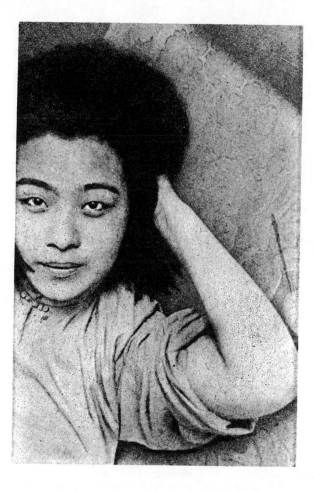

Dawn.

. . . This is a bustling city, a semi-colony where people of many different countries and races live together, an area governed by these several nations for their own benefit. For this reason, when the sun's first rays emerged from the eastern sea, the full spectrum of colors and hues were washed and highlighted beneath that pale blue sky shared by all. In one area tall buildings many stories high lay quietly, each pointed tip silhouetted against the sky like a cubist painting, made all the more so for the thin smoke rising from smokestacks like a painter's added embellishment.

Within the square rooms those enticing yet slightly lewd red lamps have just been extinguished. Beautiful glasses that held sweet liquor for the drunken guests and an assortment of cigarette butts are scattered in complete disarray on top of the exquisite tables. Easy chair cushions are strewn everywhere. Having become tired, these people have gone to sleep wherever they pleased, their indolent limbs sprawled akimbo on smooth soft bedding. Made of raw materials from the Far East that were processed by Western workers, this fine bedding had passed through several storms at sea and been handled by hands of several different complexions before finally being placed in this building. Here it is used, for the most part, by some potbellied yellows, whites who like to wear top hats, drunken foreign soldiers, and women with long drawn eyebrows and faces soiled by rouge.

At the end of the long broad street made so dark by the screen of tall buildings, young girls who failed to do any business walk with slow steps. Sighing deeply as their bodies sway to and fro, they return dejectedly along this street where the streetlamps still glint to their small rooms.

In another area, beneath the shadows of a forest of large black smokestacks, small shacks housing hundreds of thousands of the yellow race are crowded together. Just now the men are getting up from where they slept beside their thin hungry wives. Using their sleeves of that coarse blue cloth worn by workers, they wipe the grime from their faces. Their hair is disheveled. Their shoes have holes in them, revealing toes that protrude through their socks. Hurriedly they leave in a mass from their homes and hurry along a muddy road skirted by a canal of putrid, filthy water on their way to a factory that makes money by crushing and squeezing them. In that foul smelling channel, many small boats are tightly packed together. The situation on them is even worse. A small number of these pitiable people have been blessed with a degree of good fortune and they thus can come forth to join those moving along the shore. With empty stomachs they rush to the factories for the morning shift.

From the factories set up by a few hundred caucasians, overseas Chinese and, of course, some of our own greedy people, all of them people who somehow had the capital to invest, the whistles send out a unified chorus of sharp sounds. The factory gates stand wide open, filled by these dirty people who crowd in. Shortly thereafter they disgorge an even dirtier group, those who worked all night without sleep in place of the day shift so that the productive machinery need not stop. The place is so noisy, with the cries of hungry children mixed in, too.

Who can think of looking at the beauty of the morning sun and the colorful clouds drifting along? Who notices the shadows of the smokestacks reclining across the ground and the thick black smoke rolling along like a galloping horse? Does anyone see that as the water in the stinking canal receives the sun's rays it reflects a pattern of rainbow colors? This is essentially all there is to life for them—these people who have been turned into deadened, robot-like things by their misery. Utterly without hope, utterly without thought, day and night they suffer. How can it be that this mass of people does not take a break from this man-killing work and establish a movement for equality, if not for their own sake, then at least for the sake of the suffering workers who will succeed them?

Other areas of the city are now also filled with the hustle and bustle of a new day. Boats prepare to weigh anchor. Cargo handlers shout. Streetcars and buses start to move their full loads of useless people about.

This, then, is the city. There are no birds or chickens dressed in elegant plumage to call out the arrival of dawn. There are no plain and simple peasants stepping out of their small comfortable thatched huts to ready their agricultural implements. There are no healthy looking young girls coming out to tend their flocks of sheep. The rising clamor of such lovable animals as the chicken, duck, cow, and dog is totally absent. Also missing are the beautiful little birds which sing happily to welcome daylight and the rising sun.

In yet another section of the city, even though it is administered by members of the white race, a large number of those impure yellow people have still crowded in to live. In an area where even poor foreigners would not care to live, large red structures of poor quality have been erected on every street. Each building houses more than one hundred families and the number of mouths in each familiy is simply shocking.

In one of these families a girl named Yi-sai is lying in bed. She had fallen asleep only a short time earlier, but when the first light of daybreak turned the glass in her window white she nonetheless woke up again. Her age is about twenty, a young woman who has long since lost her innocence. Due to a lack of fresh air her skin color has changed from yellow to a very pale white, a sickly appearance. She has not been roused from her dreams by the sun shining on earth and the beautiful morning that has come nor have her sleeping eyes been gently opened by the moist morning breeze fragrant with the fresh odor of grass and shrubs. No, she has developed the bad habit of waking up at the slightest sound. For example, sounds to which ordinary people would not pay the slightest bit of attention, such as the child next door crying again or the racket made by the people across the hall when shifting their mahjong tiles a bit exuberantly, are sufficient to wake her. At this time, and every day at this time, the sound of the garbage cart with its big wheels squeeking along the asphalt street could be heard. Then from a small alley would come another iron cart. The man pushing it shouted loudly and in each household a maidservant would hastily jump up from a dark dingy bed underneath a stairway. A foul stench would then begin to rise from between these tall buildings located so close together and would spread rapidly in all directions. Soon the sound of hundreds of bamboo brooms scraping savagely against the inside of the wooden chamberpots and swooshing

them out with water would shake the thin walls in every building. Every morning Yi-sai was awakened and put into a foul, cranky mood by the punctual and entirely predictable commotion set up by this daily emptying of the excrement buckets.

Gradually the sound of the cart receded into the distance. The maidservants crawled back into their beds to sleep and all was very quiet. The occasional honking of a car far away was the only sound to be heard. Yi-sai, however, could not go back to sleep.

As it became lighter outside, Yi-sai's thoughts turned, as usual, to that iron cart now far away. Where will it be pushed to? After it has arrived at its destination, what will be done? She thought once again of what she had frequently seen, couples, husband and wife, pushing these carts together. Their entire life is built around this. Their children and their grandchildren will do this same work and not feel tired. They have no hopes other than whatever hope is to be found in doing what they do. They have no dreams other than whatever dreams can be put into this. Yi-sai saw the faces of these people—so filthy. Their hands are so frightfully dirty. The women? Straggling hanks of hair hanging down from the loose bun in back. Their socks are wrinkled up around their insteps. They run along quickly. She thought of what conditions are like when they return home—no interesting conversation, just dull stares as they eat with their filthy hands and then fall dead asleep in each other's arms.

This life is so frightening to Yi-sai. She thinks that if she were with them she could add something to their lives. She could make them realize that they're human beings, that they should live like people. But, then she thinks, what about all those people wearing very clean and fresh clothing with their moronic thinking, their purely selfish aspirations? How could they make others feel that what they represent is life as it should be lived? Everyone is letting life slip away day by day without doing anything of the slightest meaning or usefulness!

Yi-sai turns her eyes toward the window. Such a beautiful blue sky. In the windows of the buildings across the street she can see the reflections of the clouds above. Sadly she turns her face back toward the inside of her room.

This city disgusts her so much, but as long as she has to stay in it, she can only wish for the kind of weather that would make her hibernate. Then she would be able to avoid the depressed feeling she has every day as she sits in her room. She imagines a dark winter day. The window shades are drawn tight. She is sitting before the stove letting the hot flames toast her body. She is so tired. Her spirit is numb. Wouldn't that be the best way to get through these unhappy times? Now, though, the weather is so nice. Good weather brings her sadness. For at these times, she cannot keep her thoughts from turning to those many other places she would like to be.

Yi-sai covers her head with her blanket. She thinks about her body. She wants to sleep. But from where she lies in bed, her thoughts jump to so many different things.

The clock in the room next door strikes eight o'clock.

Eight o'clock. During the past ten years had not this been the time when she would be happily entering a classroom arm in arm with her friends, all of them singing and making noise together? So far away—those happy days of childhood. She wished fervently that they could come back again—arms around each other's shoulders, everyone full of girlish innocence, all rushing wildly to some other place. But . . . she became sadder.

Like bees, ideas swarmed into her mind. She couldn't stay lying down in bed. She struggled up. The narrow street was noisy again. Peddlers were coming and going, some calling out their wares, others using bells or brass gongs to gain attention. She had long ago recognized from their voices that there were more than ten of them, including those selling used goods. The children in each family can never sleep a lot, of course, and now, having been excited by the sight of all different kinds of things to eat, they stand by the back door of every building either laughing or crying. Some have achieved their goal and are in high spirits. Others are dissatisfied and are still loudly clamoring for something.

The maidservant comes in to perform all the miscellaneous tasks for Yi-sai. Such a disgusting face! So many times Yi-sai's idealistic dreams had been knocked to pieces by the stupid yet cunning expression on this face. Despite all Yi-sai's efforts at putting up with frequent irritation this servant caused her, she had been unable to establish any friendship between them. She had tried every conceivable way to win her over and to gradually dissolve the servant girl's hostility, but the end result had been to only upset herself more. Now she looked at those expressionless eyes and told her softly that she wanted to do these things herself. After mumbling a few words, the maidservant walked out.

Yi-sai strode back and forth, back and forth in her little room. She did a few odds and ends. She washed a tea cup; it took two minutes. But even as she worked so diligently, she sighed and lamented her lack of patience. Others didn't know that she'd really like to take all of these things and smash them to bits. She would never, though, have the nerve to let herself go and do it. Thus, she once again turned willingly to some meaningless thoughts and let them cool her angry heart. It is almost as if she has never thought of letting something besides daydreams comfort her. Frequently, while in the middle of cursing something or someone, she would begin to daydream. Then, right in the midst of her daydreaming, she would start to curse again.

Yi-sai ate lunch with three very vain and shallow relatives. Soon afterwards, her friend Wei-li stopped by. A young man with long hair, his talents as a conversationalist were as great as her abilities to give herself to flights of fancy. He often dropped in to pass an afternoon. She did not tell him not to, nor would she do anything to stop him from showing off a little and enjoying himself. As his foot crossed the threshold he called out, "What a great day!"

She knew very well that what he said was usually an exaggeration of what he was feeling, so she asked with a smile, "Why aren't you outside having fun?"

Sighing, he told her that he really wasn't in the right mood for it, and said with a mocking laugh, "The revolution has not yet been completed."

He flipped his hat onto the bed and proceeded to sit down on the rattan chair in front of the desk. Stretching one leg out in front of him, crossing the other leg over it, Wei-li began to tell her his latest love story.

But everything was just too predictable. She understood him too well. As always, he was too long-winded. She wasn't getting a thing out of this. When he looked at her inquiringly, she would nod her head in approval of what he'd said, but in her heart she wanted to give him just the opposite response. Not wishing to start an argument, however, she kept quiet. She really liked him a little, too. He had his own amusing nature, and, actually, she had to be grateful to him for coming over so often and helping the time to slip by more easily.

Yes, she must thank these people for coming to see her. Yet, what does she gain from these visits? What meaning is there in these days? Do her friends do anything besides prove that in such an atmosphere of relentless, fixed boredom everything is hopeless? It is only in her unbridled illusions that she can achieve a kind of wild and reckless emotion. She talks with her friends, but when these conversations are over, she feels that her illusions are without any foundation. Such first-hand contrary evidence makes her depressed and lonely. Thus, she very often has the feeling that if no one came by to visit her at all she might really be somewhat better off.

Yi-sai, this pale girl, yawned slightly, lifted her face up, and let her head rest against the back of the chair. Wei-li noticed and stopped speaking immediately. He looked at her and asked, "Are you tired? You ought to rest." In her heart Yi-sai was very happy. Now he would be going. All she did, however, was nod her head lazily in indication that she really was tired. She didn't want to say directly that she wanted to sleep. Then, contrary to all expectations, Wei-li said, "It's best not to sleep during the day. If you do, you may become giddy and lightheaded." Besides this, he sat down again in the rattan chair, stretched out his arms, and began to tell some interesting stories about their friends.

After a bit a girl friend who comes by to visit Yi-sai everyday stopped in. This girl friend always brings a frightening sense of gloom with her, and when she leaves, a thick cloud of melancholy always remains behind. She entered the room quietly, glanced at the talkative Wei-li, and smiled cooly to Yi-sai. Yi-sai invited her to sit down and she took a seat in front of the desk facing Wei-li.

"How are you? What have you been doing at your home lately?" Yi-sai asked.

The girl shook her head without speaking in response to Yi-sai's question whereupon Wei-li changed the subject. He said that Chinese people are very deficient in the ability to express their emotions. According to him, one should let all of one's feelings show. Excessive reticence, he added, can only make others feel uncomfortable.

Yi-sai's girl friend frowned and listened to what Wei-li had to say. She did not reply. She only asked Yi-sai a few unimportant questions before becoming bored and leaving. All she said as she went out was "See you tomorrow."

And so evening arrived. It was a bright evening. The dirty people wearing blue clothing rested their weary limbs. Upon the wrinkles of their ashen faces bitter smiles appeared. Young girls were walking quickly along the streets. Under the combined glow of the sunset and the shining street lights they cast knowing smiles. Everything had changed. It was just the opposite of morning. Only the noise and shouting down along the river and the creaking and clattering of the moving vehicles went on unchanged, a manifestation of this never-stopping world.

By now the room was dark. Wei-li had gone, too. Yi-sai lay silently in bed, her head spinning, her spirit exhausted. She wasn't thinking of anything. She was just listening to the many different sounds of the city that came to her from near and far. Shortly afterwards she fell into a deep sleep.

Tomorrow the cycle would be repeated once again.

1930

Introduction to Mao Dun's "In Front of the Pawnshop"

The appearance of "Dangpuqian" (In Front of the Pawnshop) in the first half of 1932 marks an important milestone in Mao Dun's development as one of the leading Chinese writers of this century. This was his first attempt to describe the hardships of the Chinese peasantry in a short story. The degree of control over narrative, his sharp eye for detail, the analytic explorations into the economic decline of the peasants and the petty bourgeoisie, his uncompromising loyalty to realism, all these aspects of his fiction were beyond the reach of most other leftist or revolutionary writers in China at that time. It was during this period that the theme of rural poverty became much more prevalent in the works being produced by writers who, although basically urban in orientation and adult experience, were attaining a more radical consciousness and were now striving for a greater political significance by depicting the desperate plight of the peasants.

Mao Dun (Shen Yan-bing) was born into a family of scholarly background but reduced economic and social status in the year 1896. A native of Tongxiang County, Zhejiang (Chekiang) Province, he attended several different schools in Zhejiang before going to Beijing (Peking) for three years of college preparatory work. Unable to continue his studies for lack of funds, Mao Dun went to work for the Commercial Press in Shanghai and emerged during the early May Fourth period as a leading editor, translator and critic. A founding member of the Literary Research Society and a leading spokesman for European realism, Mao Dun was also somewhat involved with the Chinese Communist Party during its earliest days in Shanghai.[1] Similar to many of his early protagonists, Mao Dun was active in both political and literary realms during the 1920s.[2]

It was only after the devastating defeat for the leftwing revolutionary forces at the hands of the Chiang Kai-shek rightwing forces in mid-1927, and his escape from Wuhan, where he had been editor of the revolutionary regime's newspaper, that Mao Dun began to write fiction. This was also the time when he adopted the pen name 'Mao Dun' (a pun in Chinese for the word for 'contradiction') by which he is best known as a writer. The first works that he wrote in the last three years of the 1920s, some of them written while he was avoiding Guomindang (KMT) persecution by living in Tokyo from 1928 to 1930, are quite pessimistic in tone and reflect

56

his disillusionment with revolution and many of the revolutionaries at that time. They probe into the psychology of the bourgeois intellectuals and young students, exposing the ambivalence and angst of modern youth in the urban areas, especially Shanghai. Although vehemently criticized by some Communist and radical literary figures, Mao Dun's early novels and short stories were immediately recognized as an important and successful step forward in the development of a more 'modern' Chinese literature. Mao Dun was proclaimed the leading chronicler of his times as well as the leading practitioner of realism.

By the spring of 1930 when he returned to Shanghai from Japan, Mao Dun had regained his revolutionary spirit and enthusiasm sufficiently to take an active role in the newly organized League of Leftwing Writers which was attempting to promote a more militant and proletarian revolutionary literature.[3] Led by members of the Chinese Communist Party, the League of Leftwing Writers advocated struggling for the emancipation of the proletariat and upheld explicitly Marxist theories on art and literature such as were being promulgated in Moscow. Interestingly, the League was opposed, among other things, to fiction which emphasized a contradiction between love (personal liberation) and political activism (collective or class struggle).[4] This particular contradiction just happened to be a distinct feature in several of Mao Dun's earliest works.[5] His basic orientation had certainly veered away from depicting bourgeois alienation, however, and he was now veering toward a more empirical, sociological and economically analytical approach to writing. He spent several months during 1930 observing the Shanghai Stock Exchange in order to gather material for his longest and most ambitious piece of writing, *Ziye* (Midnight), which was not completed until the end of 1932. Having come to grips with the fact that the largest and most oppressed segment of China's population was the peasantry and that a main goal for the revolutionary writer was to better acquaint his middle class readers with the suffering of the rural poor, Mao Dun was now confronted with the problem of how a writer committed to realism was to write about things which he had not personally witnessed or experienced. How could he, the bourgeois intellectual and sometime revolutionary who had been living in big cities for more than fifteen years, fulfill his revolutionary obligation without abandoning his artistic practice of realist writing and his increasing emphasis on sociological investigation as the basis of his realism? The resolution to this quandary was provided by an unexpected catastrophe: In January 1932 the Japanese bombarded the Chinese districts of Shanghai with extensive loss of Chinese lives and great damage. Mao Dun left to return to his native town in Zhejiang for a few months and it was from the experience and insights encountered during his stay in that once-familiar area that he obtained much of the material used in the stories he now began to write with a rural setting, "Dangpuqian" (In Front of The Pawnshop) among them.

In the subtle yet vivid descriptions in this particular story there may be found a model for a more artfully didactic style than was fashionable among the proletarian writers of the day. At the same time, it must be admitted that the very extensive vocabulary and quite ornate syntax employed by Mao Dun was difficult for all but the highly educated to read. As in many of Lu Xun's short stories, Mao Dun is content to point out the evils and social injustices of the time without affirming any explicit solution.

After the fiction, essays and one play produced in the next dozen years, Mao Dun's literary activity as a creative writer began to decrease. With the establishment of the People's Republic of China in 1949, he moved from Hong Kong up to the capital, where he assumed a high position in the new government as Minister of Culture and simultaneously served as one of the leading editors and literary celebrities. Mao Dun dropped from public view with the advent of the Great Proletarian Cultural Revolution and has only recently reappeared in the role of Vice-Chairman of the National Committee of the Chinese People's Political Consultative Conference. And as has been the case since he stopped writing fiction, he is using his real name, Shen Yan-bing, instead of his better known pen name.

John Berninghausen

Notes

1. Chang Kuo-t'ao, *The Rise of the Chinese Communist Party/1921-1927*, Volume One of the Autobiography of Chang Kuo-t'ao (University Press of Kansas, Lawrence, 1971), pp. 104-108, p. 224.

2. For a biographical sketch of Mao Dun's life, see Ye Zi-ming, *Lun Mao Dun Sishinian de Wenxue Daolu* (Discussing Mao Dun's Forty-Year Literary Path) (Shanghai Wenyi Chubanshe, Shanghai, 1959), pp. 3-6.

3. Ting Yi, *A Short History of Modern Chinese Literature* (republished by Kennikat Press, Port Washington, N.Y., 1970), Chapter 2; also see Marian Galik, *Mao Tun and Modern Chinese Literary Criticism* (Franz Steiner Verlag, Wiesbaden, 1969), tenth chapter.

4. Galik, p. 113.

5. See John Berninghausen, "The Central Contradiction in Mao Dun's Earliest Fiction," in Merle Goldman, ed., *Modern Chinese Literature in the May Fourth Era*, forthcoming.

In Front of the Pawnshop

By Mao Dun

translated by John Berninghausen

It was just turning light to the east when the whistle on that small steamer delivered up its hooting blasts as it came up the narrow river just beyond that village. For five or six years now small inland steamers had been plying this river and the two large waves that curled out in the wake of these river craft to crash resoundingly against the earthen dikes built to protect their rice paddies had brought anguished cries from the local people. Year before last, during high-water season, the river steamer had malevolently hurtled past them at full throttle. Then it had seemed that the water dragon had been roused what with the three- or four-foot waves that swept over their dikes to flood their fields.

It was this which led the villagers hereabouts to fly into a rage everytime they had heard that boat's steam whistle. During high-water season, they had thought up every possible way of preventing that steamer from using this stretch of river. First they walked several miles just to raise a stink at the local office of the Inland Navigation Bureau. There they had been told by someone that they should take a petition to the district government office located in the big market town quite a distance farther away but it had not done any good. After that experience, they resorted to direct action. Mobilizing all fifty to sixty men in the village, they had waited for that steamer to come by and when it did they let loose with a barrage of stones and dirt clods. Hooting like crazy, the steamer beat a hasty retreat. Sure enough, they did not hear the steam whistle's eerie cry all the next day. But the following day, someone was sent out from the district government's office to warn their village of severe punishment for anyone engaging in acts of violence. On the day after that, there it came, chugging up the river, but this time there were guards standing on deck, rifles held at the ready. Naturally the country people well understood that bullets have it all over stones. Add to this the fact that the district government was ready to have people arrested, there was nothing for it but to swallow their anger and rebuild their earthen embankments day after day.

However things were different this year. The steamer had changed its schedule and now it chugged past at dawn, just at the right time to wake them from their slumbers. The boat itself was a smaller one, a very nifty little craft that was called something like "diesel boat." Due to an unseasonably early drought, the river was shallow and only this diminutive boat was able to thread its way up and down the river. Not that the villagers gave a damn, but it also happened to be true that business for the steamer company was down, consequently even the cargo space in the hold of this small vessel was most likely empty. Be that as it may, the little river steamer did come past just at daybreak and the hooting of its whistle was a providential substitute for the cocks that had once crowed there to announce the coming of each new day. To these villagers, who had been living on pumpkins and taro roots since the beginning of spring and who had long since sold off the last of their poultry, the sound of this whistle they had always hated before was now actually of some use.

The sky appeared a bit hazy as no breeze stirred the air. That ear-splitting hoot from the whistle fell upon the village and as if having taken a tumble, rolled into every nook and cranny. Like a heavy great millstone, its reverberations ground and grated the souls of sleeping villagers.

In a cramped and squat little house at the east end of the village flickered some candlelight. An inch and a half of white candle stub as big around as a large copper coin was silently shedding its waxen tears. At the very first blast of the whistle, Wang the Eldest, resident of this squat little dwelling, had leapt up from his bed like a man struck by a stick. He was now hurriedly tying up a small bundle by the light of the candle. Were it not for their desperate sense of urgency, how could Wang and his wife have been willing to burn this precious candle? This treasure had been brought back by Wang the Eldest from the house in the big town where he had gone to help out for three days with the work connected with a funeral for which he had received free meals. Although there had been no wages gained from that piece of temporary work, yet he had been able to fill his belly and this was so noteworthy that the other villagers spoke of it often, even now marveling with no little envy at Wang's good fortune in finding such work, to say nothing of his having brought back such a big thick candle to boot! But it had been three months since that time and the same stomach that Wang had stuffed to the bursting point during those three days working for the bereaved family had long since shriveled up with hunger. Yesterday they had consumed the last remaining pumpkin and taro root. Now he was bundling up several pieces of worn clothing with the notion of taking them to the pawnshop in the big town.

"Take this as well!" said Wang the Eldest's wife dolefully, throwing him a semi-new quilted jacket of homespun cloth.

"This too? What'll you wear?" As Wang answered, he picked up the fairly new quilted jacket and just held it, unable to decide what to do.

"Ai!" was all the woman sighed while hunching up her shoulders in a gesture of helplessness and waving the garment away.

Reluctantly, Wang the Eldest untied the bundle and went through the little stack of used clothes it contained one by one, his fingers trembling uncontrollably as he did so. Each one of these pieces of clothing had its own individual sad story. The blood stains, for instance, on this blue jacket with a lining had been acquired that time last year when he had gone with the other villagers to raise a fuss at the office of the Inland Navigation Bureau and somebody's fist had bloodied his nose for him. Then there were these women's trousers of printed fabric which his wife had begged off the woman for whom she had gone to be a wet-nurse the year before last—in hopes of earning a little money to help out with their expenses and repayment of their debts, his wife had hardened her heart to drown their newborn second daughter at that time—whenever she saw these trousers of printed fabric, she still could not help shedding tears. Besides these garments, there was that pair of quilted trousers soft as silk which they had stripped from the corpse of their thirteen-year-old daughter,

Zhaodi, who had starved to death during the floods of that same year.*

This tiny bundle of clothing was a history of their wretched life of suffering! But these few things, virtually their only souvenirs of this wretched life, as well as the only things they still possessed, would perhaps *not* be worth a single dollar in the eyes of the pawnshop owner. With a few burbling noises from Wang the Eldest's nostrils and with trembling hands, he again picked up the semi-new jacket his wife had tossed to him and blinked back his tears. The quilted jacket still emanated the warmth of her body and that special smell of sweat. Suddenly he felt as if his heart had been pierced; embracing the jacket in his arms, Wang the Eldest began to weep. The woman, however, did not cry. Her eyes were opened wide in a dazed stare. She, too, had recalled her second baby daughter, its life stifled out of its body, that she had been forced to drown in the toilet pail and her heart seemd to have frozen solid.

With a sudden lurch, a spasm which shook her whole body, she rushed over to the bed and plucked up a young baby from where he had been nestled in a heap of torn cotton waste there. She held him tightly to her breast, seemingly afraid that someone would snatch him away from her.

"Hon-ah! Hon-ah!" whimpered the baby, its voice sounding as if it came from the hoarse throat of a kitten. The woman loosened her clothes and stuffed a withered breast into the baby's mouth, rocking her body gently from side to side. Sucking on her nipple, the baby was quieted.

"Pack them all together and get going! If you get there late and you don't get into the pawnshop, there'll be nothing for us to eat today!" said the woman softly in the direction of her husband. The candle flame flickered, then sputtering sank lower and lower just as the pale light of day crept in through the crack in the door.

Raising his head, Wang sighed and put his wife's quilted jacket in the bundle. He took off his own tattered lined jacket and threw it on the bed beside his wife, then turned away and opened the door.

"It's worse outside! Won't you be very cold in just your shirt? You wear it!" she said, her throat all choked up. The woman jumped down from the bed with the child in her arms. Wang the Eldest didn't answer. A puff of wind rushed into the dwelling, blowing out the white candle. Wang the Eldest and his wife both shivered in the cold as the infant at her breast suddenly began to wail again. Her dried up breasts could not satisfy him. Wang turned woodenly back to give the child a glance, then gritting his teeth, he put the bundle under his arm and strode off.

The woman also went out to call something to her husband from beneath the eaves but she went no further, the tears filling that doleful pair of eyes. Automatically switching her baby to suckle at the other breast, she went back inside to sit down upon the broken bamboo stool. As cutting as scissors blew the wind. She was so cold her lips felt numb. Closing the

door and pulling the tattered lined jacket her husband had left for her round her shoulders, her whole body was still wracked with shivering. Then she thought of that small bundle of clothes her husband had taken with him and of the rice they would buy; surely the used clothes would fetch several coppers with which to buy rice, she thought, and smiled wanly. Just then she realized that her milkless nipples were hurting from the ravenous sucking of her hungry baby. She clasped the child even tighter and felt a bit warmer. As she stared fixedly at his thin face, the wrinkles frowning in the tender skin of that tiny forehead made the baby resemble a little old woman.

After Wang the Eldest had hurried along his way for half an hour, the sky had grown quite bright even though there was still no sunlight. Because he had been trotting along at a fast clip, he was not feeling at all cold; in fact, there were beads of sweat on his forehead. However, his stomach had begun to growl with hunger. He paid no attention at first, but after a while, with it growling more and more insistently, his legs gradually grew heavy. Swallowing down a few mouthfuls of his own saliva, he walked at a much slower pace.

Moving along the road at this slow pace, he just did not seem to be someone who lives in a rural area. Three or four peasants from neighboring villages who were also heading for the town overtook him and went on ahead. Reaching the graves of the illustrious Ma family, Wang the Eldest sat down to catch his breath on a stone bench that had collapsed. Sitting there in front of a grave mound with some cedar trees rising straight into the sky above him, some reddish cedar leaves fell beside his feet. He picked one up and popped it into his mouth, chewing on it while the sparrows twittered in the trees overhead. Wang swallowed the bitter juice of the leaf and tilted back his head to gaze up at the sparrows. A long ways off was a bridge and he could see the houses standing in dark clusters beyond it. Those houses marked the edge of the big market town he was heading for.

"Bwah! Bwah! Bwah!" came the haughty cry of the steam whistle at the mechanized grain mill in the outskirts of town.

"Gu! Gu! Gu!" growled his stomach with increased ferocity, moreover his ears could perceive contained within these sounds the echo of his new-born son's hoarse crying. Hurriedly jumping to his feet and clutching the bundle of clothing tightly beneath his arm, he set off toward the town at a run.

"If you get there late, and you don't get into the pawnshop, there'll be nothing to eat today!" rang his wife's words again in his ears. He tightened up his belt a bit and ran for all he was worth, overtaking in turn a lot of the peasants who had been ahead of him. Like a crazy man, Wang ran and ran without stopping all the way up to the main gate of the pawnshop.

Even though the two darkly gleaming doors of the pawnshop's main gate were still locked tight, there was already a goodly number of people waiting outside them. The day's activity in town was just beginning at this time when within a few shops the clerks were up and dragging their slippers across the floor to open the shop door partway, sticking out their heads for a look, coughing up some phlegm and spitting it out on to stone paving right in the middle of the street. The apprentices, looking for all the world like little beggars, were taking their own sweet time as they went by carrying buckets

---

* It was the custom among these villagers that a dead person must not appear naked before Yan Wang, Lord of the Nether Kingdom, thus even the poorest families had to dress the corpse in quilted trousers before placing it in the poor thin coffin. Lest these good trousers rot away in vain, however, it was permissible to reopen the coffin two or three days later and remove the valuable quilted trousers so that some living person could use them. Nonetheless only those families compelled by the most drastic poverty would do this.

of water for the day's use. The "early bird" vendor of steamed cakes, his steaming round bamboo trays stacked high, stopped to hawk his wares in a penetrating and unceasing cry: "Cakes, yah!, cakes and rice dumplings, yah!," blinked his eyes rapidly, then hurried away on his rounds.

The ranks of the poor waiting outside the pawnshop were increasing minute by minute. They were now squeezed so tightly together in that particular stretch of road that there was not any space left among them. All gazed steadily at the glistening black doors and each tried to squeeze a little closer to them. Wang the Eldest with his bundle of clothes held beneath one arm was likewise trying to force his way forward amid the jostling crowd. Beside him was an old lady with red eyes who was carrying a roll of homespun. Her withered old lips opened and shut ceaselessly and she seemed to be chanting Buddhist prayers at the same time she too was trying to press forward toward the gate.

A fishmonger whose voice had been audible from some distance off yelling out his wares now suddenly arrived on this scene. The carrying pole he had balanced over his shoulder had a wooden tub brimming with water and live fish hanging from the front end and a large open basket full of muddy oysters suspended from the end of the pole behind him. He needed to somehow thread his way through the throng packed together in front of the pawnshop and he let his big tub full of fish swing from side to side in order to clear a path through the crowd. This gave rise to no small disturbance amid all those people. The old woman with red eyes was singlemindedly trying to squeeze forward when the end of the fishmonger's carrying pole came out of nowhere to strike her quite by accident on the side of the head and knock her down. The water in the tub sloshed out onto the street and three of his live fish were flopping around on the stone paving.

"An old woman's been knocked down! Hey, everybody stop pushing!" yelled Wang as he used his back and buttocks to hold back the pressure of the people pressing in on them.

"Aiyaya! Please don't trample on my fish!—This is a public road for everyone to use, you know!" Quickly setting down his load, the fishmonger shouted out at them while bending over to grab his fish from among the many legs. The old woman, however, had already scrambled to her feet and was slapping her hands together and scolding that fishmonger:

"What's the matter? Have you gone blind?" In a while she remembered her bolt of homespun cloth and hastened to reach down and rescue it from the ground. What had been white homespun was now a dirty gray color. The old woman's scolding instantly turned into crying, nevertheless all the people around her continued to press forward just the same. Thus she did not even have a chance to have her cry; hemmed in by the throng, she too began to push forward once again while also feverishly trying to wipe clean the soiled part of the fabric against her ragged clothing.

It most certainly had not been easy for Wang the Eldest to struggle his way forward to the front of the crowd up by that raven black gate. His whole body was drenched with stinking sweat and his stomach could do nothing but growl and growl. Sitting on the ground there with her back against the pawnshop door was a young woman whose face had an unhealthy pallor. Her frightened eyes were staring vacantly up at the sky. There were peasants from the countryside as well as townpeople on either side of her, all of them sticking very close against the gate.

"Ai! It doesn't get this crowded even outside the charity soup-kitchen!" sighed someone close beside Wang's ear.

"Well, it's a time of famine, isn't it?—When does the pawnshop open up?" Wang stretched and loosed his own sigh, apparently answering the voice that had spoken near him. Although still somewhat worried as he asked about the time for the pawnshop to open, actually his tone of voice betrayed that he was feeling much reassured. After all, he had not gotten there too late and the door still had not opened by the time he had forced his way up to the front, so perhaps he would be able to exchange his little bundle of garments for some money without any hitch.

"They say it won't open until nine o'clock!—Hey, isn't it nine o'clock by now?" chimed in the young woman sitting on the ground, her eyes now directed at Wang the Eldest. Wiping the sweat off his brow with the back of one hand, Wang answered:

"It's already past nine, no doubt about it. Now that I've come more than four or five miles on the run to get here, who'd have imagined they would still be closed?"

"More than four or five miles, huh? But what about me? I've been sitting here waiting since before daybreak this morning! Those people there got here practically as early as I did. We've been waiting so long and we're all mighty hungry and cold. Nevertheless this strong main gate's locked up like a prison and now there are *so* many people here!" complained the young woman fiercely while banging several times on the wooden door with her elbow.

"Still haven't opened yet? Open up!" the others up front began to shout and many fists beat a deafening tattoo on the gleaming black doors of the main gate. Wang the Eldest's fist could not quite reach the door, so he contented himself with joining in the shouting. After having had a good shout, he felt that his stomach's growling was not quite so bad as before. The people to the rear were yelling too, but instead of yelling

"open up!" they were shouting "push forward!" Wang the Eldest would have liked to move forward but in front of him was the young woman and behind her was the door itself, thus all he could do was use his back and buttocks to push back against those who were crowding forward.

All the shops along the road were opening for business at this time and the clattering and banging of the wooden planks which protected the store fronts at night being taken down was audible to the people waiting outside the pawnshop. Wang the Eldest also heard it, nevertheless that pair of raven black doors he was facing stayed tightly closed. Wang turned his head for a look behind him. The people were standing there, packed together and many layers deep. Although there were some flushed red faces to be seen among them while others stood out for their pallor and gasping, all of them were noisily shouting curses and full of hatred at the pawnshop for not being willing to open up a bit early.

"Ai, ow, ooh!" the young woman suddenly wrenched out some grunts of pain, her teeth biting into her lip and clutching her belly with both hands. However the waiting people were only clamoring for the door to be opened and no one paid her any mind. Because he was standing directly in front of her, only Wang saw clearly that the exertions of her intense pain were a little out of the ordinary. He recalled having seen someone holding her belly and groaning like this before, but he couldn't quite place it. The woman moaned a little longer and was then quiet again. When she slowly lifted up her face, the veins in her forehead seemed about to burst beneath the beads of sweat as big as soybeans. There were deep teethmarks in her lip and her eyes were clouded with fear.

She looked at Wang the Eldest, then looked first to one side and then the other as if she wanted to say something, to tell someone something if only she could find the right sort of person. Just at that moment, the crowd abruptly set up a roar: "They're going to open up!" A crack of light glimmered and then widened between those two gleaming black doors before him which brought another great shout from the waiting crowd and Wang could no longer stand fast against their shoving. He was impelled forward several paces in a dizzying blur, yet he distinctly heard an ear-splitting cry of agony. Before he knew it, he found himself already inside the raven black doors of the gate as there came a frenzied voice from some man behind him, screaming:

"Oh, no! Oh, God! A woman's been trampled! A pregnant woman!" Wang the Eldest began to tremble all over like one plunged into ice water. He tried to stand still but it was simply impossible. The people came surging through the main gate like a tide which carried him relentlessly right up against that very high counter of the pawnshop where he was pinned against it so tightly he could hardly breathe. Countless hands were holding up every kind of used clothing and small bundles over the edge of the high counter. Instinctively, Wang freed the hand that carried his bundle to thrust it forward into that forest of hands. For the time being, even he had completely forgotten that ear-splitting scream and the face of the young woman wracked with pain. He, too, followed the example of the rest of the people and craning up his neck, lost himself in yelling out:

"Mr. Pawnbroker, sir! Mr. Pawnbroker, sir!"

Wang saw a pawnbroker approaching him, but that pawnbroker took things from the hands of others. On his left,

he saw another pawnbroker behind the counter wrinkle up his eyebrows into a frown and throw several pieces of blue-colored clothing right back into the crowd with a loud voice shouting out:

"Junk! We don't take junk like that!"

After this, Wang saw the pawnbroker just across the counter from where he was standing grab up two silken pieces of clothing and call out:

"One dollar!"

"Two dollars, wouldn't that be all right, huh? Gee, they're both new!" Someone near Wang was standing on tiptoe to stretch forward and pleading over the counter. The pawnbroker did not give any response except to throw the two silk garments back out again and reach immediately for a bolt of silk white as the shining snow being offered up in someone else's hand. Hefting it in his hand for its weight, the pawnbroker called out again:

"One dollar!"

The owner of the silk hesitated ever so slightly before giving his answer and that bolt of silk was likewise instantly cast aside. At this point Wang the Eldest saw his chance and thrust forward his own bundle of clothing to the pawnbroker, his heart fairly pounding in his chest.

"What! You can't be serious! You're bringing stuff like this to pawn?" snarled the pawnbroker who was holding his nose as soon as he had gotten the bundle untied and who wasted no time in throwing it back over the edge of the counter at him.

Wang the Eldest stood there like a man who has been clubbed over the head, utterly stunned, with no idea of what to do. He bent down automatically to pick up those few treasured garments from among the sea of legs. Simultaneously the sounds of his wife's weeping, his baby son's crying, his stomach's growling reverberated in his ears.

After he had picked up their few pieces of clothing from the ground, he decided on the plan of going to a different spot along the counter in order to try again. But just as he had picked out a different pawnbroker with a friendlier face whom he thought he would try his luck with, he heard voices being raised in heated and incredulous protest:

"Come on now! Not even the time it takes to smoke a pipe and you're not going to accept more than 120 dollars' worth of business? What do you mean you're not going to accept any more articles to be pawned until some have been redeemed? What is this?"

Wang the Eldest let out a long sigh. He now knew that having run all this way today had been for nothing at all. As if in a trance, he allowed himself to be pushed and jostled back out through the gleaming black doors of the main gate by the movement of the crowd. Chancing to look down, he noticed a shallow pool of purplish-black blood had spread its stain across the stone threshold. Instantly the young woman's piercing shriek of agony rang again in his ears as he finally was gripped by the sudden recollection of the way his wife had clutched her belly and groaned just that same way when she gave birth to their son last year beside the treadmill water-lifting wheel at the river's edge. His mind jumped from this to thoughts of his half-year-old son with no milk to drink, his wife who was now nothing but skin and bone with her dried-up withered breasts, and Wang the Eldest's heart grew heavy like a piece of stone in his chest.

1932

Introduction to Zhang Tian-yi's "Hatred"

Zhang Tian-yi (1907-   ) was one of the most popular and prolific authors of China's revolutionary literature during the 1930s. From 1928 to 1959 he wrote over a hundred works; aside from the 90 or more short stories, he produced a few novels, plays and some juvenile fiction. The decade from 1928 to 1938 was his most productive period; tuberculosis kept him from writing during the next decade; after Liberation in 1949 he devoted himself to works for children. In 1957 he became chief editor of the monthly *Renmin Wenxue* (People's Literature).

In the general view of China's critics, Zhang Tian-yi's early fiction burst upon the scene like a bombshell. Just as it was appearing in 1928, two major types of story popular in the Twenties were losing their readership: one was the sloganeering fiction full of purely verbal enthusiasm for revolution, which had permeated literary circles since the May Fourth Movement; the other was the formulaic fiction of love-and-revolution already recognized as a cliche. In the first decade of his career, Zhang Tian-yi's stories have five major concerns:

—a satire on the faddish May Fourth literary styles and intellectuals in general—their superficial zeal for revolution, their wavering, egotism and melancholy, their trivial love affairs and empty lives;

—satiric treatment of social climbers in city and village;

—exposure of the structure of rural exploitation with its combination of landlords, loansharks, strongarm men, clan system and religion;

—sympathetic portrayal of unvarnished lower-class life, in which the victimized protagonists are positive figures—rural hired hands, soldiers, the urban unemployed, beggars, orphans, apprentices, prostitutes;

—vivid depiction of the development of class consciousness and consequent rebellion among the oppressed.

The historical period spanned by these stories, roughly 1911 to 1938, reflects the China of the bourgeois revolution, the May Fourth Movement, the period of conflict among warlords, the Northern Expedition and the war against Japan. His depiction of rural and urban social relations focuses on class struggle. In other words, Zhang Tian-yi's earlier fiction deals with the times in which he lived, particularly the immediate past. His work was noted for its linguistic innovations. Zhang Tian-yi went further than most May Fourth writers in rejecting the Westernized Chinese that had passed for the literary vernacular since the early Twenties. He brought the language of workers, soldiers and peasants into fiction and used it with a skill unsurpassed by his contemporaries.

"Hatred," first published in *Xiandai* (Modern Times) 2:1 (1932), is an example of the victim theme and represents the first appearance of peasant figures in Zhang Tian-yi's fiction. Though shocking, the story is a fair reflection of the horrors of interminable civil wars among the warlords, and of the immense if undirected popular rage against social conditions. One of this story's distinctive features is the use of collective characters—the protagonists are groups rather than individuals. The narrative makes extensive use of represented discourse: setting, for example, presented by the narrator, is always described in terms of the peasants' perception of it. Such a narrative mode is a characteristic of modern fiction.

This translation has been made from *Qiren Ji* (The Eccentrics), a collection published in Shanghai in 1945 by Liangyou Tushu Gongsi. A French translation, "Haine," can be found in Martine Vallette-Hémery, *De la révolution littéraire à la littérature révolutionnaire* (Paris, 1970).

Shu-ying Tsau

Hatred

By Zhang Tian-yi

translated by Shu-ying Tsau

The ragged tattered mass of people are making their way across the dirt: the men walk up ahead, the women and children following.

They take a look at the road ahead: a long long road.

They've been walking this road for three days and two nights. From the sun they can tell they haven't gone the wrong way. The road is endless. They look and it seems they have already reached the limit, but then somehow or other the road has been stretched out even longer.

"How long before we get to Liu Village?"

"Should be tomorrow."

With its dips and rises the dirt rolls like waves from the roadside. The sun is buried in the dirt, glowing a flesh-pink.

Even so the sun is roasting with a will; their skins have turned a deep purple from the roasting, there even seems to be an odor of something burnt.

"Will there really be food when we get there?"

Everyone's heart leaps. Everyone is starving; they only have some water with them. There was no food at home: their homes have become cannon fodder. Several men at home were hauled off by some Joint Anti-Rebel Force as labor conscripts. With their own eyes they saw their entire crop of wheat trampled flat by those forces.

"What'll we do in Liu Village?"

"Who'll feed us?"

"Might as well die early, damn this agony," a hoarse

throat, tears in the voice.

The women whisper:

"Old man Hai is crying again."

"I'll fuck every damn one of your ancestors . . . I live all by myself, all by myself. . . ." Old Hai is hoarsely muttering. Ever since the death of his girl, Da-niur, he has been crying and swearing to himself.

"If I ever get hold of one . . . just one . . . I'll fuck every damn one of your ancestors, any soldier that I get hold of, our Da-niur . . . You . . . you . . ."

The children see how funny his crazy features are, but they're unable to laugh. The adults keep their silence. It was they who carried his Da-niur back that day: no jacket, no trousers. Her face was grey, her thighs and lower belly were covered with blood. Before they got her home she had a few spasms and went to her final rest. Some of the men think of their own wives who have disappeared without a trace: their faces darken.

Whether it is the heat or what, their hearts are pounding, their legs go soft. They grit their teeth.

A strange odor is streaming out of the earth: maybe gunpowder, maybe the stench of corpses, but there is nothing to be seen. The sun-baked horizon is smoking. It seems that the horizon is slowly moving: oh, the edges are curling up under the sun's baking, like baking flatcakes—flatcakes are baked and baked until the edges curl up, aren't they?

Everyone is silent. There is only the sound of feet on grit. The dry grit is like riverside mud, take a step and the foot sinks in, it requires some effort to lift the leg out.

"Who's that crying?" a child suddenly asks, pointing his finger.

His mother scolds: "None of your nonsense!"

The women are afraid of meeting ghosts. In the whole world there is only this group of people, only the sky full of dirt, the land full of dirt, the flesh-colored sun. There isn't another living thing. Who could be crying, still hanging around this world . . .

But the child won't concede. He keeps his mouth shut a while, then speaks in a low voice: "There really is."

Really, there is someone moaning.

Ghosts in broad daylight! — A shudder runs through the women.

"Neighb . . . neighb . . . sorry to . . . I need . . . I need . . ."

"Who's that?"

The men look around.

"Over here!"

They climb the knoll. A man is lying beneath a small tree: his pants are tattered, his torso is bare. His whole body is black.

"Finish me off . . ." It costs the man quite an effort to get such a sentence out. "I'm too . . . I'm too . . ."

"Who wants to kill you?"

"Finish me off . . . Do a good deed . . . I'm too . . ."

One good look at what made the man's whole body black, and their intestines quiver. On the man's back and chest are seven or eight gashes, the bloody red flesh pushed out and exposed. Millions and millions of ants swarm over the length of the wounds, swarm inside the several red troughs, picking his bloody flesh with their pincers; it's hard to make out how deep the wounds are. The rest of his body is crawling with ants. They seem busy, communicating with each other by

means of feelers. The ants had come from a small hole beside a root of the tree, still crawling in an unbroken column up to the wounds, they squeeze out a spot for themselves among their companions or go crawling from one wound to another. But it isn't easy to get positions for themselves, they are all taken. Ants that have crawled through a wound have legs and feelers dyed with blood. It is the ants that have turned this man into a black person. And this man isn't dead, with ants biting every ridge and hollow of him.

"Do a good deed . . . I'm too . . . I'm too . . . I . . ." gasping for breath. The man's breathing is too weak.

They're all looking at each other not knowing what to do. Everyone's flesh crawls: it seems as if their own heart and brain matter are teeming with so many ants.

"What are you?" asks a quavering voice. But he immediately has the feeling that the question is out of place.

"Labor conscript . . . They hauled . . ." the man's mosquito-whine of a voice.

A big guy takes a deep breath and blows on the conscript, and soon many people are helping. The ants begin to scramble, creating black waves on the back and chest of the conscript, billowing like black ink poured from a bottle into clear water. A few million ants are running, dropping: some burrow deeper into the wounds, some, their legs clotted in place, are unable to move.

The conscript is moaning desperately. Gasping for breath he tells them: He was hauled off as a conscript, grew weak from exhaustion and, as they horsewhipped him, answered back, for which he received these several knife gashes. He's been lying here maybe three or four days, he can't remember the date. At the end he asks them to do a good deed, to finish him off quick.

"Do a good deed, I'm too . . . I . . ."

He wants to get a look at them, but can't make his eyelids open.

The children, who have also climbed up to the knoll, are stamping on the scattering ants. The women also go up for a look, gasp hysterically, and covering their eyes with one hand, drag the children back down with the other.

The men get busy washing the conscript's wounds with water. Water mixes with blood to form several streams of pale red which rapidly drip to the dirt. "Carry him down."

It is the only thing they can do. But to carry him with them just like this? A look all around: it is still the same long interminable road. Brown sky and brown earth; flesh-pink sun. The horizon is smoking. In the whole world there is only this group of people alive; besides them, no person, no chicken, no dog can be seen. But to carry him with them just like this down the long interminable road?

The conscript is still begging the others to finish him off.

"Do a good deed . . . Neighbor, let me . . ."

They carry him down from the knoll anyway.

"This neighbor here has hard luck just like us, I'll fuck every damn one of your ancestors. . . . Well, mates, life we have to live together, death we'll die together. . . ."

While he's speaking, someone takes off a jacket and puts it over the conscript: the salt in the sweat-drenched jacket hurts his wounds even more. He doesn't want it.

At the thought of the conscripted husbands who have disappeared without a trace, several of the women start crying and muttering curses, while the men clench their fists so rigidly their fingertips go cold. If a troop of soldiers should appear ahead, heedless of the soldiers' swords and rifles or even cannon bombarding them, they would still make a charge, get their hands around those men's necks, and use their teeth to bite those men's flesh.

The sun moves westward. They have come to a place where three roads meet. Here is a dilapidated roofless temple front of which they sit down to give their feet a rest. The conscript has a trace of warmth only in his chest; even his breathing is likely to give out.

Silence. Not even the sound of moaning. The men set their jaws and form a circle around the conscript, watching. The women are all breathing hard, but carefully so as not to make any sound. The children know that something messy is up and stand on tiptoe to see what it is inside that circle of adults, but people are in the way.

The conscript's lips have turned grey.

Suddenly Old Hai with a mournful face and hoarse voice yells:

"Damn it, look at that, look at that! . . . Fuck every last one of your ancestors, any soldier that we get hold of . . . our Da-niur . . ."

No one listens, but deep inside they all listen to him: it isn't only this conscript, not only his Da-niur. Everything they had: their daughters, sons, wives, their houses and crops, everything is like Da-niur, like this conscript. . . .

They keep thinking one thing, any soldier that crosses their path . . .

At this moment, if not for the dust in the air, they would see on the other branch of the road three black pole-like objects moving in their direction. That road is lower than here; the three black poles are laboriously climbing this way. They are three men in tattered uniforms.

Piles of dirt here and there, spun up into a dust devil by the wind, go whirling like a top in front of the three men: now the three are invisible, now they reappear, but always they keep getting closer.

The middle one, wounded in the thigh, is propped up on either side by a skinny man and one with a swollen face. Swollenface turns his bitter glance toward the higher ground and suddenly stops in his tracks.

"Civilians!" breathing rapidly.

The other two go numb with fright.

"Done for!"

They know they can't expect any consideration from civilians. But where can they go to hide? Should they go back along the same road? — They have been walking this dusty road for two nights and a day without a bite of food, without a drop of water, simply licking the sweat from their lips.

"Fuck it all, if they hadn't seized that submachine gun, who'd be afraid of lousy civilians!"

The battle had been lost, the army was scattered, and a perfectly good submachine gun was gone.

"Nothing but frigging hard luck," Skinny's voice is shaking. "Fear the enemy and fear civilians too."

Among the ragged tattered mass of people is one who spots the three of them.

"Soldiers! — There!"

As if on command every head turns in unison—there seems to be a single audible sound.

Then the men go racing down as if they were out of their minds. They charge at the three. A young guy racing in the lead slips and falls, rolls all the way down and with a grab

gets hold of Skinny's legs. Skinny falls to the ground, the young guy gets him in a bear hug and bites his shoulder in a frenzy: he wants to bite a piece of flesh out. He has sunk his teeth well in, any deeper and he would hit the bone. Skinny wants to struggle but his arms and legs are held tight, even to turn his head and give the young guy a bite is impossible. Swollenface and the one with the leg wound have also been thrown to the dirt and a hail of fists is falling on them.

"Skin him alive!"

"Pour it on, slug him, mates!"

"Slug the lousy bastards!"

"Slug him to death!"

One of the men stops hitting.

"Why slug him, bury him alive," he shouts.

They all look at the man who said it, and the punches somehow grow lighter. Old Hai, weeping and sobbing, says:

"Butcher them . . . Fuck every damn one of your ancestors, butcher, cook and eat him . . . butcher him, damn it! . . ."

Maybe it is a good idea.

"Good food, you mothers!"

"Meat to eat . . ."

Meat to eat! But there is no pleasure in the sound of their voices, just a certain fury.

The one with the leg wound presses his cheek into the dirt, his chin jerking convulsively, a row of yellow teeth protruding as if detached from his mouth. Some sand has gotten into his mouth, sand as scalding as just-fried lima beans.

"Butcher me first, neighbor," whispers the wounded soldier.

"Why should you be first?"—a malignly smiling face.

The flesh on his face trembling, the wounded soldier says with effort:

"I'm half dead . . . I . . ."

"We won't butcher you, first we'll see you in agony."

"It's our turn to see you in agony. . . . Fuck every damn one . . . You used to . . ."

"They must have stolen some silver dollars."

"Search him!"

But these three stiffs have nothing on them except for a pair of dice in Swollenface's pocket.

"Their socks! Their socks!"

They know that once a battle is lost these stiffs put bills and anything they've stolen into their socks.

Apparently the socks have been on for a long time: stripping them off, a layer of skin peels off with them.

"Nothing, what else did you expect?" says Swollenface in a low voice.

The children get some dirt from the ground and pour it over the three of them.

"Fuck it all, these brats!"

Each time the dirt pours down they turn their heads away. The children laugh, but it doesn't sound the way they used to laugh. The dirt comes pouring down with more force: it pours into the ears, noses, mouths of the three stiffs.

"Ha ha ha!" the adults start laughing too.

"Damn, they used to be bigshots, but now . . ."

"Careful, don't let them run away!"

"They can't run."

"Fuck every damn one of your ancestors! They've lived like lords long enough . . ."

"Let the women slug this stiff, too."

"Righto, drag them up and let the women take it out on them, damn it!"

"Drag them up!"

"Come on, mates!"

In an uproar they drag the three toward the crossroads: the legs trailing on the ground plow furrows in the dirt.

The wounded soldier almost passes out; his mouth and eyes gaping half open, he just lets them drag him. Swollenface doesn't seem so willing; who is willing to just die? What, will they just die without even a drink of water or half a piece of bread? How they've suffered these last few days, escaping enemy fire, getting onto this endless road, parched and starving; being baked by the sun, what is it all about — what else but to stay alive? Now—

"Fuck it all, we've had it!"

They knew long ago that civilians hated them and would give it to them good at first sight. But here is something a little confusing: Why do these people hate them as much as all this? They don't remember how they themselves got into hurting other people. They are suffering themselves. They often go hungry. They practically haven't had any women for months and years. They went to the front, charged, got bayonetted, stopped bullets; whoever couldn't take it and deserted was caught and used for target practice. They don't know where their families ended up, they miss them: parents, wives, children. Yet the civilians hate them.

Swollenface looks at his buddy with the wounded thigh and looks at Skinny. Skinny's face has been beaten black and blue, and blood drips from his cheekbones and down off his jaws. Both of his eyes are wide with fear; how strange, for he had no fear at the front. At the front, though, they all had weapons in their hands.

"That damn submachine gun is a crying shame!"

With that article, let anyone make a move! Instead, damn it, there'd be heads bowing and tributes of food and drink. And then those women. . . . Damn it!

"Now we've had it, fuck it all. . . . What is all this! . . ."

The ground is smoking. Their buttocks and legs are dragging in the dirt; skin gets rubbed off. Blood seeps into their grey cotton pants.

"Bury 'em alive!" an old woman yells sharply, tears rising to her eyes.

"Committed so many sins!" mutters a dark-complexioned woman. "They committed so many sins . . . so many sins . . ."

The women think of their own husbands and their children. They want to pinch the three stiffs, to bite them, to pick their bones. Yet once the three are dragged in front of them they don't make a move, but completely at a loss, only cry.

"Bury 'em alive!"

The three prisoners look at the roasted dirt. Are they to be buried in this scorched dry dirt, and go to their final rest without a drink of water? They lick the sweat on their lips, sweat so salty it is bitter.

"Give us some water . . ." Says Skinny as though begging the gods. "Give us some water before we die. . . ."

"Water?" an old man jumps up like a madman. "Drink water! Fuck your mother, drink would you!"

"Gonna pick your flesh! . . . Butcher you! . . ."

"Fuck every damn one of your ancestors, our Da-niur . . . she . . ."

While speaking he suddenly dashes over to the three of them, raises his dry reed of an arm and starts punching.

Swollenface gets another blue spot on his cheek. Then all around Skinny's mouth a gluey saliva appears and worms its way down his face.

They want to struggle, but several young guys are holding them down.

"Army slobs are no good," says the woman with long loose hair sitting behind them, foam at the corners of her mouth. "Army slobs are all . . ."

Skinny wants to turn his head to see the person who spoke, but his head isn't free.

The one with the leg wound half shuts his eyes and, cheek twitching, says in a trembling voice: "Give it to me quick . . . Neighbor, neighbor . . ."

No one seems to have heard.

"Neighbor, neighbor," he moans again. "Quick . . . quick . . ."

"You can't have it your way!" Old Hai spatters flecks of saliva.

The other makes an effort to hold his eyelids open so he can look straight at someone and ask a certain favor, but all of the faces are so weird. After a fearful moment, he half closes his eyes again. With all his remaining energy, he says:

"What's today, neighbor? . . . This day next year I'll be dead a year . . . Tell my old mother she shouldn't cry . . . my mother . . . She still doesn't know . . . Tell her not to worry about me . . ."

The dark pair of hands that hold him down tremble.

These stiffs have old mothers too and are afraid of suffering? They . . .

"Quick . . . quick . . . In my next life, neighbor . . . I . . ." More spit spurted onto his face.

"The next life! . .,. With a gun in your hand you'll fight your damn wars, murder . . . Fuck every damn one of your ancestors, war is how you make your money . . ."

Skinny wrenches his head around and gets a good look at Old Hai's face. The cheekbones protrude like camels' humps. Dark circles around the eyes. Dirt is stuffed in his nostrils, caked under his nose, laced among his wrinkles like an actor's mask, and in his deadfish eyes a fire is burning: his look shows him ready to stuff these three pals into his mouth, chew them up and swallow them. What kind of look is that, what kind! Who made any fucking money?—They also have the same hard luck, they also suffer pain, they also hunt for things to eat and drink. Why do people have to take it out on them alone when there's nothing between them? In frustration Skinny shouts hoarsely:

"Fuck your mother, did we want to fight? . . . When did we live like any shitty lords?"

"Ha, you're a fine one!"

"When the Commander says fire you fire. And we . . . and we . . ."

"Don't listen to him!" the women shout. "They killed all those people. . . . Army slobs don't have any . . ."

"We . . . we . . ."

They were once civilians themselves and hated army slobs: they once belonged among people like these, found hunger unbearable and ran off. Maybe their parents now are just like this ragged tattered mass of people, chasing all over a brown heaven and earth, hating them, ready to catch them on sight and bury them alive, to butcher, cook and pick their flesh. They have been driven out of their own world. Their parents would disown them. Brothers, sisters, wives won't

accept them any more. Their buddies are defeated and scattered. They are three solitary men in this baked scorched world.

"We . . . we . . ."

Suddenly the skinny one is shedding tears like a baby.

"Crying!" It gives the children a scare. What, these stiffs who murder and loot can even cry!

The pockmarked big fellow holding Skinny down, constantly watching him, slowly relaxes his grip and the sweat of his face falls drop by drop onto Skinny.

The sky thickens with dirt, the color of the sun goes from flesh-pink to purple. A boiling hot grit-bearing wind is whirling, making breathing impossible.

"Who enjoys fighting a war," Swollenface mutters. "Even a soldier has a mother. . . . At home . . ."

"Where are you from?"

"Mule Junction."

"And you?"

"They're both from Zhou's Inn," Swollenface answers for them.

"What did you do before?"

"Farmed," in anger, "the whole family . . ."

Silence.

"I'll be damned, farmed! Then what do you do this shitty stuff for, who told you to enlist!"

Swollenface glances at the speaker then cautiously, softly, lets out what is pent up inside:

"Who do you think enjoys doing all this stuff! . . . How about you, with no food, wouldn't you?"

Wind is blowing, grit scrapes. The horizon gets blurred, there's no telling which is earth, which is sky: it must have melted the sun.

Women, men and children keep their mouths shut and look at the three buddies. They always imagined that army slobs were like something from another world. But how come these slobs say they used to farm . . ."

"Used to farm!" the same idea flashes through everybody's mind.

These stiffs are army slobs, so how come they're people just like themselves?

"No food, so you just murder and loot," the women's voices.

"Committed sins and don't even know it . . ."

"Used to farm, eh, so why always make us . . ."

Don't shout, the slobs are going on with their story.

Their families were starving. They meant to go on living. But where would they find any food?

". . . sure the world is full of food, but there are owners for all of it. . . ."

Well, to just plain starve to death is no way to go. So last year, uh, the year before last, they enlisted. They expected to fight, be promoted, and have food and drink in times to come: when their commander said cut up the enemy, what did they care what his name might be, he'd be someone practically like themselves anyway. They didn't know why they had to go into battle; maybe this commander was pissed off at that one for some reason or other. The civilians hated them but they had nothing against the civilians. When they lost the battle the three pals ran for it: everyone has to live. But . . .

"But we've had it. . . . Bury us alive, butcher us, it's up to you, anyway . . . who gives a fuck."

When he's finished his mouth is still open, yellow teeth

sticking out. A pair of dozing eyes.

Their mouths hang open, gaping; they look at each other. The lives of the three stiffs are in their hands. They have to let off steam. But should they take it out on these three—these three who farmed, who have fathers and mothers, who are people like themselves after all?

They keep looking at each other. No one can come up with an idea. The former excitement is gone from every sallow face, but here is something messy: really some mess, so who should they take it out on? They themselves are starving and in pain, and the three stiffs likewise had to get along with nothing to eat or drink. They themselves wanted to live, and the point for the three was to live too. Are they to take it out on the three?

Those holding the three down let go.

"I'll fuck every damn one of your ancestors, I'll fuck every damn one of your ancestors . . ." Tears are flowing in streams from Old Hai. He wanted to take something out of the hides of these three, but now it is a little mixed up: he doesn't know who to take it out on, no chance to get the whole mess out of his system.

The slob with the leg wound is moaning, his cheeks in violent convulsions.

"What's up, Wu Da-lang?"*

The men come close to laughing out loud: how did he get that funny name—Wu Da-lang!

"It hurts!" Wu Da-lang whispers as if afraid others will overhear. The wound on his thigh hurts so much that the whole left side of his body is aching. It feels like something is crawling around in the wound. "Damn it, how it hurts! It must have gotten more of those . . ."

Dozens of pairs of eyes are on Wu Da-lang's wounded left leg. Wu Da-lang rolls up the leg of his pants. The wound is wrapped in a dirty strip of bandage, blood has seeped through the grey cloth and the red is flecked with yellow.

"It must have gotten more of those . . ."

Fingers trembling, Wu Da-lang unties the grey cloth. But it won't come off: it sticks fast in blood.

"Damn it, what a mess!"

Swollenface glances at them all, thinking he'll ask for some water, but doesn't dare speak up.

"Don't touch it, don't . . ." says Swollenface.

"But it hurts," his lips are trembling.

"If we had a little . . . a little . . ." but Swollenface doesn't pronounce the word "water."

Wu Da-lang spits five or six times on the grey cloth around his wound. The spit is a gluey yellow and gritty.

"The lousy . . ."

Bracing himself, he takes the grey cloth sticking to his flesh and tears it off. Over an inch of skin and flesh flanking the wound is ripped off with it, and blood drips down his thigh and onto the ground, forming little black pellets in the dirt.

"Ugh, maggots!"

---

* Wu Da-lang is also the name of a short ugly character in plays, oral tradition, and the widely popular novel *Water Margin*.

The wound is the size of a teacup. Thousands of maggots are crawling in the red opening; they have eaten themselves white and fat, pus and blood all over them. Crimson blood and pale yellow pus have been mixed together. Once the grey cloth is off, the fat white maggots begin to burrow and scatter as if terrified. Several crawl out of the wound and working their backs crawl arc by arc onto Wu Da-lang's hand, painting it with red meandering lines. Several arc along carelessly, fall to the ground and struggle in the boiling hot dirt.

The people watching clench their teeth: to help seems like a poor idea, not to help is no better.

With yellow teeth Wu Da-lang bites his lower lip till it hurts. He crooks his fingers rigidly, and after a moment like this, he holds his breath and then digs his fingers into the wound.

"Damn! . . ." he is still biting his lip, and the voice seems muffled in blankets.

The maggots he comes up with he flings violently to the ground. In the wounded spot, at the touch of his fingers salty with sweat, the rotten flesh hurts till his bones shake.

He digs his hand in again for a second batch. . . .

Maggots by the handful are squirming in the dirt. Some of them stick to Wu Da-lang's fingers, wriggling on his black fingernails: it takes him quite an effort to get them off.

Then the third batch. The fourth batch, the fifth batch. At each dig his whole body shakes as if shivering with cold.

"Still more."

Swollenface wonders: should he ask them for water or not? But the others hate them, and mean to see them in agony. He raises his eyes to look at Wu Da-lang's face. Wu Da-lang's cheeks keep trembling, both hands keep scooping maggots out convulsively, throwing them in handfuls of pus and blood onto the ground. Swollenface shivers. If he had that submachine gun in his hands, for sure he'd send Wu Da-lang to his final rest. . . .

There are still several maggots in the wound; Skinny helps him by picking them out, whispering as he does so:

"Does it hurt?"

Everyone stares idiotically with jaws set. They are thinking of the gashes and the biting ants. The skinny one is bound to drop dead—let him do it quick, don't keep making him suffer. But what about this one?

"What do you call this, what? Why does everyone have the same hard luck?"

With the utmost care the skinny one is still picking maggots out for Wu Da-lang.

"All gone."

Pus and blood are flowing steadily from the wound. Wu Da-lang spits some saliva onto it and binds it again with the dirty grey cloth.

"It's no good without water," says a big guy.

Water? The three slobs give the fellow a stunned look. Where to get water? Having walked this smoking dirt for two nights and a day, the sun has drawn all the water from their bodies. With nothing even to drink, where is the water to wash wounds? They feel as if they haven't seen water in decades, nothing but bitter salty sweat. The brown earth and sky, and the purple sun, boiling hot wind, can there be water in such a world?

The three pals lick the sweat on their lips.

Old Hai draws a long breath.

"Fuck every damn one of your ancestors, how come you

have hard luck too . . ."

"Plenty of hard luck," Skinny's eyes are fixed on the ground.

"They have it the same way, the same way . . ."

Both these and those used to belong to the same world. Both these and those found it equally hard just to live, but they became each other's enemies. What is behind it all? Once again both these and those have run into each other, once again they belong to the same world, a world that has only brown earth and sky and a purple sun but nothing to eat. The three army slobs even—

"How many days have you gone without water?" asks the big guy.

Three pairs of eyes turn a blank stare on the fellow. The three mouths are mute: throats are so parched they can't make a sound, it seems as though tongue and gullet are glued together. They feel a constant irritation: whether hunger or stomach cramps, who could tell.

The big guy walks away stiff-lipped. Watching speechlessly, everyone makes way for him.

Silence. At the stillest moment, a muffled sound of something cracking seems to be audible: it must be the ground, baked to a crisp in the sun, splitting apart.

Before long people part to let the big guy back in; in his hand he carries a jar.

"Fuck it, man, drink it!"

What, what's this?

The three pals are baffled and simply stare wide-eyed. Suddenly they throw their arms around the big guy. Tears well up in their red eyes. They desperately drink the water in the jar. And Wu Da-lang even drips some onto his wound, well, what kind of a world is this?

Everybody breathes again. Everybody thinks it's a good idea to help the three pals, but no one lifts a finger. Knowing that the three are the same kind of people as themselves, it seems they should all treat them as their own. They no longer think of taking it out on these three men: they've had hard luck too, haven't they. But no one has lifted a finger to do anything for them: to change the former mood of hatred to affection just like that seems a huge embarrassment. Odd, always gaping like that, watching others endure thirst, endure pain?—These three used to be their own kind. Everyone glances at the big guy. He was the first to give the three pals some help: he broke out of the bind. At this they all felt an enormous load was taken off their minds, and each person is thinking about how he should do something for the three men.

"Thank you . . ." pants the one with the swollen face. "In my next life I won't forget you, neighbor . . . . Now I've had water. . . . In the next life I won't forget you. . . ."

The big guy turns his eyes away, scanning the horizon.

"Fuck it, man, don't say that," he seems afraid the others might mention some of the shameful things he'd done. "Anyway everyone is . . ."

The three pals wonder if they're dreaming.

"We all have the same hard luck, we have it the same, the same . . . We . . ."

He says "We!" In the talk between the two groups this is the first use of the word—"We!"

Wu Da-lang suddenly keels over, his head falling against a boy of fifteen or sixteen. The boy supports Wu Da-lang's head in both hands not knowing what he should do: he glances from one person to the next as if he is holding some

tremendously valuable thing, deadly afraid that one false move will shatter it.

Skinny and Swollenface look at each other for a while but, feeling ill at ease, they turn their heads to watch the sky.

"Hey, hey! . . . What's his name?"

"Wu Da-lang!" Swollenface helps to call him.

"Wu Da-lang! Wu Da-lang!"

Wu Da-lang's head slides from the hands of the boy to the ground. The boy is shocked, as if to say: Oh no, it did get broken! and glances at many faces for forgiveness.

A dirt-caked withered hand feels Wu Da-lang's forehead: "Fever!"

"Uh . . . uh . . ." Wu Da-lang lies there as if he doesn't ever want to get up. Both hands are digging grit, scratching deeper, apparently meaning to plant both arms in the dirt like trees. Mouth ajar, the row of yellow teeth rests on the grit. The eyes, not quite shut, show slivers of bloodshot eyeball and the smaller half of the inlaid pupil. He sees many whirling multicolored designs. He sees his own home town: starvation, his old mother crying. . . .

"Uh . . . uh . . ." He's chewing the dirt in his mouth.

"Drink some water. Wu Da-lang!"

The wind whirls up a dust devil. It spins crazily over their bodies. The wind has been fried in a pan; it scalds them, back and face: they think they can smell a burnt odor from their own bodies. The hot air is practically visible, pouring like rain down from the sky, spewing out of the ground, racing this way from the horizon.

Only half of the purple sun remains: the other half is covered with dark brown gauze.

The children notice something funny about the conscript and whisper: "He . . . Look! . . . He . . ."

The conscript has stopped breathing.

"Might as well go early to heaven, he suffered enough." Blessing him in tears, the women lower their heads.

The whole world is dumb.

Quietly the men go to dig a pit by the roadside; they make no noise, as if for fear of waking the conscript.

But the conscript suddenly moans again. He is racked by spasms, bathed in cold sweat. The lines on his forehead grow knotted. He tosses, his frightful eyes open wide, and moans still louder.

The diggers all turn their heads. Skinny and Swollenface remember their submachine gun again, they feel there is something blocking their hearts and the blood stops circulating through their veins.

"Might as well go early to rest . . ."

The conscript calms down. His chest heaves and falls a few times, then there is no further movement. The lines on his forehead are still knotted. The eyes are not quite shut. The mouth is turned down at the corners. The hands and the feet are twisted. With care they carry him over to the pit, with care they cover him with dirt.

"Might as well go early to heaven . . . We'll remember today's date, and next year . . ."

Next year: Where will they be themselves next year? . . . But they have to go on living, they have to hunt up something to eat and drink.

Uprooting a sapling, they stick it into the earth beside the mound as a marker.

"Where are you headed?" they ask Skinny and Swollenface.

"Who knows! . . . ran away from the front . . . gotta find some food . . ."

"Let's go together, to Liu Village, then we'll see."

The mass of ragged tattered women, men and children and the three pals take to the endless road once more. The big guy and a pockmarked man support Wu Da-lang. Several dozen pairs of feet plunge into the scalding dirt and tug out again, and so step by step they move on. As the women and children listlessly drag their steps over the grit, the dust rises up around their feet.

Wu Da-lang's face has turned grey; he can't hold out any more. The arms supported by other men's shoulders slip down, his knees buckle and he sinks to the ground. He lies with his face in the dirt, gasping, the sand near his nostrils hopping up at every breath.

"What's wrong with you? . . . Wu . . . Wu . . ."

"Give it to me . . ." Wu Da-lang parts his lips that have turned black, and foam pushes out. "I can't take it . . . Neighbor, give it to me . . . Neighbor, neighbor, neighbor! . . ."

Many people stop in their tracks.

"Neighbor, neighbor! . . ." cries Wu Da-lang in anguish, "Good buddies, . . . you . . . I can't take it, can't take it! . . . Uh, uh, good buddies, good buddies! . . ."

The sun sinks toward the west. No one can tell how much time passes before they go to dig another pit by the roadside: they lay Wu Da-lang peacefully inside. Swollenface takes the pair of dice from his pocket and places them beside Wu Da-lang. His tears fall as he says inaudibly:

"You used to ask for them, I wouldn't give them up. Let me give them to you now. . . . Your mother back home . . . You said to her I should tell her . . ."

Staring at the dice and seeming worried, he picks them up again and slips them with great care into Wu Da-lang's pocket.

The big guy and the pockmarked man feel something is missing from their shoulders. Their noses ache as if they had just been pinched, their nostrils flare and flare again. They look up at the sky to keep the tears from flowing.

Old Hai speaks with tears in his voice: "Fuck every damn one of your ancestors, we all have hard luck. . . . Our Da-niur . . . Fuck every damn one of your ancestors! . . ."

"What dopes we were!" Skinny shouts hoarsely.

No one says anything, everyone understands.

"Who can say there isn't more hard luck on the way."

"They seized the submachine gun, fuck it all! With an article like that, forget the hard luck!"

Brown earth and brown sky. A crimson sun. The horizon has been baked until the edges curl. Together they pick up their blistered feet and make their way onward over the roasting hot grit. Whether there will be food at Liu Village doesn't seem to be on their minds. They are simply walking. There is a constant hoarse-throated line:

"Fuck it all, that submachine gun . . ."

Introduction to Ma Ke's
"Man and Wife Learn to Read"

By David Holm

Man and Wife Learn to Read (Fu qi shizi), a yangge play written and composed by Ma Ke, was originally performed at the 1945 Spring Festival in Yan'an.[1] I have chosen this particular yangge play first because it is a farce, and farce comes across well in translation, and secondly because it is an excellent example of light drama as written and performed by intellectual cadres in the heyday of the Yangge Movement. Unlike many plays that were written towards the end of the war, *Man and Wife Learn to Read* remained very close to North Shenxi folk yangge in form while introducing "new content" in interesting and ingenious ways.

What came to be called the Yangge Movement got under way in North China in areas under the control of the Party around 1943, and became the CCP's first systematic attempt to reform Chinese opera. Yangge, a kind of folk opera and dance which I shall discuss shortly, was made the nucleus of annual campaigns at the Spring Festival (the old New Year) to use dramatic genres current among the common people as a means of carrying the Party's message to the widest possible audience. Thus first of all the Yangge Movement was an attempt to cast Party propaganda in a form that the peasants knew, loved and understood. The fundamental difference between this and earlier attempts by the CCP to make use of "old genres" as media for propaganda and agitation (cf. the use of folksong and *huagu xi* during the Jiangxi Soviet) was that in Yan'an following the victory of Mao and his followers over Wang Ming and the Internationalists in May 1941,[2] a systematic effort was made to involve writers and artists with cosmopolitan city backgrounds in the creation of a new "national opera" on the basis of indigenous dramatic forms.[3] Yangge plays of the new type were to combine the form and style of folk opera with internationalist content, and were to be at once popular and serious.

But intellectual leadership was regarded only as the first stage: like other campaigns fostered by the CCP in the wake of Rectification, the Yangge Movement was also intended to be a mass movement, with yangge troupes in the villages participating in the reform of their own repertoire and the creation of new plays. The introduction of new content reflecting village life in the Resistance War was also regarded as the start of a dialectical process: the new yangge, on one hand, was to be used as a tool to raise levels of education and culture in the villages and, in conjunction with other campaigns, to stimulate production and urge the reform of the agrarian economy; at the same time, gradually improving conditions in the villages would lead to the transformation of yangge and other folk arts into higher and more modern forms.

One should perhaps note here that the use of popular and folk forms as vehicles of moral influence by the scholars and ruling classes has a very long history in China. It has been argued for instance that some of the odes in the *Shijing* were composed in the royal palace, in imitation of the popular style, and were sung afterwards in the villages of the various fiefs as a means of reforming morals.[4] Similarly, the vernacular tales and *shan-shu* of more recent times were composed as a rule by low-ranking literati for the edification — as well as the entertainment — of the lower orders. Conversely, folk and popular forms have also been used as vehicles of social protest by the common people themselves, and a great deal of work has been done in recent years by Chinese scholars to document this tradition. Particularly relevent here is the connection between secret society activity and the popular stage. The Boxers, for instance, made extensive use of local opera and puppet shows to make propaganda among the peasant masses,[5] and similar activities can probably be documented for almost any political mass movement in modern Chinese history. On a deeper level, traditions of Taoist mystical boxing that formed such a prominent part of much secret society activity and ideology were closely linked with the theatre.[6]

Yangge is a type of folk dance accompanied by short plays and was performed in celebration of the New Year and Lantern Festivals. Until the reforms of the 1940s, at least, it was a religious observance. Throughout North China regional and local variations in performance were quite pronounced, but generally yangge included a procession through the streets, a "large dance" (da yangge) performed by the whole troupe, a series of "little dances" involving two or so dancers, and a number of short plays. Yangge was often accompanied by variety acts such as "dry boat" and "bamboo horse."

In North Shenxi a yangge troupe usually consisted of anywhere between fifteen and thirty dancers. Musical accompaniment was provided by an orchestra of five or six men: two of these played suona (a double-reed instrument with a brass bell) and the rest played percussion. Da yangge, the most typical item in yangge performances throughout North China, was traditionally distinguished by its overt sexuality and general atmosphere of excitement and enthusiasm. A rare eye-witness account from Yan'an in the early 1940s brings out these qualities well:

> I have seen the old yangko dance of Yan'an several times.
> Once I saw it near the new market-place: the leader
> (lingdui) was holding an open umbrella, and there were
> around twenty troupe members. Boys and girls danced in
> pairs, and the girls were boys dressed as girls. There was a
> clown, and a priest holding a tortoise in his hand. When
> they danced the boys and girls flirted with each other and
> the atmosphere of eroticism was very thick. This kind of
> yangge is no longer seen this year. Another time I saw
> yangge at Qinghuabian: this was organised by the peasants;
> the leader was the parish head and he held a bushel lantern
> on top of a long pole. There were ten-odd dancers who
> wore flowery costumes and had huagu (also called yaogu,
> "waist-drums") hanging at their waists. Their movements
> were crude and vigorous, the beat was pronounced, and
> their voices were loud and clear, full of the health and
> happiness of the working people.[7]

The focus of most of the Party's attention, however, was on yangge plays, yangge ju. The old yangge ju in North Shaanxi was a relatively simple affair. Sometimes performances were given in the middle of the procession, but more often in the open area (on the ground, not on stage) where the yangge dances were performed. Often there was no story-line, properly speaking, and no fixed relationship between the characters. Usually the plot was conveyed by alternate singing (duichang) and question and answer. Usually too there were only two or three characters in a play, most frequently one dan (female role) and one chou (clown). The scenes presented in these plays were based on everyday life in the villages, and plots often centered on flirtations and jealous quarrels. The most widespread of these plays were Ju dagang ("The Tinker"), Xiao fangniu ("The Little Cowherd"), Xiaogu xian ("The Virtuous Daughter-in-Law") and Xiazi suanming ("The Blind Fortune-teller"). The play Ju dagang was one found all over North China, and the Dingxian collection contains a text of this play.[8] Ju dagang is mainly a lewd comic dialogue, full of double-entendre, between a housewife and a tinker about how to mend the holes in her pots and pans. In Xiao fangniu a young country girl loses her way and asks directions from a sly young cowherd. He deliberately makes things difficult for her and she, not to be outdone, talks back and makes fun of him.

Scenes such as these led more perceptive writers in Yan'an to observe that in yangge ju the content, village life,

appeared entirely in the form of burlesque (naoju). Characters were portrayed in an exaggerated and satirical manner in order to provide material for mirth. According to one writer this was partly because yangge was performed at the New Year, when a light and happy form was most appropriate, and partly because the peasants could not, in the old society, describe the circumstances of their lives or express their emotions in a straightforward manner.[9] Such an interpretation of yangge drama, which implied that it contained elements of realism and was consequently a serious art form worthy of attention and meriting reform, was by no means the majority view in Yan'an intellectual circles.

It was partly this opposition to the use of "feudal" and "superstitious" forms that explains the long interval between the time the Party leadership first came out in favor of using folk literature and the active and extensive prosecution of the policy after 1942. But time was also needed for preliminary investigations: one of the first steps along the road that led to the production of new yangge plays at the Lu Xun Institute was a series of field surveys, undertaken largely after 1939. The eminent musicologist Lü Ji and his colleagues collected well over a thousand folk songs from North Shenxi, including many that dated back to the period of land revolution under the Red Army of Liu Zhi-dan. Extensive collections of yangge and theatre music were also undertaken, probably slightly later. These materials were reproduced on mimeograph at the Lu Xun Institute and used as teaching materials. Later they were supplemented by old artists who were brought to the Institute to teach.

By 1944 the directions in which the old yangge was to be reformed were more or less established. In the yangge dance the display of sexuality was to be eliminated and the motley crowd of comic characters in the old processions — the fool, the priest with a big head, the old woman, the fisherman, the firewood gatherer — were to be replaced by dancers representing workers, peasants and soldiers. In this way it was intended that da yangge be transformed into a dance of solidarity, with only positive characters taking part. In yangge drama, too, the element of sexuality and the old comic roles, particularly that of the clown, were to be eliminated, and positive characters representing the "new masses" were to take pride of place. Everything else, including the old music, was to be salvaged: songs sung to the old tunes made the new words easier to remember. The Party workers were particularly anxious to retain the traditional form of comic dialogue, as this was the basis of much of yangge's mass appeal. Since the traditional roles did not fit neatly into either positive or negative categories, a certain amount of juggling was necessary, especially in plays of the one dan and one chou type. If both the man and the woman were positive characters, representing the new masses of the Border Region, how was a plot to develop? The general formula developed to deal with this problem was to have one of the positive characters pretend to be backward, and thus act as a "feed-man." This formula is quite apparent in Man and Wife Learn to Read and is used to good effect, but it should be pointed out that there was not an infinite number of variations that could be worked on this theme. This leads me to suggest that the contradiction between national or folk form and internationalist content had to be resolved on the level of artistic practice; that is, it had to be resolved afresh with each new play.

Apart from the comic dialogue, there are quite a number

of other features of *Man and Wife* taken from the old North Shenxi yangge. The whole play derives a lot of its appeal in performance to rhythmical effects, and in my translation I have tried to retain as much of this "fresh and lively Chinese style and manner" as possible. This attention to rhythm is particularly evident in the prologue, which is cast in a traditional form of recital in verse called *lianzi zui,* or "patter-mouth." This form was current in the region around Zizhou and Wubao counties to the north of Yan'an, and it was meant to be performed at breakneck speed, as indicated by its alternative names *jikouliu* and *jikouling,* "torrent-mouth." There seems to have been a close connection between *lianzi zui* and yangge performances in these areas, so the use of *lianzi zui* in the prologue of this play may be seen as a reflection of traditional practice. Then there is the music. Ma Ke was a musicologist and composer at the Lu Xun Institute of Literature and Art, and during the early 1940s he was active in field surveys of local opera genres organized by the Chinese Folk Music Research Society.[10] I presume that the three tunes used in *Man and Wife* were collected by Ma during these surveys. Two of the tunes, "Ornamented *gangdiao*" and "Playing on the Swing," are melodies taken from Meihu, a popular form of "little theatre" (*xiaoxi*) that was current in the south and west of Shanxi and most areas of North Shaanxi south of Suide and Mizhi. In these areas Meihu plays were often performed along with yangge at the New Year. Thus Ma Ke's use of Meihu tunes in this play also reflects traditional North Shaanxi practice. Ma Ke also composed the music for a five-act yangge play *Zhou Zishan,* published in 1944,[11] and in the first half of 1944 collaborated with Zhang Lu and others on the score of *Baimao nü.*

We may conclude that *Man and Wife Learn to Read* is a fairly clear-cut example of the policy of "from the people, to the people" in the sphere of art and literature.

The play was written and composed as propaganda for the new mass education movement.[12] The drive for mass literacy had been under way particularly since the Conference of Senior Cadres of early 1943. The production drive launched at that conference required that a "peasant household production plan" (*nonghu jihua*) be drawn up for each family, and this in turn necessitated a wider dissemination of literacy. After 1943 earlier attempts to introduce romanization were replaced by teaching, in part-time "winter schools," a basic vocabulary of Chinese characters that would be of immediate use both in production and for political education. At the same time the drive was not to interfere with the production movement itself. A typical solution was for the names of standard farm implements, for instance, to be carved on their handles so that characters could be studied while at work. An additional aspect of this campaign was the fiercely competitive spirit injected into it by the labor hero emulation campaigns. Objective standards were set for the achievement of tasks (of the number of characters to be learned, for example) and used as the basis for widespread contests and "declarations of war" between individuals or groups.

As a piece of propaganda the play combines agitation with education. One of the main aims of the play was obviously to drum up enthusiasm for the mass literacy campaign: this was done both by the vivacity of the performance and by a fairly straightforward appeal to peasant self-interest. In the prologue, for instance, the immediate advantages of literacy are pointed out by negative example in Liu Er's satirical self-criticism. Possible reasons for lack of enthusiasm among the masses for the literacy drive are also alluded to (chiefly lack of time and energy after a hard day's work), but only when the characters are speaking in their "negative" or backward roles, hence no solution is proposed. The comic dialogue that forms the bulk of the play is heavily and unashamedly didactic. This approach was designed to make maximum impact on an audience of peasants and townspeople, most of whom were illiterate. The audience is given explicit instructions in the play on how to go about learning to read and write Chinese characters, and comic reversal is used as a mnemonic device to facilitate the repetition of these basic practical instructions without altogether breaking the dramatic illusion. Setting new words to old songs is another way of making sure that the message reverberates long after the performance has ended.

The text of *Man and Wife Learn to Read* was originally published in *Liberation Daily* (*Jiefang ribao*) on February 28, 1945. In September of the same year it was published as a separate booklet: this was a clear indication that the play met with the approval of the Party's literary authorities and that it was intended to distribute it more widely among yangge troupes in outlying districts. The present translation is based on the text in Zhang Geng, ed., *Yangge ju xuanji* (A Selection of Yangge Plays), Peking: Renmin wenxue chubanshe, 1958, pages 221-233.

My thanks are due to Dr. Charles Curwen of the Department of History at the School of Oriental and African Studies for help with the translation of some of the more difficult North Shaanxi expressions.

Notes

1. Zhou Er-fu, "Yangge ju fazhan de daolu" (Yangge Drama's Path of Development), in Qunzhong zazhishe, ed., *Yangge ju chuji* (A First Collection of Yangge Plays), Chungking: Xinhua ribao tushuke, 1945, p. 12.

2. See Tetsuya Kataoka, *Resistance and Revolution in China* (Berkeley: University of California Press, 1974), p. 228.

3. Zhou Er-fu, pp. 7-8.

4. Marcel Granet, *Fêtes et chansons anciennes de la Chine* (Paris: Editions Ernest Leroux, 1919), pp. 11-12.

5. See photographs in Beijing lishi bowuguan, ed., *Zhongguo jindaishi cankao tupian ji, zhongji* (Pictorial Reference Materials for Chinese Modern History, Volume 2) (Shanghai: Shanghai jiaoyu chubanshe, 1958), p. 116.

6. Displays of military arts frequently accompanied the performance of yangge during the New Year in rural districts of North China, and many of the dance movements and variety acts in yangge are taken directly or indirectly from *wushu.*

7. Ai Qing, "Yangge ju de xingshi" ("The Form of Yangge Drama"), in Ai Siqi et al., *Yangge lunwen xuanji* (A Selection of Essays on Yangge), (Dalian: Dalian Zhong-Su youhao xiehui, 1947), pp. 23-24.

8. Li Jing-han and Zhang Shi-wen, ed., *Dingxian yangge xuan* (Shanghai: 1933).

9. Zhang Geng, *Yangge yu xin geju* (Yangge and the New Opera), (Dalian: Dalian dazhong shudian, 1949), pp. 6-7.

10. Published as Zhongguo minjian yinyue yanjiuhui, ed., *Yangge quxuan* (A Selection of Yangge Songs), (Yan'an: Xinhua shudian, 1944), and (same ed.), *Meihu daoqing quxuan* (A Selection of Meihu and Daoqing Tunes), (Yan'an: Xinhua shudian, 1945).

11. Ma Ke et al., *Zhou Zishan,* (Yan'an: Xinhua shudian, 1944).

12. On education in the Yan'an period in general see Peter J. Seybolt, "The Yenan Revolution in Mass Education," CQ 48 (Oct-Dec 1971), 641-69.

Man and Wife Learn to Read

By Ma Ke

translated by David Holm

Dramatis Personae
LIU ER, a young peasant   LIU'S WIFE

Enter Liu Er

LIU ER: *[recites* lianzi zui—*"patter-mouth"]*

Talking 'bout change, change,
Making people's customs change,
Studying culture, learning to read.
I, Liu Er, used not to read,
In three days twice I'd look the fool.
I went to market in Qianzhuang,
Cotton my wife told me to buy.
A brand new thousand dollar note
I spent as a fifty. So . . .
The crowd did laugh,
My wife did scold,
You tell me I'm not a pumpkin-head,
You tell me I'm not a pumpkin-head!
This year we made output plans,
The public sent a man to help.
I speak up, he writes it down,
Once he's gone, I've forgotten it!
Other people's plans were set,
I thought a plan was too much sweat.
Black little words on paper white,
I could not make them out aright.
Other men did things to plan,
Output got on really grand.
I'd not a plan of any kind,
People said I'd got just one hand.
My output's faulty compared with them.
The crowd did laugh at me,
The wife she scolded me.
I went home and looked at the plan,
White paper, black words—what a drag.
I couldn't make them out aright.

The crowd did laugh at me,
The wife she scolded me.
You tell me I'm not a pumpkin-head,
You tell me I'm not a pumpkin-head!
Study culture! Study culture!
Be a word-blind man no longer!
Reading squads, newspaper squads,
Just give your name, participate!
Little boys, little girls,
Old men, women too,
You teach me, I'll teach him,
As happy and lively as one family.

[gradually faster]

Now that I've got culture in my belly,
Everyone says that's really jolly.
Now this word-blind man can see,
The world's getting wider in front of my eyes.
I can read the papers,
I can write letters,
I can reckon bills,
I can keep accounts.

[sings yangge-diao—*"Yangge tune"]*

From now on, let's raise up our culture, a great *fanshen*,
Muddleheads, become clever men.
Of our food and clothes we've guarantee,
No man of us will suffer poverty.

My name's Liu Er. Tonight our village is electing its model reading student. I'm going home to tell my wife to come to the meeting.

[sings huayin gangdiao—*"Ornamented* gangdiao"]*

I, Liu Er, walk along, feeling very fine.
I take out my reading book and read a few lines:
"Being a farmer's preferable to commercial trades,
For each seed in the ground, in the barn ten thousand laid.
Diligently plough and plant, make hay and store grain.
Three years plough, put one aside, prepare for lack of rain."

Exit

Enter Liu's Wife

LIU'S WIFE: *[reading aloud]*

"Produce, produce. Have food, have clothes. Study, study. Read books, learn the script. In production be a model. In

74

study strive to be tops."

Somebody's asking who am I. I'm the wife of that Liu Er. Me and my man have made out a plan for learning to read. The two of us compete, and we've got to learn at least two characters a day. While I've been spinning thread I've also memorized these two characters—I wonder if he's memorized his? Ah! Just let me quickly hang up the reading board. Then when he comes home, if he recognizes them well and good; if he doesn't—hmmpf! I'll see to it that he gets nothing to eat, gets no sleep, and spends the night kneeling on his knees till daybreak! Then we'll see if he don't pay attention.

Enter Liu Er

LIU'S WIFE: *[coughs]*

Heh! Speak of the devil, here he comes. Let's pretend I haven't noticed.

[sits on the ground and copies characters from the reading board]

LIU ER: *[comes in; sees what his wife is doing; makes an ugly face; then comes up to her and gives her a shove]*

Hey, look here when a body's been out working all day, and he comes back home, you don't raise your head, you don't say a word . . . just a clay idol in a temple. Which god are you pretending to be?

LIU'S WIFE:

Ai! What are you playing at? Where've your eyes got to? Haven't you noticed that somebody's *studying* here?!

LIU ER:

Never mind your studying. I'm asking you, have you boiled up the pig-swill yet?

LIU'S WIFE:

Boiled it up long since.

LIU ER:

Have you fed the piglets?

LIU'S WIFE:

Fed 'em long since.

LIU ER:

Have you led the livestock in to their stalls?

LIU'S WIFE:

They're led in.

LIU ER:

Have you brought the coverlet and blanket back into the cave?

LIU'S WIFE:

They're brought in.

LIU ER:

Have you shut up the pigs and sheep?

LIU'S WIFE:

They're shut up.

LIU ER:

Have you shooed the hens and ducks into their nests?

LIU'S WIFE:

They're shooed in.

LIU ER:

Have you fetched the water?

LIU'S WIFE:

It's fetched.

LIU ER:

Have you cooked the dinner?

LIU'S WIFE:
It's cooked.

LIU ER:
Well bring it in, then.

LIU'S WIFE:
Bring what in?

LIU ER:
The food.

LIU'S WIFE:
Oh you don't mean to say you want to eat?

LIU ER:
What is she playing at! A man that's been working hard all day, why he'll just starve to death if he don't eat.

LIU'S WIFE:
So you want to eat?
[pulls Liu Er down to the reading board]

LIU ER:
What're you doing?

LIU'S WIFE:
Learning to read.

LIU ER:
You can't eat learning to read!

LIU'S WIFE:
Don't act stupid. Just let me test you: have you forgotten the two characters you memorized today?

LIU ER: [aside]
Hai (sigh), I've taken her . . . Look at my wife now, studying culture. She's altogether enthusiastic! Let me search her out a bit.
[towards Liu's Wife]
Well now, my baby's mother, you see I've been out working all day, and when I got back I went to the mutual aid team meeting. I haven't even had time to catch my breath, so where would I get the time to learn characters?

LIU'S WIFE:
You haven't learned your characters?

LIU ER:
I haven't!

LIU'S WIFE:
That just won't do!

LIU ER:
Won't do? What're you going to do about it?

LIU'S WIFE:
Do about it? You learn those characters for me. Learn them off, write them down. Write them down, memorize them. If you can recognize them, well and good. But if you can't recognize them, I'll see to it that you get nothing to eat, get no sleep, and spend the night kneeling on your knees till daybreak! Then we'll see if you don't pay attention!

LIU ER:
Very well now, wife of mine! Look, today I've worked all day long, I'm dog-tired, and that's it for today. Tomorrow I won't go out to the fields: I'll wrack my brains for you learning characters at home.

LIU'S WIFE:
Eh?

LIU ER:
No, no. I'll learn characters for *myself.* I'll learn ten in the morning, ten in the afternoon, and carry on at night and learn another ten.

LIU'S WIFE:
That won't do, that won't do! You should do *both*

productive labour *and* learn to read. Then you won't get into the red by learning to read. So be serious and squat down there and learn those characters.

LIU ER: [Sigh!]
Just let me eat and then I'll learn the characters.

LIU'S WIFE:
Nope.

LIU ER:
Really no?

LIU'S WIFE:
Really no. I'm not fooling.

LIU ER:
Just let me . . .
[raises his fist and pretends to hit her]
(Sigh!) Alright I'll learn those characters for you.
[the two sing alternately xi qiuqian—"Playing on the Swing"]

LIU'S WIFE: [sings]
Just as in the pitch-black sky . . .

LIU ER: [sings]
Little stars appear,

LIU'S WIFE: [sings]
Words on the blackboard . . .

LIU ER: [sings]
Shed their light far and near.

LIU'S WIFE: [sings]
Written words . . .

LIU ER: [sings]
Shed their light.
The two words we've studied I've got quite clear.

LIU'S WIFE: [sings]
Got quite clear,

LIU ER: [sings]
Got quite clear,

LIU'S WIFE: [sings]
You should explain their meaning here.
Why should a farmer man learn to read?

LIU ER: [sings]
If he doesn't he won't know 'bout great events and deeds.
In the old days, we couldn't read.
Fumbling in the dark we'd be taken in.

LIU ER & LIU'S WIFE: [sing in unison]
Now though we have all turned over,
Laborers have become householders.
As word-blind men how can we live?
Ai-yo studying culture is most imperative *en-ai-yo.*

LIU ER:
Baby's Ma, have a look at these two characters: one of them's the character *xue,* for study, and one's the character *xi,* for practice. Isn't this right, would you say?

LIU'S WIFE:
You're just talking off the top of your head. If you have a wild guess and happen to get it right, that doesn't count.

LIU ER:
Why doesn't it count?

LIU'S WIFE:
If you can remember them but can't explain them, it's as if you hadn't remembered them. If you can explain them but can't write them down, it's as if you hadn't explained them. You've got to write them down as well.

LIU ER:
I've got to write them down as well?

LIU'S WIFE:

That's right, you've got to write them down as well.

LIU ER:

Very well, Baby's Ma, I'll write them down for you.

LIU'S WIFE:

O.K., you do it then.

LIU ER:

A dot . . . a line . . . a hook . . . a basin . . .

[pretending he can't write the character, sneaks a look at the reading board]

LIU'S WIFE:

You mustn't look, you mustn't look!

[runs over and stands in front of the reading board]

LIU ER:

Who's looking? A dot . . . a line . . . a hook . . . a basin . . . a hole-in-the-ground here . . . a fork there . . . Is this right or wrong would you say?

LIU'S WIFE

It's wrong.

LIU ER:

Which one is wrong?

LIU'S WIFE:

This character *xue* is wrong.

LIU ER:

How is it wrong?

LIU'S WIFE:

You have a look at that character *xue* on the reading board. Long strokes, short strokes, there's bound to be ten-odd strokes in all. It's not easy to write, for sure. Now this character *xue* of yours, it's got the character *xiao* for "small" on top, it's got the character *zi* for "son" on the bottom: you've cheated on your contract and sold us short on the building materials, so it doesn't look a bit like that character *xue*.

LIU ER:

Oh my aren't you clever! The character written on the reading board is in longhand. The one I wrote is an abbreviated character. They're the same.

LIU'S WIFE:

They're the same?

LIU ER:

They're the same.

[Liu's Wife kneels on the ground and writes the character xue*]*

LIU ER: *[aside]*

Just look at that woman. She's made me jump through hoops, now let me give her a test as well.

[to Liu's Wife]

Hey, you've examined me, now I want to test you, too. Those two words we learned yesterday, have you forgotten them yet?

LIU'S WIFE:

Oh dear! Yesterday's words I'm afraid I still haven't got memorized into my bone-joints yet.

LIU ER:

If you can remember them, you read them out to me. If you read them out correctly, well and good. But if you don't read them out correctly, I'll see to it that you get nothing to eat, get no sleep, and spend the night kneeling on your knees till daybreak! Then we'll see if you don't pay attention!

[turns reading board around]

LIU'S WIFE:

Ah! "Zhu Bajie strikes them down with a single stroke of the rake."[1] You haven't been taken in at all! Alright, Baby's Pa, you listen while I learn characters for you!

[sings xi qiuqian—*"Playing on the Swing"]*

This reading board of ours is like a lamp so bright.

LIU ER: *[sings]*

These words here on the board . . .

LIU'S WIFE: *[sings]*

Let's memorize by heart.

LIU ER: *[sings]*

Which words have you memorized by heart?

LIU'S WIFE: *[sings]*

"Out-put" 's what these two characters do spell.

LIU ER: *[sings]*

What does this word output mean?

LIU'S WIFE: *[sings]*

Of ten thousand different things it's the start.

LIU ER: *[sings]*

Men, do your cultivation in work teams,

LIU'S WIFE: *[sings]*

Women, weave cloth and spin thread.

LIU ER: *[sings]*

Both feed pigs, and herd sheep,

LIU'S WIFE: *[sings]*

Oxen and donkeys fill the pen.

LIU ER: *[sings]*

On sunny slopes . . .

LIU'S WIFE: *[sings]*

. . . cotton grows,

LIU ER: *[sings]*

On field's edge . . .

LIU'S WIFE: *[sings]*

. . . peach trees, pear trees, apricots, date trees—plant them out, pot by pot.

LIU ER: *[sings]*

Wintertime's the season slack,

LIU'S WIFE: *[sings]*

Drive on the donkey,

LIU ER: *[sings]*

Gee-up, girl!

LIU'S WIFE: *[sings]*

Transport salt.

LIU ER & LIU'S WIFE: *[sing in unison]*

With well-set peasant household plans,
"Plough three, leave one" 's a great advance,
Big stores are piled high and small stores full of grain,
Pleased are we to have sufficient clothes and sustenance,
Study culture—the reason's plain,
Ai-hai ai-yo study culture—the reason's plain.

LIU'S WIFE:

Look, Baby's Pa, this is the character *sheng,* and this is the character *chan.* Put them together and it's out-out-put, put-put-out, out-out-put-put, put-put-out-out—is this right or wrong would you say?

LIU ER:

Ha! The blind man recognizes the needle. It doesn't count

---

1. Zhu Ba-jie: the character "Pigsy" in the 16th century novel *Journey to the West* (tr. Arthur Waley, *Monkey,* Penguin Books, Harmondsworth, Middlesex, 1961). A rake was his customary weapon.

if you guess.

LIU'S WIFE:

Why doesn't it count?

LIU ER:

If you can remember them but can't explain them, it's as if you hadn't remembered them. If you can explain them but can't write them down, it's as if you hadn't explained them. You've got to write them down as well.

LIU'S WIFE:

I've got to write them down as well?

LIU ER:

That's right, you've got to write them down as well.

LIU'S WIFE:

You watch, Baby's Pa, I'll write them down for you.

LIU ER:

O.K., you do it then.

LIU'S WIFE:

A dot ... a line ... a hook ... a basin ... a hole-in-the-ground here ... a fork there ... Is this right or wrong would you say?

[Liu Er coughs]

LIU'S WIFE:

That doesn't count, that doesn't count!

[hurriedly rubs out the characters and writes them out afresh]

A dot ... a line ... a hook ... a basin ... a hole-in-the-ground here ... a fork there ... Is this right or wrong would you say?

LIU ER:

I'd say they're wrong.

[rubs out the character sheng *in the lower part of the character* chan *with his foot]*

LIU'S WIFE:

Ai! It really was wrong.

LIU ER:

Ai! Yep, and you said you were able to do it! Let me be teacher for you: the character *chan* with this element *sheng* is read "*chan*," and if it don't have this element *sheng* it's still read "*chan*"—that's an abbreviated character again. They're the same.

LIU'S WIFE:

They're the same *again*?

LIU ER:

They're the same.

[Liu's Wife writes the characters on the ground]

LIU ER: *[seeing what an activist his wife is, smiles]*

To look at her studying so enthusiastically, she has it in mind to be a Reading Hero. I'll even cast a vote for her at the meeting tonight.

[to Liu's Wife]

I've got some good news to tell you.

LIU'S WIFE:

What good news?

LIU ER:

Tonight the village government is holding a meeting to elect model reading students. Let's hurry up and get ready to go, and let's also send the whole village a challenge to compete with us.

LIU'S WIFE:

Right! Let's get ready to challenge and compete.

LIU ER:

I've got some more good news to tell you.

LIU'S WIFE:

What more good news?

LIU ER: *[takes out his copy of "Farming Vocabulary"]*

What do you think this is?

LIU'S WIFE:

That's a little book. Where did you get it? Give me it, give me it!

LIU ER:

I bought it in the co-op in the street market.

[imitates Liu's Wife]

"Give me it, give me it!" Do you know what book it is?

LIU'S WIFE:

What book is it?

LIU ER:

It's called "Farming Vocabulary." You listen and I'll read it for you.

LIU'S WIFE:

Alright, you read it then.

LIU ER: *[sings "Ornamented* gangdiao*"]*

"Being a farmer's preferable to commercial trades,"

LIU'S WIFE: *[sings after him]*

"Being a farmer's preferable ..."

[to Liu Er]

What?

LIU ER: *[sings]*

"... to commercial trades,"

LIU'S WIFE: *[sings]*

"... to commercial trades,"

LIU ER: *[sings]*

"For each seed in the ground ..."

[Liu's Wife gets ready to grab the book]

LIU ER: *[sings]*

... *ai-ai* "in the barn ten thousand laid."

LIU'S WIFE: *[sings]*

"For each seed in the ground, in the barn ten thousand laid."

LIU ER: *[sings]*

"Diligently plough and plant, make hay and store grain,"

LIU'S WIFE: *[sings]*

"Diligently plough and plant, make hay and store grain,"

LIU ER: *[sings]*

"Three years plough, put one aside, prepare for lack of rain."

LIU'S WIFE: *[grabs book and walks off with it]*

We women in the spinning and weaving squad are going to learn to read!

LIU ER:

Our mutual aid team is going to learn to read!

LIU'S WIFE:

You go buy one at the market.

LIU ER:

That won't do, that won't do!

LIU'S WIFE: *[pretends to throw the book far away]*

There! I've thrown it away.

[runs off stage]

[Liu Er runs to the spot, finds it isn't there, and turns round and chases after her]

Finis

Note: Musical Scores

The system of musical notation used in these scores is the tonic sol-fa system used in the original published version of *Man and Wife Learn to Read.* Tonic sol-fa notation was originally introduced into China by Christian missionaries, and because it was easy to teach and easy to print, it was adopted for use in the numerous song booklets (*changbenr*) and other musical materials published in the Border Regions during the war. This system is retained here for ease of printing.

In tonic sol-fa notation *relative pitch* in the major scale is indicated by number: 1 is *do*, 2 is *re*, 3 is *mi*, and so forth.

Yangge diao   -   "Yangko tune"

x O   x O | x   Ox | x   x   x   x | x   x x | x   x   x x |
From now on, let's raise up our culture, (a) great fanshen, Muddleheads, become

x x   x | 1   1   1   1 | 1   2 16 | 6 5   5 | 6 1   3 5 |
clever men. (Of our) food and clothes we've guarantee, No man of us will suffer

1 5 6 | 5 - |
po - verty.

Huayin gangdiao - "Ornamented gangdiao"

Key of G

6 6   1 6 5 | 6   1   3 | 5   1   6   3 | 5 - | (1 1 1 6 5 |
I, Liu Er   ,   walk a - long fee- ling ve- ry   fine.
Be-ing a farmer's prefer-a - ble   to com- mer-cial trades, (instrumental
Di-li - gently   plough and plant make hay and store grain.

3 3 3 5 | 3 2 1 1 | 2 · 3 | 2 -) | 3   2 3   5 | 6   1   3 |
interlude)   I   take out (my) rea-ding book
                                            For   each seed   in   the ground
                                            Three years plough (have) one to   spare

     5   5   6 | 3 · 5   1 | (3 3 2 3 | 5 · 1 | 6 5 1 6 |
(and) read a   few lines   -
      in the barn ten thou-sand laid.
      pre - pare for lack of   rain.

5 · 1 | 5 -   )
po -

79

In "Ornamented *gangdiao*" below, where the key of G is indicated 1 is G, 2 is A, and so forth. A dot above the number makes the note an octave higher; a dot below makes it an octave lower. O stands for a rest, while a horizontal bar indicates the prolongation of the note. X indicates percussion or speaking tone.

Length is indicated by lines below the notes. No line below indicates a quarter-note, one line below an eighth note, two lines a sixteenth. The symbol = with a number above it indicates a grace note.

Most other symbols are the same as those on staff notation. All the tunes below are in 2/4 time.

For further information on how to read music in tonic sol-fa notation, see Zenyang shi jianpu bianxiezu, ed., *Zenyang shi jianpu* (How to Read Simplified Scores, pub. Shanghai renmin chubanshe, 1972).

Xi qiuqian — "Playing on the Swing"

Just as in the pitch-black sky , little stars ap-pear , Words on the

black - board shed their light far and near . Written words shed their light.

(The) two words (we've) stu-died I've got quite clear. Got quite clear,

got quite clear, You should explain their meaning here. Why should a farmer man

learn to read? If he doesn't he won't know 'bout great events and deeds.

In the old (days) we couldn't read, Fumbling in the dark we'd be taken in.

Now though we have all turned o-ver, La-bourers have be-come househol-ders.

As word-blind men how can we live? Ai - yo - stu-dy-ing culture

is most im-perative en-ai-yo - .

Silence

By Qin Zhao-yang

translated by Jean James

On an afternoon in late autumn, I rode on a bicycle to Li village, which is roughly six miles from the county seat, to call on the head of the agricultural cooperative and collect some information. Half way there, I encountered a line of large carts which appeared to be the better part of a mile in length. All the carts were empty. I jumped off my bike and began chatting with the drivers. I found out that they were heading back to Li village from the Grain and Foodstuffs Bureau at the county seat. They had gone there to turn in the government's share of the harvest. They were all from Li village because it had over one thousand households in it. What was so peculiar was that the line of carts was moving so slowly, as if they were afraid of stepping on ants. Probably right after having eaten breakfast, these drivers had hitched up the carts, weighed the load, loaded up, gone straight to the door of the Grain and Foodstuffs Bureau in town, unloaded, weighed the load, got their receipts and had stored the grain away in the

Introduction to Qin Zhao-yang's "Silence"

"Silence," by Qin Zhao-yang, written under the pseudonym He You-hua, appeared in *Renmin Wenxue* (People's Literature) in January 1957. Qin was the editor of this periodical and an adherent of realistic fiction rather than socialist realism. He published Wang Meng's story "The Young Newcomer" and wrote a number of stories and essays attacking party bureaucrats and bumbling cadres.

"Silence" is a fairly subtle story; while apparently a study of human nature, it also draws attention to the persistence of attitudes of mind characteristic of the old society which still afflict the populace. Qin explicitly criticizes both the District Chief who bullies and intimidates the villagers, while implicitly reproving the villagers, who let themselves be bullied and intimidated. Such attitudes are remnants of the old society and must be changed. One cannot help but be convinced that the District Chief is chastened and silenced solely because Fang Guan-fang is the wife of a party official. He backs down not because her cause is right but because her position is high. Fang Guan-fang, on the other hand, is struck dumb with rage and disillusionment that persons such as the hooligan and the District Chief should have any influence and authority at all. The villagers have not yet learned to speak up for themselves.

Such situations should not arise in the new China, and clearly, implies Qin, there remains much to be done.

Jean James

Bureau's granary. Soon it would be dark, so how could they not be tired and hungry? Furthermore, the sky was clouding over, probably it was going to rain, they were still about ten li from the village, so why wouldn't they be getting anxious? Therefore they were cursing furiously and continuously, some even going so far as to whip the donkeys and horses, but not for going too slow, rather the drivers were put out with them for being in a hurry to be fed and wanting to go fast, even to the point where their forelegs were constantly knocking into the rear of the cart ahead, making a hollow thudding noise. The cart ahead would get bumped and then the cart ahead of it got bumped. The animals' legs were sore from knocking into things and what with putting up with the drivers' curses and whippings as well, they became even more upset and angry; they began to rear, and bumped into the cart ahead again.

Because my pace was faster, I had already reached the middle of the line.

Suddenly, the fellow driving the lead cart stood up and looked back, tilted his head and guffawed, then pounded his chest and yelled at the men behind him, "What are you all complaining about, are you thinking of not submitting to my 'leadership'? I want to go very slowly today. If any of you has the skill, let him pass me!" And then, without further ado, he stood on the back of his old brown ox and made a face at the others, swearing and gesticulating at them.

All the rest of them starting shouting. So, the truth was that what had been holding up the line from moving quickly was the deliberate nastiness of this one fellow.

I quickly pushed my bike on along the ruts, intending to ask that guy to stop his troublemaking and hurry up a little. Suddenly, I heard a woman's voice call out up ahead.

"Uncle, pass him! Don't hesitate, pass him!"

Then I saw a woman sitting in a cart with an old man. With a length of white woolen cloth around her head and wearing a long dark coat, she looked just like the ordinary farm village woman. When I got up close to her, I realized she was Comrade Fang Guan-fang, the wife of the Secretary of the Party County Committee. I knew her from County Committee meetings. She had impressed me as being a person of enthusiasm and liveliness; slim and short, she was over thirty but looked twenty. Although ordinary village women liked to dress like cadres, she, on the other hand, always wore the rustic jacket and pants of a village woman. Her forehead stuck out a little; when she was speaking to someone, her bright and shining eyes always looked him straight in the face. Besides, I also knew that she had been transferred to the county seat not long ago, and was in charge of instruction at the high school. Oh, it then occurred to me, she had also told me that she was from Li village, so she was probably hitching a ride home to visit.

I began to talk with her. Very angrily she told me that that rotten lout in front who was acting up was a well-known ruffian in the village, he'd joined the collaborators and fought with the Japanese. She also said this "no passing" was the District Chief's rule. When they went to town the strong animals from the co-op went in the lead and moved very fast. Now, coming back, the tail end had become the front end; the weak beasts from the individual farms were in the lead and this roughneck in front was going slow on purpose. The more she talked, the angrier she became. She turned again to the old man who was driving and said, "Uncle, you can see with your own eyes how the animals are all injuring themselves, can't you? Pass him! I'll take responsibility for it with the District Chief!" Her round face was red and shining, her bright eyes now even brighter.

This old man was over sixty, he had a head covered with white hair. Although his face was dark with rage, he still hesitated. He said that what with the District Chief living right there in the village, no one dared to break his firm rule. This was no laughing matter! But he didn't wait for Fang Guan-fang to urge him a third time, and with all the drivers behind and ahead urging him on too, he finally made up his mind, jumped down off the cart, brandished his whip and cracked it twice. His dark brown donkey immediately turned and pulled the cart over to the side of the road and then flew on ahead. The carts behind all followed closely. I got onto my bike and rode right after them.

It was dark by the time we got to the village. I went to a small eating place for a bowl of noodles first and went to the office of the co-op afterwards. I found the place packed with people all standing silently; a harsh ear-splitting bellowing came from the vicinity of the lamp in their midst.

"I'm asking you, a man of your age, didn't you grow up eating food like everyone else? So how come you can't understand even this one little point? You've lived all these years without learning a thing, haven't you?"

I had some trouble squeezing my way through to the *kang* [raised heated bed common in North China]. I got up on to the *kang* and then I could see the District Chief. He was a short fat middle-aged man with a thick red neck, a shiny bald head and an inflamed purplish fat face; his appearance was really quite frightening. He was raging at the old man who had driven the rule-breaking cart. The old man's face had turned grey, his white beard was shaking, he stared at the floor. That trouble-making hooligan was standing next to him and was grinning crookedly, probably because he had done the accusing and was feeling very smug right now. Fang Guan-fang was sitting on a stool next to the table, fury swelling her face, chest rigid, her eyes glinting with an extraordinary light. She stared at the District Chief's fat face without moving a muscle.

"You!" the District Chief continued, "Why are you so lawless and heedless? Why do you so casually break the government's laws? I made it absolutely clear to all of you before you left," he glared balefully around the jammed room, "no matter what, you were not allowed to pass another cart! It was because I was afraid you'd endanger things, what with everyone fighting to get in front until carts would get overturned and the animals injured. So why did you just

ignore my rule? Why? Is what I, the District Chief, have to say still going to count for anything after this? I . . ."

"District Chief!" There were two men in the crowd wanting to speak.

"I just got done telling you, there's no need for any of you to say anything!" He turned around furiously to stare in the direction of the speakers. "Who are you calling District Chief? Do you still take me for your District Chief? Since what I say doesn't count, does that make me seem like a District Chief?"

He went on harshly reprimanding them, it seemed as if he would never be able to stop. I couldn't stand it and was considering breaking in and putting an end to this wrangle when I saw Fang Guan-fang stand up and go over to face the District Chief. Obviously suppressing the fires of rage in her heart, she spoke in a low, slow, but rather shaky voice.

"Haven't you berated them long enough? Will you let me say a few words?"

"I already told you, it's still not for you to chip in your two cents worth!" roared the District Chief, his voice like a clap of thunder.

"I cannot allow you to treat people in this way! You're no District Chief at all!" Fang Guan-fang suddenly blew up, her voice rose very high, even the light from the lamp on the table began to quiver in the blast.

"Ha!" he shouted evilly, took two steps back and gave an appraising glance at the way she was dressed, then began to laugh coldly. "Ho ho! You people in this village are really something special, even a housewife is such hot stuff! So I'm no District Chief? *You* won't allow . . . is that what you said?"

"That's what I said!" Fang Guan-fang spoke menacingly.

"By what right do you say that?" Even his eyes were red.

"To be a District Chief and intimidate the people in this way, is this the law of your government? Why don't you let them tell the whole story? Do you know who this lout is?" Fang Guan-fang pointed to that ruffian and said, "He is a hooligan, he was with the collaborationist army! Hey, Louse, are you named Louse? As a matter of fact, a louse is just what you are! You needn't be so smug, you needn't smile, I've heard all about all the rotten things you've done!"

"You get the hell out of here!" the District Chief roared again.

Suddenly the people in the doorway began to move about; a big tall man of about forty with a heavy growth of beard came shoving his way into the room. He was Yang Yin-ming, the head of the co-op, the man I'd come to see. (I'd seen him once before at a joint meeting of the co-ops in the county.) He looked at the District Chief and then at Fang Guan-fang and stamped his foot. "Ah! This is my fault for coming a little bit late!" He grabbed hold of the District Chief's sleeve. "Out, outside . . ." and pulled him out of the room.

Everyone in the room looked at each other in amazement. Fang Guan-fang was probably stupefied with fury, and actually seemed not to realize that there would be a change in the situation. Still bursting with rage, she sat on the bench, waiting for the District Chief to come back. Most likely the hooligan did not recognize Fang Guan-fang either, possibly because it was a large village and also because Fang Guan-fang was usually away, so his eyes passed over her face without pausing, without ever realizing who she was.

The village head finally came back, but his head was down. He went to the front of the table, stood there a while, then sat down on a chair, a hand groped for the edge of the table, his eyes stared at the lamp, he didn't move an inch; that face, never in my life have I seen such a red face!

Silence, silence, everyone there was silent.

Suddenly the District Chief waved a hand. "Get out, all of you. Get out!"

Once again they stared at each other. Some seemed to understand something and to be privately amused by something. Following the others out the door, I was the last one out. Turning back to look at Fang Guan-fang, I realized that she still seemed not to understand. She was sitting there by herself, catty-corner from the District Chief, looking at him in a baffled way, her lips moving. Just as she was about to say something, the District Chief said hoarsely, "Just now, I let my temper get the best of me. I didn't know you were . . . his wife. We've never met."

Fang Guan-fang suddenly looked startled. She stood up, eyes gleaming, but silent, chewing her lip, her face wore an angry and pained expression that meant she had something to say and was not able to say it, and also it was as if her anger and pain were so great that she did not have the words to express them. When she turned around and started for the door, I stepped without a word out the door. I, too, felt very bad.

1957

Introduction to Zhou Li-bo's

"The Guest"

Zhou Li-bo (1908-   ) was born in Yiyang, Hunan Province, about 175 miles north of Xiangtan, the birthplace of Mao Ze-dong (Mao Tsetung). As the youngest son of a village schoolteacher, he was able to finish junior middle school. He left for Shanghai in the turbulent year 1927 and managed to enter the University for Workers in 1929 only to be expelled eight months later because of his revolutionary involvement.

From 1931 to 1932 he worked as a proofreader in a printing shop. There he took part in a strike, and was arrested and imprisoned for two and a half years. Not long after being released from prison in 1934, he joined the League of Left-wing Writers as well as the Chinese Communist Party. During the Yan'an years he was active as a writer, lecturer, war correspondent and editor of newspapers and magazines. He also headed up the Editing and Translating Department at the Lu Xun (Lu Hsün) Institute of Arts and Literature located in Yan'an.

Zhou Li-bo's early writing was primarily in the form of essays on literature, life and revolution which he collected in a volume entitled *Sixiang Wenxue Duanlun* (Short Essays on Thought and Literature). *Baofeng Zouyu* (The Hurricane), describing the land reform movement as carried out in the liberated areas of Northeast China (Manchuria), was completed at the end of 1948 and published shortly before the founding of the People's Republic of China in the autumn of the following year. This novel won wide acclaim, was given a Stalin Prize for Literature and was translated into English, Russian, Hungarian, Czech and Japanese.

Zhou continued to write about this theme of agrarian revolution in *Shanxiang Jubian* (Great Changes in a Mountain Village) which depicts the consolidation and expansion of an agricultural co-operative in a remote Hunanese village. Although Zhou Li-bo also tried his hand at portraying workers in his novel *Tieshui Benliu* (The Molten Iron Flows) and in some short stories collected under the title *Tiemen Li* (Inside the Iron Gate), he was more at home in delineating characters from a peasant background and in reflecting the tremendous economic and social transformation of the countryside.

Among his other works the most notable are *Hechangshang* (On the Threshing Ground), a collection of short stories, and the *Zhou Li-bo Xuanji* (Selected Works of Zhou Li-bo). He has also translated several Western and Russian classics into Chinese, including Pushkin's *Dubrovsky* and Sholokhov's *Virgin Soil Upturned.*

Zhou's style is distinguished by precision and economy in his use of language. His consummate use of patois—Northeastern in *Baofeng Zouyu* and Hunanese in *Shanxiang Jubian*—further enriches his narratives and greatly contributes to the authenticity of his works. "Xinke" (The Guest), which appeared in the February 1964 issue of *Renmin Wenxue* (People's Literature), is one of his finest stories and also one of his last to be published. He has not published since the start of the Cultural Revolution and has dropped from view entirely (in so far as can be ascertained from outside China).

Joe Huang

The Guest

By Zhou Li-bo

translated by Joe Huang

The day after the Mid-Autumn Festival, just as the *dongnian** turned a ripe yellow and the tea plants were in blossom, a guest arrived in the home of Wang Gui-xiang, a production team leader and Communist Party member. This was soon known to everyone in the team and aroused great interest among them. The old men who no longer went out to work in the field, the women and the children all came by in droves to take a look. The kids were the most dedicated. They hung on the windowsills or thronged at the door, curiously studying the stranger from another village and softly offering their observations. One lad, after standing at the door for a while, walked away, declaring with indifference:

"What's there to look at? The eyes are horizontal and the nose vertical just about the same as anyone else."

People were still watching, some making comments on the guest's looks and behavior and others scrutinizing a flower-painted, oil-paper umbrella she was carrying with her.

The guest, a girl of about eighteen or nineteen, was now sitting on a broad red-lacquered stool in Mother Wang's room. She was dressed in a red jacket printed with small white flowers and blue trousers. This outfit was very becoming, revealing her slim, well-shaped figure. She wore a pair of small blue canvas shoes. Her hair was held with a black clip on each side, and trimmed into loose bangs to cover her high forehead. Seeing so many people outside the window and the door, she casually flung back her long glossy black plait, a smile lighting up her comely face.

"Girls nowadays are really something," an old woman outside the window commented in a low voice. No one knew whether she intended this as praise or criticism.

"So self-assured and unabashed." Sister Guo, the next-door neighbor, was favorably impressed by the girl.

"Too unabashed! In the old days an unmarried girl was not ever supposed to be seen by her future in-laws before the wedding," the first old woman quietly retorted.

"Not supposed to be seen? But what if someone were matching you up with a pockmarked girl?" a boy was quick to ask.

"Then," replied the old woman, "you'd have nothing but your own fate to blame."

"Here comes the team leader." Sister Guo looked in the direction of the threshing ground.

Everyone turned round to see a lean, middle-aged man, a hoe on his shoulder, coming unhurriedly from the threshing ground. He wore his workaday old blue clothes. His pants, although neatly rolled up to the knee, were amply dotted with mud splatters.

"Team leader Wang," a little boy rushed to deliver the message, "you've got company."

"Your daughter-in-law's here," added another.

"You're lucky, team leader," said Sister Guo, "your daughter-in-law is clever, friendly, just smiling all the time."

"By the same token, if the daughter-in-law should happen not to smile, this means the father-in-law is ill-fated, right?" asked one impish boy among the youthful crowd.

"You little devil, you always love to play games with what others say," Sister Guo shot back at him, "just see if I don't go tell your mother!"

The team leader grinned and entered his house with the hoe still on his shoulder. As he was putting down the hoe, he heard a feminine voice clearly calling "Hello, father." He turned round to see a face, its attractive contours like that of the melon seed, beaming at him. He was going to answer but did not know just what he should say, then somebody was throwing a new blue tunic over his shoulders.

"Change into this," his wife, Mother Wang, urged him from behind.

"What for?" Wang Gui-xiang was by nature a modest man, and felt more at home in his old clothes. He often said, "New clothes make you uncomfortable."

Mother Wang faced him, signalling to him by means of a quick glance in the direction of the guest. Getting the message, he could do nothing but put on the new tunic. When he had finished buttoning it up, he grinned at the girl, trying to say something to bid her welcome but unable to think of some appropriate words. While he was absorbed in this effort, somebody outside the paper window inquired:

"Is the team leader home?"

"Yes," he answered and rushed out, feeling quite relieved at being rescued from his predicament.

"Do you know where the broad-bean seedling bed is?" asked the man outside the window.

"The seedling bed is at the outskirts of the village," the team leader answered, "I'll go with you to take a look."

"No, you've got a guest today, you shouldn't leave."

"No, I must go have a look." As always, team leader Wang never forgot his responsibility.

Inside, Mother Wang opened the red-lacquered chest with an award certificate pasted on its cover, took out two new blue tunics and put them on a square stool next to the bed, and then went back to the kitchen to get down to her cooking. The onlookers gradually dispersed. Sister Guo stayed behind, just in case Mother Wang would be unable to cope

---

* A kind of glutinous rice mainly for making rice cakes.

with everything all by herself, and she did help out by lighting up a fire under the stove. The two women chatted as they worked.

"What's her name?" asked Sister Guo in a low voice.

"Her family name is Wu, and she is called Ju-ying."* Mother Wang answered also in a low voice.

"Must have been born in September. Has a date been set yet?" asked Sister Guo again, her voice even lower.

"Not yet. The matter has been raised with the other side," Mother Wang said softly. "Our silly fellow won't agree; he says he won't get married for eight more years."

"Aiyah, what kind of talk is that? Wouldn't this long wait make one get a bit old?" Sister Guo was an advocate of early marriage.

"Our silly fellow says that nowadays the government is promoting planned production." Mother Wang meant to say "family planning" but had inadvertently used the very similar phrase "planned production."

In came a young man carrying two empty buckets used for collecting night soil. He was twenty years old or thereabouts, stoutly built and ruddy-faced. After entering the house, he put down the buckets, walked over to the big crock of tea always kept by the stove, ladled out a bowl of cold tea, and stood there guzzling it down in large mouthfuls.

"Da-xi, look who's here!" Sister Guo beamed, pointing at the door to the main room.

The young man walked to the door with the tea bowl in hand, and glancing through it into the room, suddenly blushed. He turned back and put down the bowl on the stove. The guest came out into the kitchen, walking up to him quite naturally, her eyes smiling at him as if she had something she wanted to talk over with him. He pulled hurriedly away and moved out through the door at a brisk pace. At first he was just trotting, but after reaching the threshing ground, he was racing, faster and faster, as if afraid someone might be running after him.

"Why run away, you?" Mother Wang rushed outside the door, a new blue tunic in hand, and let rip with a good scolding. "Dumbbell, good for nothing." When the scolding was over, she could do nothing but return to the house and set the new tunic down again.

Just at this time a boy of eleven or twelve rushed in from the door behind her. Seeing the girl visitor, he did not recognize her and was at a loss.

"Call her elder sister, Little Er-xi. She is your brother's future wife," Sister Guo urged with a smile.

"Sister," the boy greeted her warmly, and unabashedly, without blushing, unlike his brother.

Before the visitor had any time to respond, Mother Wang came out from the bedroom with a slightly smaller blue tunic and told the boy to put it on.

"Why do I need to wear this?" asked the boy, refusing to change into the new tunic.

"Are you going to wear it or not?" Dealing with her younger son, Mother Wang's tone was quite firm.

"All right, if that's how it is, then I'll put it on. What else can I do? From the looks of things, you want me to show off for the benefit of my new elder sister, don't you?"

"In fact, there's a lot to be shown off," Sister Guo broke

in. "Mother's a model, your father's a team leader and a good one at that, kind at heart and good in leadership, and you can count all the merits. We've suffered such a drought this year, yet he still has led our production team in bringing in a bumper crop. Shouldn't such a family be shown off?"

"Showing off is backward and being modest is progressive, understand?" The young lad availed himself of one of the progressive ideas he had recently learned to bluntly admonish this member of the older generation.

"It's just that you love to shoot your mouth off, you young rascal." Seeing that there was a strained look on Sister Guo's face, Mother Wang promptly scolded Little Er-xi. "Get out of here right now, or we'll see if I don't give you a good thrashing."

The boy took to his heels, and Mother Wang dropped the subject. Walking to the wooden counter, she started washing some white chard. Sister Guo remained at the stove keeping the fire going. The dark bluish smoke rose to the tiled ceiling, then scattered into thin columns like dispersing soldiers to quickly find its way out through the skylight or tile joints; what remained inside the house was the thick smell of burnt firewood. The guest also came in to the kitchen, and seeing everyone busy, she rolled up her sleeves and helped with washing some vegetables.

"Oh, leave them, child." Calling her "child" in an affectionate tone, Mother Wang added, "You don't want to get any stains on your clothes; I can manage just fine." Wu Ju-ying would not listen, but kept on washing.

"Girls nowadays behave so well, as eager as can be to lend a hand," Sister Guo expressed her approval.

The guest just smiled and went on washing the vegetables.

"Just look at this young woman, she's quite something, smiling and giggling all the time," Sister Guo said again. "But you know, dear, you're still a guest yet to be married."

Hearing this, Ju-ying made a great effort to refrain from chuckling. After a while, when Sister Guo said something funny, or something more or less funny, she chuckled again, forgetting her status of "guest." Sometimes she giggled so hard that she had to lift her hand, which had turned red after being immersed in the cold water, to politely cover her mouth with the back of it.

The three finally had the food ready. In the upper corner of the kitchen which also served as the dining room there was a large square table. The table was set with cups and chopsticks, and the dishes of food were set on it one after another—altogether nine dishes including smoked fish, mandarin fish, preserved pork, steamed pork, dates stuffed with pork, braised soy sauce chicken, scrambled eggs with green onion, and cabbage soup. In the Wang household this amounted to a more than adequate display of hospitality.

"Mother Wang, your larder is indeed well stocked," said Sister Guo glancing at the table as she rose to leave, "the table looks just grand."

"To tell you the truth, all these are just leftovers from the festival," replied Mother Wang. "You mustn't go. Stay here to help keep our guest company. How can you even think of not staying?" Mother Wang pulled at Sister Guo's arm, but could not detain her. According to the local custom of mutual help, neighbors do not expect to join the family they have helped for a meal after the work has been done.

Team leader Wang and his two sons came back one after

---

* The character *ju* in Ju-ying's name means chrysanthemum, an autumn flower.

another. Da-xi also had put on his new clothes, so the three were all wearing their same new tunics of bright and gleaming blue. All were seated. Da-xi sat kitty corner across from the guest, not daring to raise his head to see her.

"Please go right ahead and make yourself at home. We have nothing very special," Mother Wang said with customary politeness, lifting her chopsticks to invite the guest to begin.

"Nothing very special? A table full of main courses, seven or eight more than usual," said Er-xi as he threw all restraint to the wind and pitched in with great gusto. "I'd love to have a meal of nothing special like this every day."

Wu Ju-ying lowered her head chuckling. As a result, a grain of rice got stuck in her throat and made her cough. As soon as her coughing stopped, she was chuckling again, and then hurriedly covered her mouth with the back of her left hand. It took her a while to stop chuckling.

Mother Wang scolded Er-xi, and at the same time stood up and leaned over to place some choice morsels of chicken, fish and lean pork in her future daughter-in-law's bowl.

"Mama, you're giving all your attention just to elder sister," said Little Er-xi.

Saying nothing, Mother Wang only shot him a fierce glance. When dinner was over, tea had been served and everyone had washed up, the guest rose to make her farewells.

"Well, Mama, I have to be going."

"Going? Not staying for the night?" Mother Wang clearly wanted her to stay.

"No," the girl said, "there are things waiting to be done in our team."

"Sooner or later you'll be moving over here. Why not stay for a night right now?" Little Er-xi stuck in his two cents' worth.

"You little devil, you're really asking for it!" snapped Mother Wang.

The guest smiled and walked out from the kitchen to the threshing ground.

"Since she really is going, you escort her back," Mother Wang told Da-xi.

"I'm not going to do that." Da-xi was blushing again.

"If you're not going to, who do you think will? Me?" Mother Wang demanded sharply.

"If he won't, I will," Er-xi said quickly, ready to move.

"Nobody asked you! What do you think, that you're as indispensable and as popular as licorice root in herbal medicine?" Mother Wang used her eyes to stop the younger boy right in his tracks.

"You're too young." Their neighbor, Sister Guo, who had popped in again, said with a laugh, "When you have a girl friend, you can see her back as far as you like. Your turn for that will come but not just yet."

At first, as she heard Mother Wang telling Da-xi to walk her back, Wu Ju-ying had paused, obviously waiting for him. When he didn't agree to do so, she turned back to thrust a pink letter into his hand, and gave him a smile.

"You open it after I'm gone."

The girl's suddenly putting a letter into Da-xi's hand out of the blue gave Da-xi's mother quite a start. Unable to guess what was in the letter, she was worried lest the girl might have changed her mind. She knew for a fact that the girl had attended one year of junior middle school while Da-xi was only a primary school graduate. By comparison with her, Da-xi fell a bit short in terms of education. Mother Wang did not

know how much ahead of a primary school graduate someone who had gone to a junior middle school was, but she was surely a little ahead. And she had often heard that a woman who has studied in junior middle school would not be willing to marry beneath herself with a primary school graduate. But was this girl getting cold feet? Who could tell? The worrying mother then cast a glance at Da-xi and urged:

"Hurry up, see her off!"

Da-xi still did not make a move.

"Please do," that incorrigible busybody, Sister Guo, also tried to help persuade him.

"See her home and be quick about it." Smoking his pipe by the stove, team leader Wang issued a succinct order.

Da-xi obeyed. Team leader Wang was not only good at work in the fields, but was also first-rate in making plans; he always took the lead in team work. As a result, he enjoyed great authority among the team members including his own sons. Da-xi followed after Ju-ying, his footsteps slow, lagging far behind. The playful girl, knowing her betrothed was seeing her off, turned round with a warm smile. This welcoming gesture further unsettled the young man whose pace became even slower. Twenty or thirty feet still separated them, so the girl deliberately slowed her steps.

"Dumbbell, you can walk a little faster than that, can't you?" From where she stood in the kitchen door, Mother Wang's voice came to prod her son along.

After passing the threshing ground and walking out on the main village road, the two still maintained a more than respectable distance between them. By the time they reached a stack of hay along the road, Ju-ying looked at the sun already sliding downward in the west and said with a twinkle in her eye:

"It's still early, let's sit down for a while. Come on, this spot is sheltered from wind." Ju-ying sat down against the haystack, and motioned to her betrothed to take a spot covered with hay next to her. Da-xi thought, "It's all right to sit down as I've something important to talk over with her." And so he sat down, but not at all close to her. When Ju-ying tried to move closer, he moved still farther away. The girl moved once more towards him, almost touching his shoulder. He could no longer steer clear of her, but his heart pounded fiercely and his face was burning. Running her eyes over him, Ju-ying drew a straw from the pile and put it between her teeth to bite. After a while, as she was about to say something, her eye happened to be caught by a tea plant with thick leaves in full blossom near a tall cedar tree up on the slope opposite to where they were sitting. In the sunlight the tiny snow-white flowers amid the dark green leaves stood out unusually fresh and beautiful. Ju-ying jumped to her feet, overjoyed.

"Look at the tea plant in such gorgeous blossom. I'll just go pluck a branch."

"Don't. If you pluck a branch, next year the team will collect a good deal less tea seed."

As soon as he said that, Ju-ying gave up her idea and sat down again.

"You're right. You show greater consciousness in protecting the collective property of the commune." Her words contained self-criticism as well as appreciation for her betrothed.

They remained silent for some time. Da-xi was thinking to himself that if he did not say it soon, he would miss the chance. Trying to marshal up his courage, his face a bright

五穀豐登
六畜興旺

crimson, he just could not find the right way to broach the issue.

"What's wrong with you?" The girl was a little surprised at his obvious embarrassment.

"I, I've something important to say, but don't know if I should say it," Da-xi finally managed to utter.

"Say what you have to say. Otherwise, it would be better to chew on it a while, let it stew inside you for the time being," said Ju-ying, half-jokingly.

"It seems to me, well, we're both young."

"Yes, we are not old," Ju-ying teasingly cut him short. "Compared to our parents, we do seem much younger, don't we?"

Da-xi, born with an earnest and guileless nature, was not one for kidding around. Right then he was concentrating so intently on what he had to say that he was not about to try and come up with any humorous touches. After lowering his head to ponder it over, he began again:

"I'm a member of the Communist Youth League, and I know you're also one. The Party and the League are calling on us to build up the countryside. In order to do this we should not be concerned solely with our private life."

"Who's asking you to pay attention only to private life?" Ju-ying demanded, her smile gone.

Da-xi avoided responding to this directly, but rather plunged ahead with what he had to say.

"We want to dedicate our youth to our beloved Party, our great Motherland."

"I seem to recall having seen this very line in the newspaper," said Ju-ying with the faint traces of a smile.

"What's printed in the newspaper is also what we have in our hearts. But my mother has a different plan."

"What plan has she got?" inquired Ju-ying, feigning surprise.

"She says she's getting on in years."

"She isn't that old; she's much younger than my father and mother."

"She said," Da-xi halted, lifting his eyes to gaze up at the emerald-green hillside.

"What did she say?"

"She said, 'Son, just do this one thing for your old mother's sake!' What she wishes . . . uhh, you know . . .'"

"I don't know. I'm stupid," said Ju-ying.

"She . . . wants us to get married soon," having plucked up his courage, Da-xi finally blurted it out, his face red as a beet. In order to reduce his tension, he rushed on, "She said, 'I'm old now and have stomach trouble to boot.'"

"What has our getting married to do with your mother's stomach-ache?"

Again avoiding a direct answer, Da-xi only kept on with what he was saying:

"She says, her stomach trouble flares up frequently and that she won't live long. I feel very bad that she's got this worrisome stomach-ache, but our marriage should not be decided on the basis of her stomach trouble. Rather it should be decided in light of agricultural development in our country."

"Comrade Da-xi, you don't have to beat around the bush with all this useless talk." For the first time Ju-ying's face turned stern, "Please tell me straight out, what are your plans?"

Da-xi stole a glance of Ju-ying's face cold as frost, and his heart seemed to sink within him. Thinking it all over at length as if gathering all his strength, he determinedly but not without a great sense of foreboding, stammered out, "I reckon, umm, I think, . . . ahh, I know, you're eighteen, I've just reached twenty, and it won't be too late if we wait for seven or eight more years."

"So what you're saying is that we'll get married, but only after seven or eight more years?" Ju-ying asked him straight out.

"Yes, not until our country's agriculture becomes modernized."

"You, you really feel this way?" Ju-ying's shining black eyes stared intently into his.

"I always say what I mean," Da-xi answered firmly.

"Is this your own idea?"

"Just wanted to talk it over with you."

"You've got everything figured out. What's there to talk about?" Ju-ying jumped to her feet and said. "It's late, and I must go. Goodbye, and I wish you every happiness in dedicating your youth to the modernization of our homeland's agriculture, Comrade Da-xi."

Ju-ying strode off toward the main village road. At the intersection, she turned round to see Da-xi still sitting beside the haystack with his head in his hands, his two elbows resting on his knees. She laughed, turned back, and stealthily skirted the haystack to stand behind him. She saw a few drops of tears

like a string of silver dewdrops trickle down to fall on the golden hay in front of him. She clapped him hard on the shoulder, squatted down beside him, held his right hand wet with tears tightly in both her hands and burst out laughing.

"Ha, ha, I saw everything." Er-xi's face had suddenly appeared from behind Ju-ying just then. Holding an elegant oil-paper umbrella, he grinned: "You two acted so proper and serious at home, not even talking to each other. Now in this out-of-the-way place, here you are holding each other's hand, sitting all snug and cozy together. I overheard all your little talk, with that stuff about agricultural modernization and mother's stomach trouble. Elder brother even cried, yet now he's already grinning. Your behavior is a scandal, elder brother," teased Er-xi. *First the tears, then the laughter, who can tell what comes after.* I'm going to tell mamma, the two of you are here talking behind her back."

The younger brother, delighted with himself to think he had uncovered a secret, set off toward home, jumping and skipping, but just as quickly came back to hand over the umbrella to Ju-ying, laughing:

"Sister, you're too happy to think of your umbrella. Ma told me to bring it to you."

Ju-ying took the umbrella and shook hands with Da-xi, adding with her warmest smile:

"This time I really have to go. Go home to read my letter, you silly man."

The girl was gone. Da-xi, too, walked back home with Er-xi. But before he got halfway there, he stopped along the roadside and opened the letter. It went like this:

Dear Da-xi:

I want to tell you something, and think you will be happy for me. The night before last our production team officially appointed me as the bookkeeper. The ten-point Guidelines stress bookkeeping as an important assignment. I don't want to let down the Youth League which has nurtured my development nor can I disappoint the members of our commune who have placed their trust in me. I must try to do my very best. The Party secretary told me that at the end of this month the commune will be sending me to the county seat for a training course in accounting. Da-xi, you don't know how happy I am. I am grateful to the Party and the people for their trust and confidence. I have made up my mind that I will totally dedicate my precious youth to the Party and to socialism. I believe that in the hands of our new generation of peasants who have had at least some schooling, China's agriculture will definitely become modernized.

I've heard that the pearl of industry in our province, the Zhexi Hydroelectric Plant, has already begun operation. Along the river not far from our village a huge electric irrigation station will be constructed, making use of electricity generated from Zhexi. Isn't this wonderful news? Before long, even if there is drought in our area, people will no longer have to sweat and toil pedaling the old water-wheels. The days of back-breaking human labor to bring water up from the river with those water-wheels will be gone forever.

But there is another piece of news I need to tell you. Your mother has sent word to me that she wants to set a date for our wedding. This would be bad for both of us, but the old folks look upon it as a good thing. If we go along with them, then I'll have to give up the work I've just been assigned. How could I face the Party and the team? People would say, "Look at this Youth leaguer; for the sake of getting married she abandoned her work with nary a thought for anything else." It is a shameful thing if we let our personal considerations interfere with the collective cause, Comrade Da-xi.

So what I've come to talk over with you is whether or not our marriage can be postponed for, shall we say, ten years until our villages are filled with the sound of motors and until electric light will shine out from the windows of every house. At that time we can take care of our own matters, all right?

Dear Da-xi, I felt my heart could belong only to you from the day I first saw you. How much I long to be with you, day and night, without parting. But for the sake of socialist construction and the great work of our Party, please accept this suggestion of mine.

I shall pay you a visit, but am concerned that there may not be an opportunity for us to have a good long talk, so I have written out this letter in advance. I fully trust that you will agree with me wholeheartedly.

Your Ju-ying
October 15

Watching his elder brother read the letter, nodding his head and grinning now and then, Er-xi figured that there must be something novel and interesting in the letter. To find out what it was all about, he asked with an ingratiating smile:

"Elder brother, can you disclose what's in the letter?"

"I'm sorry, it's confidential and can't be made public right now." Da-xi folded the letter and carefully put it into the pocket of his tunic.

"Later?"

"Not even later."

"All right, I'll repay in kind," vowed Er-xi.

"What have you got to repay?" Da-xi asked with a rather condescending tone.

"Someday, when I have a girl friend and receive a letter from her, just see if I'll let you look at it. I mean what I say, you wait and see if I don't!"

The two brothers walked, one behind the other, along the narrow path, and chatted with a cheerful heart. As they got to the kitchen door, their mother, that hard-working, thrifty Mother Wang whose acquaintance we have already made, issued an irreversible order: "Take off your new tunics!" They obeyed, removed their tunics, folded them, and put them back into the red-lacquered chest. As she was closing the chest cover, the two brothers saw the large certificate of merit awarded by the Party Committee of the commune to Mother Wang: printed on beige paper was a design with a red flag, a peony, an ear of wheat and a magpie, and at the center were written seven Chinese characters in a calligraphy reminiscent of Chairman Mao's:

"A Model for Thrifty Management of Household."

February 1964

Debut

By Hao Ran

translated by Wong Kam-ming

I

Zao-hua lived in the Baicao Mountain Range for two days and learned a lot of skills from the model workpoint recorder Gao Xiu-zhi. Her little brains, like well-oiled cogwheels, were filled with drive and enthusiasm.

Happily she set out for home, sorry only that she couldn't fit herself with a pair of wings, to fly back to Guozi Valley. She wanted to work in the same way as Xiu-zhi; she wanted to be a Gao Xiu-zhi-style workpoint recorder. She felt that all she had to do was to make up her mind to take the same road as Gao Xiu-zhi and to work hard, and she would definitely be able to catch up with Gao Xiu-zhi.

It was late autumn. Most of the crops on the land had been completely harvested. Only a few commune members were digging white yams on the terrace fields. Suddenly, someone called out in front: "Hey there! Is that Zao-hua?"

Zao-hua raised her head to take a look. An old man was standing on the road. He was short and had a small, narrow face. Squinting his eyes, he was smiling out of the corner of his mouth.

This man's name was Liu Lao-zheng ["lao" = old, "zheng" = upright]. It was quite a nice-sounding name. At fifty-five he was "lao" all right. But there was something not quite "zheng" about the way he did things. In Guozi Valley, whoever mentioned this old middle peasant would get something of a headache. This was because he was always up to his tricks. He was very close to the former workpoint recorder, always trying to curry favor with him and "to lure him into a trap." It was his doing that the workpoint recorder had gone astray and was in the end dismissed from his job. Everyone knew how that whole affair had come about.

Zao-hua took a look at him and, quickly sizing up the situation in her mind, responded: "Uncle Liu, been visiting your relatives?"

Liu Lao-zheng sidled right up to Zao-hua and said: "That's right. I went to Beijing [Peking] to visit with my daughter. Zao-hua, I hear that you have become the workpoint recorder."

"Uh-huh."

"Good! Uncle supports you. To be a workpoint recorder you have to learn to use the abacus. You haven't got an abacus, have you?"

"No."

Liu Lao-zheng pulled out an abacus from a sack he was carrying over his shoulder. "Huala, huala," he shook it several times and said: "I bought one in Beijing. I'll lend it to you to use."

Zao-hua glanced at that glossy new abacus and shook her head. "That's not necessary. When it is time to go to the market, I will ask my dad to get me one."

Liu Lao-zheng did not press her, put the abacus back in the sack and said: "Anytime you want to use it, just come to my place and take it. Whether it is yours or mine, it is the same thing. Don't stand on ceremony. It's just that I'm fond of you. You can tell what a child will be at three years of age. When you were still in your mother's arms, I already told her: 'In the future, little Zao-hua will certainly be somebody.'"

Listening to these words, Zao-hua found them quite pleasing to the ear. She raised her head, and saw quite a few commune members on the terrace fields stop what they were doing. Pair after pair of eyes was fixed on them.

Liu Lao-zheng went on: "To be a workpoint recorder, it matters little whether or not you are educated, resourceful or experienced. The most fundamental requirement is to unite with the masses. Zao-hua, you must think of ways of uniting with the masses. You mustn't offend anybody. Once you offend anybody, it will make your job difficult. Then even if you want to stay on your job, you won't be able to do it for too long. Quitting halfway, what a loss of face!"

Listening to these words, Zao-hua found them quite reasonable. She again raised her head and looked. People on the terrace fields were whispering to one another. Some were beckoning to her.

Liu Lao-zheng wanted to say something else. But Zao-hua was already climbing towards the terrace fields.

The commune members formed a circle around Zao-hua, speaking all at once, to "disinfect" her.

"Zao-hua, don't listen to what Liu Lao-zheng says. There is poison in his honeyed words. If you listen to them you will get into trouble."

"All he thinks about is money, never socialism. All he does is take advantage of the collective."

"You come from a family of poor and lower-middle peasants. You must do things in line with our thoughts and feelings."

Zao-hua listened and listened. Her head, grown warm with Liu Lao-zheng's honeyed words, slowly cooled off, as if a spring breeze had blown through it. She said: "Please don't

worry. This time I found a living example in Baicao Mountain Range. I will definitely become a good workpoint recorder like Gao Xiu-zhi."

II

Indeed, Zao-hua followed the example of Gao Xiu-zhi and started on her job. In the morning she dug white yams with the commune workers; in the afternoon she sorted white yams with the commune members; at dusk, she went to the fields and to the barn, to assess work and record workpoints; finally, she went to the threshing ground to collect grass.

The greater portion of manpower of the entire production team was taking part in the cutting of mountain grass. The grass was cut so that in the winter they could help the dairy farms outside the mountains feed their cows and help people on the plain in making their fires and cooking. Moreover, they had to keep a portion of it for use in the team. This sideline production was very important. It was quite a large source of income.

The sun descended behind the mountains. The shadow of the mountains lengthened. One after another the mountain grass cutters returned. One load after another of golden kindling grass, mottled here and there with red and green, was carried to the threshing ground.

Zao-hua borrowed a big hand scale from the stockroom. As soon as a load arrived, she weighed a load by hoisting it up with whoever brought the grass. Then she put down in her account book the number of pounds each load weighed. She also put it down in the commune members' workbooks. In weighing she was conscientious and meticulous; in recording she was also conscientious and meticulous. Never sloppy in the least.

So she weighed and recorded, working straight through till the moon rose above the mountains.

Zao-hua was extremely tired. Her waist hurt and her legs grew numb. Her upper and lower eyelids constantly came together. At that moment, nothing would have been more wonderful than to lie down on the *kang.* Even if there were an opera being performed at the east end of the village, or a movie being shown at the west, Zao-hua would not have wanted to see it. She had to go to sleep.

Carrying the big hand scale on her shoulders and treading the after-dusk moonlight which was not yet fully bright, she walked exhausted through the north entrance into the village.

Someone was calling her from behind, with a very small voice: "Zao-hua! Zao-hua!"

Zao-hua stopped, turned around and looked. It was Liu Lao-zheng.

Liu Lao-zheng was bearing a split-bamboo carrying pole on his shoulder. A bundle of rope dangled from his hand. Dust covered his body; sweat hung on his face. "Huchi, huchi," he was panting hard. From the way he looked, one could be sure that, having done some heavy labor and walked a long distance, he had just come back.

Zao-hua asked him: "Uncle, are you calling me about something?"

Smiling with glee, Liu Lao-zheng said: "In these few days you have really done your job. Not only did you take part in labor, you also recorded workpoints, doing everything that needs to be done in both. The contributions you have made to the team are indeed great. I said you would become somebody; and you have really become somebody. Unfortunately, there are people with dust in their eyes. No matter what you do, they look down on you. They were saying behind your back that you could not stay on your job for too long. How I quarreled with them! I will never allow anyone to look down on our Zao-hua. Zao-hua is tops! . . ."

Zao-hua was terribly embarrassed by all this praise. Hastening to put an end to what he was saying, she asked: "Uncle, haven't you gone up to the mountain to cut grass today?"

Liu Lao-zheng shook the split-bamboo pole on his shoulder, jerked the rope in his hand, and said: "I have! I have! Except when something special comes up, I never miss work. No matter which day it is, not only do I go to work earlier than anybody else, I also come back later than everybody else. To work for socialism, how can anyone not put his all into it! In cutting this grass, we are not only laying in winter fodder for the cattle of our commune, we also have to sell some to the supply and marketing co-op, to help our country. In doing this kind of thing, can uncle fall behind others?"

Listening to Liu Lao-zheng, Zao-hua found what he said pleasing to the ear and felt that he was not as backward as others had made him out to be behind his back. So she went on to ask: "Where is the grass you cut?"

Liu Lao-zheng said: "I unloaded it on the haystack."

Zao-hua got agitated: "Huh! We have not weighed it yet; nor have we recorded it. How come you put it in the stack?"

Liu Lao-zheng said: "I just went to the threshing ground to have a look. You were not there. I thought you had already gone home to sleep. Ai! You have worked all day. You must be very tired. For a trivial little thing like that, and you live so far away, is it really worth all that trouble to drag you back here from home! Uncle is concerned about you. So young and frail. Mind you don't overexert yourself. If you overwork and damage your health, it will be a problem for life!"

Zao-hua said: "If we don't weigh it and don't record it, it will mean that you have worked a whole day for nothing, won't it?"

Smiling, Liu Lao-zheng said: "Zao-hua, don't you let your uncle work for nothing! At his age, it is not easy for uncle to climb all over the mountains. Hmm, you really know how to tease an honest fellow like me . . ."

Zao-hua wondered: "Then what can we do?"

Liu Lao-zheng said: "At any rate, I always cut that much any old day. To save both of us trouble, let's write down yesterday's total for me and call it that. So what if it's a bit more or less."

Very seriously Zao-hua said: "That will not do! If we record less, you lose out. If we record more, the collective loses out. It doesn't matter which side loses out, it still means that the workpoint recorder has not fulfilled her duty. I must do it in such a way that neither the collective nor the individual would lose out.

Liu Lao-zheng said: "Zao-hua, don't be such a stickler for the rules. No matter what we do, we must adapt ourselves to circumstances. In doing your kind of work, you should be all the more flexible. If you are flexible, it will make things convenient for both of us . . ."

Resolutely Zao-hua said: "No, no, I am the workpoint recorder. My duty is to record workpoints. I cannot opt for

convenience."

Liu Lao-zheng said: "Ah, it's just a bit of reed kindling. It's nothing like gold twigs or silver sticks. Why must you be so pigheaded?"

Zao-hua said: "This is what the leadership has put me in charge of. Even though it is just reed kindling, we must treat it like gold twigs, like silver sticks."

Startled, Liu Lao-zheng took a look at Zao-hua. Suddenly, his manner changed, and, holding up his thumb, said: "Right, Zao-hua! What a good model you are! Uncle admires this kind of conscientious, responsible spirit of yours. Of course, a workpoint recorder must seek truth in actual facts! Whatever you say we should do, uncle will follow suit."

Zao-hua said: "Let's go to the threshing ground and weigh it. Whatever it is—that's what it will be."

Liu Lao-zheng said: "Good. Let uncle and you do just that."

They turned back. As they walked, Liu Lao-zheng endlessly praised Zao-hua, saying how good she was in this, how good she was in that, his mouth filled to overflowing with butter.

Liu Lao-zheng walked onto the threshing ground where the hay was stored and made a beeline for the new stack which had been stacked up only that afternoon.

Zao-hua asked: "Uncle, where did you put the two bales of grass you cut?"

Liu Lao-zheng raised his hand and pointed to the stack: "I put them right there."

Moving two bales of hay, Zao-hua again asked: "These two bales?"

Liu Lao-zheng hurriedly nodded and said: "Right, that's it. I cut them on the Sun Slope. See how tall this grass has grown. It was really difficult to cut. Ai, it pricked my hands so that they still hurt."

Zao-hua brought down the two bales of hay and, hoisting them up with Liu Lao-zheng, weighed them. One bale was fifty-nine catties, the other sixty-three [1 catty = ½ kilogram or 1.1 lbs.]. After that, she very carefully recorded the workpoints for Liu Lao-zheng. She also recorded them in her own account book.

As Liu Lao-zheng was shoving his workbook into his pocket, he couldn't help but feel elated. Speaking non-stop, he praised Zao-hua: "You are a wonderful workpoint recorder. You're really conscientious and responsible. Uncle supports you all the more. Well, well, well, from now on, you should always keep it up like this."

Zao-hua lifted the two bales of hay and placed them securely on the stack. As she was putting the hand scale together, she told Liu Lao-zheng: "Uncle, from now on when you come back after cutting grass, you must never dump it on the stack yourself. I don't mind being tired; nor do I mind the trouble. You can come get me anytime. You must never again do things this way."

Liu Lao-zheng was chock-full of promises: "Right, right, see you tomorrow." He turned his face to hide a grin, and beaming with glee, went home.

Zao-hua also set out for home. She felt that she had treated this incident in accordance with Gao Xiu-zhi's living example and had succeeded in taking her own work in every way as seriously as possible. Doing it this way, her mind was at ease. And Liu Lao-zheng, as a member of the massees, was also satisfied. From now on, she should always try to act like this.

III

Zao-hua arrived at the doorstep of her home. Lightly she pushed open the door, strode across the threshold, and once again closed it. She raised her head and looked. There was a bright moon again today.

She recalled the other night when she and Gao Xiu-zhi, treading the moonlight, went to the East Valley. Today, she had herself done a similar thing: she had not listened to Liu Lao-zheng; she had not allowed him to get things done in a sloppy way.

As she was thinking like this, her heart suddenly skipped a beat. Without knowing it, she came to a halt in the courtyard. No, no, in what Liu Lao-zheng did today, there must have been something wrong. There was no telling whether those two bales of grass were actually cut by him. He must have cut two small bales, tossed them to the top of the stack and laid false claim to two big bales. The commune members had all told her to watch out for this "old but crooked" selfish fiend. Liu Lao-zheng cared only about money, not about socialism. His head was full of fiendish schemes!

The more Zao-hua thought about it, the more reasonable she felt her suspicions were; and the more reasonable she felt they were, the heavier her heart grew. Her face burned, and her heart thumped. Stamping her foot, she decided: "That

won't do! I must go get him and get to the bottom of the whole thing."

She pulled open the door, went out of the village, and ran towards the south. She thought of the group of commune members in the white yam fields who had told her to be careful; she also thought about the old branch secretary, the team leader, her father, her mother, and moreover about Gao Xiu-zhi and Gao Xiu-zhi's father and mother. . . .

Zao-hua wanted to find Liu Lao-zheng at once, to make him tell the truth, to track down the two bales of grass he cut, and once more weigh them for him. She wouldn't put down a catty or an ounce more than was his due. She couldn't allow him to take advantage of the collective. She was bound and determined to do just that.

She went running toward the south and saw the south hills still a great distance away. She saw the woods on the hills, the small courtyard in the woods, the windows half showing above the courtyard walls, and the lamplight shining through the windows.

As if someone had just warned Liu Lao-zheng on the phone, he was again putting on his act. He thought: "That girl Zao-hua is quite sharp. On her way back to return the scale, she might run into the team leader; or on her way home to go to sleep, she might run into other commune members. What's more, in her family there are her father and mother. If by any chance Zao-hua mentions to them what had just happened, it's

95

hard to say whether someone wouldn't get suspicious. It's quite possible that Zao-hua might come looking for me . . ."

Thereupon, he turned the whole thing over several times in his mind, thought up an idea, and stopped at his door, smoking his pipe as he waited for Zao-hua. When he saw at a distance a small form moving toward him, he hurriedly knocked off the ashes, and, taking big strides, broke into a run to meet Zao-hua.

When Zao-hua saw Liu Lao-zheng running like that, she thought something urgent had happened.

Without letting Zao-hua open her mouth, Liu Lao-zheng started to speak first: "Aiya, Zao-hua, I was just going to look for you. That grass of mine, we just weighed the wrong bunch!"

Zao-hua was taken aback. Then she let out a sigh of relief. She thought to herself: "He did something wrong. Now he feels bad about it." So she said: "Right, right, I also thought something was wrong."

"Did you think so yourself?"

"Ai, I thought something was wrong."

Liu Lao-zheng rolled his eyes once in the dark, then energetically nodded his head and said: "Right, right, something was wrong. Think about it. Today I got up earlier than usual, went up to the mountain real early, and found a place thick with grass. The cutting went so well that I didn't rest for a minute. Not even to fill my pipe and have a smoke. I was also the last to come back. . . ."

Zao-hua interrupted him and anxiously said: "It looks to me like the weight of your grass must have been a mistake. This won't do . . ."

Liu Lao-zheng also said with anxiety: "Listen to me. It must have been a mistake. Think about it. I was not only early but also fast. And I didn't even take a rest. I should have cut a lot more than usual. But, according to the number you wrote down for me, it was only a little bit more than usual. Think about it. Isn't that so?"

Zao-hua was baffled by what he said: "What! We have given you less than your due?"

Liu Lao-zheng said: "That's right. Otherwise would I come looking for you in such a hurry?"

Zao-hua said: "How could it be less?"

Liu Lao-zheng said: "We must have mistaken the small bales for big ones."

Zao-hua said: "It couldn't be. I think we have given you more than your due."

Liu Lao-zheng said: "How could it be more?"

Zao-hua said: "We must have mistaken the big bales for small ones."

"Ha, ha," as if unable to hold himself in any more, Liu Lao-zheng burst out laughing: "Aw, come on now, a kid like you, you really know how to tease your old uncle."

In all seriousness Zao-hua said: "What I said is serious business. Who's teasing you?"

Pretending to be not the least bit concerned, Liu Lao-zheng gave a wave of his hand and said: "Forget it. I have said just now that it was neither gold twigs nor silver sticks. Just a bit of reed kindling. More or less hardly makes much difference. From now on, we will pay a little more attention and that's that. You better hurry home and go to sleep."

Zao-hua was dumbfounded. She was a youngster with very little experience. How could she match wits with the "old and crooked" Liu Lao-zheng?

In the moonlight Liu Lao-zheng threw a glance at Zao-hua. He saw Zao-hua frowning and stunned and thought that Zao-hua was worried about the mistake she had made. Secretly he was delighted. His thinking then took a new turn: "From now on in my work, there is no avoiding dealing with the workpoint recorder. If I can lure her into my trap, from now on it will be far easier to take advantage of the production team. No matter what, youngsters are easier to handle than grown-ups. Why not take this opportunity to set her up?" As he was thinking about this, he became all the more elated. Immediately he put on a show of extreme concern and said: "Zao-hua, don't be afraid. It doesn't matter. It's just that uncle is fond of you. Do you suppose uncle would tell the team leader on you? This whole thing, if you don't tell anybody and I don't tell anybody, who will know about it? From now on, the two of us, you and me, will have to cooperate hand in glove. Uncle will protect you, and make you a first-rate and permanent workpoint recorder. Nothing can go wrong. Well now, you haven't eaten yet, have you? Come, come, let's go to my house and have something to eat." As he was saying this, he started pulling Zao-hua towards the courtyard.

Forcefully Zao-hua flung off Liu Lao-zheng's hands. She was so angry that she was shaking all over.

Liu Lao-zheng urged her: "Don't be so dead serious. In doing your kind of work, you have to be a little more flexible. No matter how capable you are, there's no use kidding yourself that you will never make mistakes. Close one eye and shut the other and everything will work itself out. If you are so dead set about your principles, you will make things inconvenient for everybody else, and you yourself will also lose out."

Zao-hua stamped her foot, turned around and ran back.

"Hmm, hmm," Liu Lao-zheng sneered behind her. He thought to himself: "This time, I gained an advantage, and on top of that got hold of someone who will be of help to me."

IV

Zao-hua was retracing her steps. She thought of the old branch secretary, thought of Gao Xiu-zhi and also thought of the commune members who had educated her and helped her. Her mind was in turmoil; her steps went from quick to slow, and again from slow to quick. Finally she started to run and charged all the way to the team headquarters.

After a while, Zao-hua came back out of the team headquarters, bearing on her shoulder a split-bamboo carrying pole and a hand scale, and in her hand a safety lamp and a rope. Once more she went back to the grounds where the hay was kept.

This was a threshing ground, situated on a piece of level land at the north side of the village. All around were open fields. The huge haystacks, crouching in the moonlight, looked like mound after mound of small hills.

A patroling militiaman, rifle on his shoulder, came over. When he made sure it was Zao-hua, he asked her: "It's already so late. What are you coming here for?"

Zao-hua said: "I have something to take care of over there in the hay storage grounds. You don't have to keep watch over there now. I'll watch it for you."

The militiaman nodded his head and, rifle on his shoulder, set out to patrol the north side.

Zao-hua arrived at the midst of the haystacks and went up to the side of that new haystack. Looking at the haystack covered with a layer of moonlight and reflecting on the sequence of events which had begun here not long ago, she was on the verge of tears. But she clenched her teeth and did not let her tears fall.

Zao-hua put the split-bamboo carrying pole through the leather trap of the scale and lodged one end of the split-bamboo pole in the fork of a small tree. Clasping two bales of hay, she brought them over and, tying them together, hooked them to the scale. Then with her shoulder she hoisted up the other end of the split-bamboo pole, and thus the bales of hay were lifted off the ground. With one hand steadying the swinging bales of hay, she moved the weight back and forth on the beam with the other.

By the light of the safety-lamp, Zao-hua put down in her account book the weight of the bales of hay. Then with a rope she tied up another two bales of hay, brought them over to weigh them and, the same way as before, hoisted them up, weighing them and recording their weight.

Bale by bale she weighed the hay; stroke by stroke she recorded its weight.

She weighed the hay till the moon climbed up to the tip of the tree.

She recorded its weight till the moon shifted directly over her head.

. . .

Rising very early the next morning and feeling extremely elated, Liu Lao-zheng shouldered his split-bamboo pole, picked up a sickle and went out of his house. He couldn't help glancing at the two huge bales of reed kindling in the shed, and he chuckled slyly. He thought to himself: "Luck is really with me. Tonight I'll do the same again."

When he reached the door and was about to step out, however, he hurriedly drew back.

At that very minute, the two of them, the team leader and Zao-hua, arrived. Huffing and puffing, they stormed into the courtyard.

Straight off the team leader said: "Liu Lao-zheng, what kind of shenanigans have you been up to again? Tell me the truth quick!"

Zao-hua added her salvo: "You are really good at pulling fast ones! Confess and own up to your mistake right this minute!"

Liu Lao-zheng backed off in fright: "Ai, ai, I must say, what is going on here? You have got me all confused!"

The team leader said: "You have not delivered a single blade of grass to the team. Why did you ask Zao-hua to put down workpoints for you?"

Zao-hua said: "You even said that you lost out. It must be your way of not wanting to do any work, but reaping all the benefits for nothing!"

Liu Lao-zheng's face instantly turned white, but he still wanted to tough it out: "Ai, ai, that's really not true! Zao-hua, last night, didn't the two of us, you and me, talk face-to-face and weigh the hay face-to-face?"

The team leader said: "Enough of your play-acting! Zao-hua didn't sleep all night. Bale by bale she weighed all the hay in that stack once over, and stroke by stroke she checked the figures on her record. When she added them all up and checked the two sets of figures one against the other, the total was exactly the same. There was none of your 125 catties at all!"

Zao-hua said: "If you don't own up, we'll weigh it all over once more, right this minute and face-to-face. We'll see whether there is any grass you cut!"

In a daze, Liu Lao-zheng looked at Zao-hua. He found it a little difficult to recognize the youngster. His two legs felt weak, and he almost fell to the floor. Hastily he leaned for support against the door frame, dropped his head, and in a voice like a mosquito's said, "I, I deserve to be hanged, I deserve to be hanged . . ."

Zao-hua and the team leader gave Liu Lao-zheng a sound scolding. They turned up the two bales of mountain grass in

his shed and, each carrying a bale, went towards the threshing ground at the north side of the village.

The team leader said as he walked: "Zao-hua, you certainly didn't go to the Baicao Mountain Range in vain. You have brought back the 'true scriptures.' You're truly a good work-point recorder! But before we get carried away, we should remember that this incident was nothing more than a small test. In the future, there will be a great many more 'big winds and big waves' waiting for you to go through. As long as you can always maintain this drive of yours, you'll be sure to come through all right."

Solemnly and full of confidence, little Zao-hua nodded her head.

At that moment, the bright crimson glow of dawn washed red the rocks of the serried mountains.

Final revision, Spring 1966

Short Annotated Bibliography

Bibliography

1. Gibbs, Donald, and Yun-chen Li, comps., *A Bibliography of Studies and Translations of Modern Chinese Literature (1918-1942)*. Cambridge: Harvard University Press, 1975. A complete, albeit not annotated, bibliography of translations of and research on Chinese literature of the May Fourth period, just published in the Harvard East Asian Monograph series.

Novels

1. Chu Po (Qu Bo). *Tracks in the Snowy Forest*. Peking: Foreign Languages Press (hereafter FLP), 1965. 549 pages.
Colorful guerrilla fighters fight the Guomindang in Northeast China on the eve of Liberation. A good example of the utilization of fairy tale traditions from earlier vernacular fiction in a post-Liberation novel.

2. Lao Shaw (Lao She). *Rickshaw Boy*. New York: Reynal and Hitchcock, 1945. 384 pages.
Probably the most "literary" of all the translations of Chinese fiction, this translation of Lao She's famous novel from the late thirties about a Beijing (Peking) ricksha puller was a Book-of-the-Month-Club selection in 1946 and is consequently still widely available in libraries and garage sales. One of the best early works portraying the hard life of the urban poor, this novel is of much historical and sociological as well as literary value. In the Chinese original, the story of Luotuo Xiangzi (Camel Happy Boy, the protagonist's nickname) has been a favorite of Chinese readers due in large measure to the author's successful rendering of Beijing street language. Unfortunately, the very pessimistic ending of the original was turned on its head as the translation concludes happily.

3. Mao Tun (Mao Dun). *Midnight*. Peking: FLP, 1957. 523 pages. Hong Kong reprint, 1976 (paper).
Considered the masterpiece of pre-Liberation novels by many Communist critics before the Cultural Revolution, this long, episodic work attempts to give a panoramic view of Shanghai society in the year 1930. Writing in a somewhat naturalistic style, Mao Dun gives a detailed description of the financial world and stock market speculators in Shanghai as well as a none-too-flattering picture of Communist-led labor unions. The central figure, Wu Sun-fu, is a capitalist trying to build up Chinese-owned industry under heavy imperialist pressures. The result of painstaking research by the author, this novel is also one of the best sociological treatises of the period.

4. Pa Chin (Ba Jin). *Family*. Peking: FLP, 1958. Reprinted by Anchor Books, 1973. 320 pages (paper).
Since publication by Anchor (with a number of passages left out of the earlier Beijing edition), this is now the most readily available modern Chinese novel in translation. A melodramatic account of a young man's rebellion from his upper-class family at the time of the early May Fourth movement. Highly autobiographical, this unsophisticated but moving work was first published in 1933 and quickly became the favorite story among Chinese youth, particularly high school students who identified strongly with the trials and tribulations of the young man's struggle for an independent identity.

5. T'ien Chün (Tian Jun or Xiao Jun), *Village in August*. New York: Smith and Durrell, 1942. 313 pages.
Village in August was the first full-length modern Chinese novel to be published in English; it tells the story of a band of patriotic Chinese guerrillas fighting the Japanese in their home area of Manchuria following the Japanese occupation of Northeast China in 1931. The author ran afoul of Party authorities twice and has not published anything since 1954. The lyrical description and revolutionary romanticism of this work presage much of the post-Liberation writing.

6. Ting Ling (Ding Ling). *The Sun Shines Over the Sangkan River*. Peking: FLP, 1954. 334 pages.
Probably the best of the novels in translation which deal with the land reform movement carried out under Communist Party auspices in the North of China during the 1946-1948 period.

7. Yang Mo. *The Song of Youth*. Peking: FLP, 1964. 599 pages.
Set in the period from 1931 to 1935, this somewhat sentimental work treats the radicalized but bourgeois students who became active revolutionaries and is a throwback to May Fourth period literature in its interweaving of a love story and revolutionary politics. As is the case with virtually all works written before the Cultural Revolution which were translated by the Foreign Languages Press in Beijing, this work was severely repudiated during the Great Proletarian Cultural Revolution and has been out of print for a decade.

8. Yeh Sheng-tao (Ye Sheng-tao). *Schoolmaster Ni Huan-chih*. Peking: FLP, 1958. 383 pages.
Published in 1928, Ye's epochal novel details the evolution of an idealistic young teacher from his youth at the time of the 1911 revolution through his growing despair while working in a rural school during the period up until the sudden re-invigoration of the May Fourth cultural revolution of 1919.

Probably the first full-length novel to realistically depict the response of the radical intellectual to the first stage of the modern Chinese revolution.

Collections of Short Stories

1. Hao Ran. *Bright Clouds.* Peking: FLP, 1974. 139 pages (paper).

The first collection of Hao Ran's stories to be published in English and one of the very few collections of new stories to come from the FLP since the Cultural Revolution. Half of the eight stories, all written between 1957 and 1964, are done in the reportage style with author present in the tale and recording events as they unfold (cf., "Silence" by Qin Zhao-yang). None of these stories contains a villain like Liu Lao-zheng in Hao Ran's "Debut," the emphasis in each being placed on the tempering of good socialists through the conquest of natural obstacles.

2. Hsia, C. T. (Xia Zhi-qing). *Twentieth Century Chinese Stories.* New York: Columbia University Press, 1971. 239 pages (paper).

This is probably the best available collection, although the last four stories have little to do with China and represent the difficulties of writers in exile. Translations of important stories by Yu Da-fu, Zhang Tian-yi, Wu Zu-xiang, and Zhang Ai-ling are definitely worth the price of admission. Nine stories altogether, written between 1921-1965.

3. Isaacs, Harold R. *Straw Sandals.* Cambridge: MIT Press, 1974. 444 pages

23 stories, one short play by Guo Mo-ruo and a poem, all from the May Fourth period. Included in this volume are an interesting description by Isaacs of the political repression by the Guomindang against the writers in Shanghai in the early 1930s and some brief notes by Mao Dun on left-wing literary magazines. Although many of these stories have already appeared in translation, there are some Communist authors here such as Chiang Kuang-tz'u (Jiang Guang-ci), Shih Yi (Shi Yi), Hu Ye-pin, and Ting Chiu (Ding Jiu), whose works are not commonly seen.

4. Jenner, W. J. F. *Modern Chinese Stories.* Oxford: Oxford Paperbacks, 1970. 271 pages (paper).

A fairly broad collection of some twenty short stories, beginning with some oral tales surviving from the Nian rebellion of the 1870s and covering several post-Liberation works. The selection of stories by the major authors of the May Fourth period leaves something to be desired, some of them being merely sketches. The most political of the currently available anthologies, it provides useful information about each of the authors represented. Important for the oral tales and the post-Liberation stories it contains.

5. Lu Hsun (Lu Xun). *Selected Stories of Lu Hsun.* Peking: FLP, 1972. 255 pages (cloth or paper).

This selection contains most of Lu Xun's short stories, some of the very best pieces of writing in modern China. Widely available because Lu Xun's place in the pantheon of revolutionary heroes in China seems unassailable.

6. Mao Tun (Mao Dun). *Spring Silkworms and Other Stories.* Peking: FLP, 1956. Reprinted at Harvard University in limited edition by the Department of Far Eastern Languages. 278 pages (reprint in paper).

Thirteen stories written between 1930 and 1943. The "Spring Silkworms" trilogy in this volume represents some of the best writing from the May Fourth left-wing fiction and several other stories are relatively successful; particularly interesting are those which portray bourgeois and petty bourgeois people, some satirically, others sympathetically.

7. Snow, Edgar, *Living China.* New York: Reynal and Hitchcock, 1937. 360 pages. Hyperion reprint, 1973

Originally published in 1937, this was until recently the best collection of Chinese short stories available in English. It includes an introductory essay by Nym Wales, largely based on information gained from personal interviews; this book is now available, unfortunately, only as an exorbitant Hyperion reprint.

Poetry

1. Hsu, Kai-yu. *Twentieth Century Chinese Poetry.* Garden City, NY: Anchor Books, Doubleday & Co., 1964. 465 pages (paper).

A fairly comprehensive treatment with a rich selection of translated examples. The translations are accurate and representative. The development of post-Liberation verse is clearly shown up to the late 1950s. The best of its kind in English.

Theoretical Writings and Policy Statements

1. Chou Yang (Zhou Yang). *The Path of Socialist Literature and Art in China.* Peking: FLP, 1960. 74 pages (paper).

An interesting discussion of the then-official view toward literature after the Great Leap Forward, the split with the Soviet Union and the deepening power struggle between Maoists and the "pragmatists." Discusses the trend toward adapting traditional forms of art and literature to needs of revolutionary ideology, attacks "revisionist" Marxist critics like Lukács and urges the combining of revolutionary romanticism with revolutionary realism.

2. Mao Tse-tung (Mao Ze-dong), *Mao Tse-tung on Literature and Art.* Peking: FLP, 1967. 162 pages (paper).

Sixteen articles, statements or excerpts from 1927 to 1957. Includes the crucially important "Talks at the Yenan Forum on Literature and Art" from 1942, "On *Let a Hundred Flowers Blossom, Let a Hundred Schools of Thought Contend,*" "The May Fourth Movement" and "The Culture of New Democracy."

3. *Summary of the Forum on the Work in Literature and Art in the Armed Forces With Which Comrade Lin Piao Entrusted Chiang Ching.* Peking: FLP, 1968.

Representative piece in which all theories advocated by former CCP literary authorities before the GPCR are attacked as

"revisionist." Extreme ideological militancy characteristic of the cultural revolution.

Histories of Modern Chinese Literature

1. Hsia, C. T. *A History of Modern Chinese Fiction.* 2nd Edition. New Haven: Yale University Press, 1971. 701 pages (paper).

A survey with critical discussion and literary evaluation of most of the major fiction writers from Lu Xun to 1949. This revised edition also includes more coverage of post-Liberation fiction and an interesting essay on the moral fervor of the modern Chinese writer's concern with China. The author's erudition and critical acumen are evident throughout the book. His fervid anticommunist perspective and hostile response to the ideological content of much of the literature discussed are also unmistakable. While this work is not likely to be superseded for some time and is the obvious starting point for future investigations of many modern Chinese writers who are still relatively ignored by Western researchers, there are many small discrepancies in it. More important, it is necessary to take the author's strong biases into account. For instance, Hsia in discussing the Yan'an Forum asserts that "in repudiating the Western tradition in modern Chinese literature, Mao Tse-tung has by fiat reversed the course of that literature and killed its potential for further experimentation and development." There are two important reviews of this book, one by Z. Slupski in the Czech journal, *Archiv Orientalni,* 32 (1964), pp. 139-152, which judiciously points out the lack of a consistent critical methodology. The other is by Professor Jaroslav Prusek in *T'oung Pao* 49 (1962), pp. 357-404, to which Hsia rejoins in *TP* 50 (1963), pp. 428-74. Despite the fact that the debate focuses more on political matters than literary criticism, this exchange represents perhaps the best scholarly dialogue on the problems of modern Chinese literature in the West to date. Whatever its faults, the scope of *A History of Modern Chinese Fiction* is large, the author's straightforward enunciation of his taste is laudable for its candor even if one disagrees with that taste, and the work is an indispensable contribution for English language readers. The second edition is to be preferred over the first and is readily available.

2. Ting Yi (Ding Yi). *A Short History of Modern Chinese Literature.* Port Washington, New York: Kennikat Press, 1970. 310 pages

Reprinted from the long out-of-print FLP translation of the Chinese original work which was put together right after Liberation, this history gives a good indication of the way Communist literary historians have written about the development of modern Chinese literature. Much discussion of the political struggles in China during the first half of this century and how modern literature related to those struggles; little attention given to the literary qualities or questions of style.

General Studies on Modern Chinese Literature

1. Birch, Cyril. *Chinese Communist Literature.* New York: Praeger, 1963. 254 pages.

Originally published as a special issue of *The China Quarterly,* 13 (Jan.-March, 1963), the articles included are the fruition of an important conference held at Ditchley Park, England in 1962. Thirteen articles dealing with various aspects of post-Liberation literature in China. Of greatest interest are those by Birch, the Hsia brothers, Li Chi, Hellmut Wilhelm and S. H. Chen. Birch's piece on the persistence of traditional forms in post-Liberation literature sets a standard all too rarely seen in studies of this type.

2. Fokkema, D. W. *Literary Doctrine in China and Soviet Influence, 1956-1960.* The Hague: Mouton & Co., 1965. 296 pages

The Dutch scholar Douwe Fokkema presents us with a study of great detail and impeccable scholarship. The general reader may wish to focus on the Historical Introduction which in 53 pages gives an overview of the period from the Yan'an Forum to the arrest of the gadfly Communist writer Hu Feng in 1955. Also the 20-page Conclusion and the very useful indices of literary terms and of titles and authors (with the Chinese characters given) at the end of the book are helpful and of interest to the scholar and general reader alike.

3. Goldman, Merle. *Literary Dissent in Communist China.* New York: Atheneum, 1971. 343 pages (paper).

Not concerned with literary analysis, this book is an account of the grim story of the repression of literature in post-Liberation China. It discusses literary policies and politics from the Yan'an (Yenan) period to the Hundred Flowers movement of early 1957 and its aftermath. Because the analogy between Chinese politics and Stalinism seems to be pressed a bit too hard, this work overemphasizes the distinction between intellectuals and the Party.

4. Goldman, Merle, ed. *Modern Chinese Literature in the May Fourth Era.* Forthcoming in 1976.

A collection of papers from a conference held in 1974, many of the studies of revolutionary writers in pre-Liberation China represent progress toward a more sophisticated methodology for studying revolutionary literature as literature. This anthology promises to be one of the more significant works on modern Chinese literature published during the 1970s.

5. Hsia, Tsi-an (Xia Ji-an). *The Gate of Darkness: Studies on the Leftist Literary Movement in China.* Seattle: University of Washington Press, 1968. 266 pages.

Largely sharing the biases of his brother C. T., T. A. Hsia combines considerable literary and historical erudition in this collection of five well-researched articles. While some of the articles seem to be motivated exclusively by partisan considerations, the book retains its value as a research introduction to the original sources of the Chinese literary scene of the '20s and '30s.

6. Huang, Joe C. *Heroes and Villains in Communist China.* New York: Pica Press, 1973. 345 pages (cloth).

An indispensable work closely examining many of the most important Chinese novels written since Liberation. Huang's study clearly shows the close relationship of each work to ideological requirements of Party policies and gives much information about each novel's political significance, the critical response it received in China, and its content, imagery, style and artistic merit.

7. Hsu, Kai-yu. *The Chinese Literary Scene: A Writer's Visit to the People's Republic.* New York: Vintage, 1975. 267 pages (paper).

A recent work and one of unique importance, this book gives many insights into the current cultural scene in China by means of honest and critical reporting of interviews with both post-Cultural Revolution literary workers and the older generation of May Fourth period writers such as Shen Cong-wen, Feng Zhi and Zang Ke-jia. Also includes translations of creative works and criticism from before and after the Cultural Revolution. Based on the author's six-month visit to China in 1973, *The Chinese Literary Scene* is one of the best reports of a "China visitor" that has been published since the opening of PRC doors to visitors from America. It is thus of interest to anyone seeking a better understanding of Chinese realities.

8. Lee, Leo Ou-fan. *The Romantic Generation of Modern Chinese Writers.* Cambridge: Harvard University Press, 1974. 365 pages (cloth).

In basic agreement with Professor Prusek that modern Chinese literature in the May Fourth period was infused with an intense subjectivism, Leo Lee's book focuses on Lin Shu, Su Man-shu, Yu Da-fu, Xu Zhi-mo (Hsu Chih-mo), Guo Mo-ruo, Jiang Guang-ci (Chiang Kuang-tz'u) and Xiao Jun, writers whose works cover a period of almost sixty years from the 1880s to the 1940s. Lee presents the thesis that this subjective tendency represents a radical break with traditional Confucian didacticism and his case is persuasively documented. Its general applicability to the majority of May Fourth writers, however, and especially to the late May Fourth and revolutionary Communist writers, would seem somewhat questionable.

9. MacDougall, Bonnie. *The Introduction of Western Literary Theories in Modern China (1919-1925).* Tokyo: Centre for East Asian Cultural Studies, 1971. 368 pages (paper).

MacDougall's book deals with this topic by means of literary schools or themes, such as "Romanticism," and clearly outlines the major trends in Western literary criticism in those years and their impact on Chinese literature and literary theories.

10. Prusek, Jaroslav.

a. Introduction to *Studies in Modern Chinese Literature.* Berlin: Akademie-Verlag, 1964. 179 pages (paper).

Possibly Prusek's most succinct and insightful statement on modern Chinese literature. His 43-page introduction combines a full appreciation of historical and contemporary social realities and their relationship to modern literature. It also devotes some attention to the debts owed by modern Chinese literature to traditional forms. The "studies" alluded to in the title are by Prusek's students. While not as interesting as later work done by the same people, the studies still merit reading.

b. *Three Sketches on the New Chinese Literature.* Prague: Oriental Institute in Akademia Prague, 1969. 149 pages (paper).

A study of several of the more important narrative works of Mao Dun, Yu Da-fu and Guo Mo-ruo. This volume integrates some of the advances in twentieth century European criticism with Prusek's long-term concern with creative literature as the most sophisticated indicator of intellectual and social history. This book is not as polished as much as Prof. Prusek's other work, as it was rushed to publication just ahead of the purge in Prague following the Soviet invasion of 1968. Since then, Prusek has been expelled from the institute which he virtually founded.

c. "Reality and Art in Chinese Literature" in *Archiv Orientalni* 32 (1964), pp. 605-18.

d. "A Confrontation of Traditional Oriental Literature with Modern European Literature in the Context of the Chinese Literary Revolution" in *Archiv Orientalni* 32 (1964), pp. 365-75.

Both of the above articles break new ground in analyzing the relationship between traditional and modern literary forms in China.

11. Tagore, Amitendranath. *Literary Debates in Modern China 1918-1937*. Tokyo: Center for Eastern Asian Cultural Studies, 1967. 280 pages (paper).

Tagore's book concentrates on delineating the complex alignments of literary societies and cliques during the May Fourth period. Since nearly every writer belonged to one society or another, the account of the disputes that raged among them given here provides much information about the critical theories and personal associations of most major writers. Also there are excerpts in translation from many of the most influential essays and polemics of the period.

Studies of Individual Writers

1. Galik, Marian. *Mao Tun and Modern Chinese Literary Criticism*. Wiesbaden: Franz Steiner Verlag, 1969. 185 pages

A scholarly and very complete account of the influences on Mao Dun's early contributions to modern Chinese letters as a literary critic, editor, translator, author of writing guides and introducer of European realism to the May Fourth generation. Occasional rough spots in the English.

2. Huang Sung-k'ang. *Lu Hsun and the New Culture Movement in Modern China*. Amsterdam, 1957. 155 pages Reprinted by Hyperion Press.

The first intellectual biography of Lu Xun in English, this work focuses on Lu Xun's ideas and their relation to the emerging May Fourth literature.

3. Lang, Olga. *Pa Chin and His Writings*. Cambridge: Harvard University Press, 1967. 402 pages

A sympathetic biography of the sentimental anarchist writer, Ba Jin, author of *Family*. The author uses Ba Jin's novels to illustrate the various stages in his life and thinking. This study clearly reveals the process whereby the hopes of non-Party revolutionary intellectuals in the Guomindang-controlled areas were necessarily dashed during the last dark years of the war against Japan.

4. Roy, David. *Kuo Mo-jo: The Early Years*. Cambridge: Harvard University Press, 1970. 244 pages

A straightforward biography which examines Guo's writings and activities before 1925 in terms of his character and personality rather than his literary role. The study unfortunately stops just at the point when Guo begins to be most active in terms of revolutionary activity and commitment.

5. Slupski, Zbigniew. *The Evolution of a Modern Chinese Writer*. Prague: Oriental Institute, 1966. 168 pages (paper).

One of the best studies to come from the remarkable group of scholars trained in Prague under Prof. Prusek, this book analyzes Lao She's literary technique using a structuralist methodology. The work of scholars like Prof. Slupski in Warsaw is a testament to the contribution of Prusek to the study of modern Chinese literature and makes the dismantling of the Prague center after Russian intervention in Czechoslovakia in 1968 all the more poignant.

Contributors

John Berninghausen teaches Chinese language and literature at the University of Vermont. His current research is focussed on Mao Dun's fiction and on the interaction between form and content in literary works of a highly political nature.

Ted Huters is a Ph.D. candidate in modern Chinese literature at Stanford University and is now writing his doctoral dissertation on Qian Zhong-shu.

Perry Link teaches Chinese language and literature at Princeton University and is especially interested in popular thought.

Donald Holoch is Assistant Professor of Chinese at York University, Toronto. His major research interests are the rise of bourgeois fiction in late-Qing China and its transformation during the Republican period.

Lars Ellström is a Ph.D. candidate from the University of Stockholm, currently studying modern Chinese literature at Fudan University in Shanghai, one of fourteen foreign students there.

Michael Gotz is a doctoral candidate in Oriental Languages at the University of California, Berkeley, and is working on a dissertation, "Images of Workers in Contemporary Chinese Fiction, 1949-1964." He is editor of the *Modern Chinese Literature Newsletter*.

Yu-shih Chen is Assistant Professor of Chinese at Hunter College. She has written on topics in Classical Chinese literature and is now working on a book on the fictional works of Mao Dun.

Paul Pickowicz is Assistant Professor of History at the University of California, San Diego. He is currently writing a book on Qu Qiu-bai and the origins of Chinese Marxist literary thought.

Gary Bjorge is a Ph.D. candidate at the University of Wisconsin, Madison, and Library Associate: Chinese in the university library. His major research interest is 20th Century Chinese literature.

Shu-ying Tsau, of Beijing, graduated from Beijing University in 1958. She is Assistant Professor of Chinese at York University, Toronto. Her main research interest is the development of China's proletarian literature, in its thematic and stylistic aspects.

David Holm is Research Fellow at the Contemporary China Institute, School of Oriental and African Studies, London. He is working on a thesis on transformation of the folk arts and popular literature in the Border Regions of North China, 1937-49.

Jean James is a graduate student in East Asian Languages and Literature at the University of Iowa and is interested in promoting translation of modern Chinese literature. His current research is on Han Tomb No. 1 at Ma Wang Tui.

Joe Huang is author of *Heroes and Villains in Communist China: The Contemporary Chinese Novel as a Reflection of Life* and is currently writing a book on post-1949 theater in China.

Wong Kam-ming teaches Chinese literature at Cornell University. His main area of interest is Chinese fiction, both traditional and modern, with special emphasis on *Dream of the Red Chamber*, Lu Xun and Hao Ran.